CHARLES DARWIN:

The Years of Controversy

The *Origin of Species* and its critics

1859-1882

Peter J. Vorzimmer

D1611410

When Darwin published the *Origin of Species* in 1859, he was convinced that he had presented the evidence to support his belief in natural selection. In 1872 he published the sixth and last revision of the work. The history of those successive editions is the history of an intellectual struggle —of Darwin's attempts to justify the inconsistencies that critics found in his work, and of his increasing frustration that he had been unable to demonstrate irrefutably that natural selection was the sole agent of evolutionary change. Although he lived for ten more years, he made no further modifications in his work after 1872 and left the verdict on his achievement to posterity.

For the first time, Peter Vorzimmer fully explores this dramatic but neglected chapter in the history of ideas. He has drawn on original material which hitherto has not been investigated, including the Darwin

(Continued on back flap)

and is co-

A Chronological History. He is currently associate professor of history at Temple University.

CHARLES DARWIN:
THE YEARS
OF CONTROVERSY

The Origin of Species *and* its Critics *1859-1882*

by Peter J. Vorzimmer

TEMPLE UNIVERSITY PRESS
Philadelphia 1970

Standard Book Number 87722–001–8
Library of Congress Card Number 73–118377
Printed in the United States of America
Copyright © 1970 by Temple University
Philadelphia—19122
All Rights Reserved

TO PROFESSOR GARRETT HARDIN,
with respect and gratitude

Contents

Table of bibliographical abbreviations
(*comprising the main sources for this work*)

LL: Darwin, Francis, ed. 1897. *Life and Letters of Charles Darwin.* 2 vols. New York: D. Appleton & Co.

ML: Darwin, Francis, and Seward, A. C., eds. 1903. *More Letters of Charles Darwin.* 2 vols. New York: D. Appleton & Co.

LLH: Huxley, Leonard, ed. 1900. *Life and Letters of T. H. Huxley.* 2 vols. New York: D. Appleton & Co.

LLJDH: Huxley, Leonard, ed. 1918. *Life and Letters of J. D. Hooker.* 2 vols. New York: D. Appleton & Co.

Origin: Peckham, Morse, ed. 1959. The Origin of Species *by Charles Darwin: A Variorum Text.* Philadelphia: University of Pennsylvania Press.

   Citations follow Peckham's own numbering (viz. Chapter 14, sentence 251 = XIV:251) followed by appropriate letter to indicate the edition (viz. Chapter 10, sentence 15 of the fifth edition = X:15.e). For full explanation of system, see Peckham.

Variation: Darwin, Charles. 1868. *The Variation of Animals and Plants under Domestication.* 2 vols. London: John Murray.

Descent: Darwin, Charles. 1871. *The Descent of Man.* 2 vols. London: John Murray.

DRC: The Darwin Reprint Collection at the University Library, Cambridge University. Each article was numbered by Darwin himself and he divided his collection into three parts: a general collection (numbers given simply as DRC #41, DRC #1132, etc.), a review collection consisting of published reviews of his works (numbers given as DRC #R 12, DRC #R 257, etc.), and a collection of quarto-sized pamphlets (numbers given as DRC #Q 322, DRC #Q 8, etc.). Unless otherwise noted, all quotations from these are those underlined or otherwise marked by Darwin himself.*

DL: Books from Darwin's Library currently at the University Library, Cambridge. These are not numbered, and therefore full bibliographic references are given. Unless otherwise noted, all quotations are those underlined or otherwise marked by Darwin himself.†

DPL: Darwin Papers and Letters in the University Library, Cambridge. Box numbers given correspond to those listed in the *Handlist of Darwin Papers at the University Library, Cambridge,* 1960. Cambridge: University Press.

* A catalogue of the Darwin Reprint Collection is available through the Anderson Room, University Library, Cambridge. It has been critically edited by this author.

† A complete list of these titles is given in a privately published list entitled *List of Books received in the University Library, Cambridge, March-May 1961,* available from the Anderson Room of the University Library. A more general list of Darwin's entire Down Library, which includes those books now at the Cambridge University Library, is contained in *Catalogue of the Library of Charles Darwin now in the Botany School, Cambridge* (Cambridge: University Press, 1908).

Chronological Table

November 26, 1859	1st *Origin* published
December 8, 1859	2nd *Origin* begun
December 18, 1859	2nd *Origin* completed
January 7, 1860	2nd *Origin* published
January 9, 1860	*Variation* begun
November 26, 1860	3rd *Origin* begun
March 1, 1861	3rd *Origin* completed
April 26, 1861	3rd *Origin* published
March 1, 1866	4th *Origin* begun
May 10, 1866	4th *Origin* completed
December 15, 1866	4th *Origin* published
January 26, 1867	*Variation* completed
February 13, 1867	*Descent* begun
January 30, 1868	*Variation* published
December 26, 1868	5th *Origin* begun
February 10, 1869	5th *Origin* completed
August 7, 1869	5th *Origin* published
January 15, 1871	*Descent* completed
February 24, 1871	*Descent* published
June 18, 1871	6th *Origin* begun
January 10, 1872	6th *Origin* completed
February 19, 1872	6th *Origin* published
November 20, 1873	2nd *Descent* begun
April 1, 1874	2nd *Descent* completed
September 1874	2nd *Descent* published

July 2, 1875	2nd *Variation* begun
August 20, 1875	2nd *Variation* completed
September 1875	2nd *Variation* published

The Origin of Species, The Variation of Animals and Plants under Domestica-tion, and the *Descent of Man* form a trilogy of Darwin's writings concerned strictly with the theory of evolution. The variations in these three works form the printed evidence of the changes made by Darwin in his conception of the mechanism of evolution. While his remaining works have some slight, secondary bearing on this study, the dates listed above are of primary im-portance in establishing the specific works of Darwin's contemporaries that can be associated with particular changes in Darwin's own printed works.

Foreword

*T*he *Abstract of an Essay on the Origin of Species* which Charles Darwin rushed to completion in 1858–59 was not very long or very logical by nineteenth-century standards in natural history; and we are all the beneficiaries. Darwin's publisher, quite sensibly, refused to try to sell to the general public a book called an *Abstract of an Essay,* and so it was issued simply as *On the Origin of Species.* The condensation which Darwin had performed on his materials produced a work capable not only of being read but also of being reprinted in cheap editions from his day to ours.

Even so, *On the Origin of Species* is more often cited than read, and more often read than understood. One reason is that it is not one book (even though one volume) but several; heated arguments can still arise when one scholar considers the first edition as pure Darwin and another relies on Darwin's final formulations in the sixth edition. This situation has been known for a long time; what has not been known is what to do about it. Professor Vorzimmer here solves this problem. Not only does he establish and explain the reasons for the changes but, in doing so, he explains the parts of the original theory more thoroughly than has been done heretofore: its strengths, but also its weaknesses. Some of these weaknesses were those of the biological knowledge of his time, of which, in such chapters as "The Study of Inheritance, 1799–1862," Vorzimmer gives valuable new views. Others were those of Darwin's own characteristic approaches to nature—that nature does not make jumps, for example—and Vorzimmer shows how these prejudices kept Darwin from accepting suggestions from his friends and supporters.

The original *Origin* was not very logical, not all rigorous. Darwin was writing to convince, not to prove. He was trying to get across his own complex vision of how the natural world operates; and he seized upon any metaphors, any analogies, any line of argument that he had on hand. We now believe that he was correct, that his vision was too advanced to fit neatly into the scientific and logical categories usually employed at the time, and that therefore he was justified in treating them casually. But this made him vulnerable to contemporary criticism and, as Vorzimmer shows, to self-doubts. His vision was an imaginative whole; tampering with it only made it more prosaic.

Vorzimmer's approach is to concentrate on the specific mechanisms of the first five chapters of the *Origin,* their contemporary scientific status, the objections raised by other scientists, and Darwin's reaction to these objections. He depicts a Darwin considerably more thoughtful than most of his critics; impervious to suggestions from his friends; conceding too much to the pressures of his antagonists; and eventually reduced to argumentative impotence. This is not the picture that most people have of the development of a scientific theory. We feel, somehow, that more evidence, more argument, more investigation should lead to an improved theory, not to one more self-contradictory. Yet modern historians of science have come to question the usual liberal notions of how progress in scientific truth comes about. Vorzimmer gives us a thorough documentation of one of the most important cases in which the liberal processes worked against progress. Is this a more typical oc-currence, at least for the great theories, than the usual picture? Only more studies of a depth and penetration equal to this one will enable us to tell. Meanwhile, Vorzimmer's study justifies the conclusion that two of Darwin's chief virtues were ones not usually praised in a scientist: jumping to conclusions which go well beyond the evidence available; and maintaining his faith in his position regardless of the valid arguments that could be brought against it.

Walter F. Cannon

Smithsonian Institution
Washington, D.C.

Preface

Certainly no one who began so cautiously with facts ever got quite so deeply involved in ideas as Charles Darwin.

—*William Irvine*, Apes, Angels, and Victorians

*T*he *Origin of Species* was the work in which Charles Darwin proposed a theoretical mechanism to account for the evolution of new specific forms. That mechanism was his theory of natural selection. But the *Origin* fulfilled a second function: it provided as well the evidence to support that theory. Fully half the work consisted of a vast assemblage of facts which Darwin culled from fields as diverse as embryology and geology, then marshaled to give weight to his hypothesis.

Yet the core of the *Origin* lies in its first five chapters—those in which Darwin described the conditions and the process of natural selection. The facts were rarely contested; the explanatory merit of the theory rested ultimately upon the processes and conditions that constituted it.

The years following the publication of the *Origin* testified to the controversy which ensued. For many, the appearance of the *Origin* precipitated renewed arguments over the fact of organic evolution itself—an issue largely irrelevant to the purpose of the work. For the scientific community, however, the book's principal value lay in its ability to explain the theory of organic change it proposed.

There is at present no work by either historian or biologist providing a detailed analysis of Darwin's theory which treats it at the same time in its proper historical and scientific setting. Moreover, in the vast literature surrounding Darwin and his theory, a large and significant part of his life has been somewhat neglected: the period following the publication of the *Origin of Species* (1859) to the time of his death (1882). Without a detailed knowledge and understanding of Darwin's thought and work during these years, no history of the Darwinian theory of evolution can be considered complete. This book is an attempt to fill that gap.

Darwin's feelings about evolution, as revealed in the letters, papers, and published works of the latter part of his life, indicate (when contrasted to the *Origin* of 1859) some fluctuation during the years. In 1859, Darwin's belief in the principle of natural selection was not merely an article of faith; it was grounded as well in the firm conviction that he had effectively demonstrated its validity. However, by the end of his life in 1882 Darwin had become, under critical attack, increasingly frustrated by his inability to prove to the satisfaction of fellow scientists that the selection process was the sole or, in some cases, the principal agent of evolutionary development. He died clinging to the belief that later scientists would prove him right. Because of the continuing attacks of his scientific colleagues on his theory, and his own attempts to meet these attacks by constant re-study and revision, a detailed look at this period has seemed a worthwhile undertaking.

Perhaps the most important impetus to this work was the rediscovery of Darwin's reprint collection in the Botany School Library in Cambridge, England.* Because the collection had been combined with that of Darwin's botanist son Francis, it had lain in obscurity for many years on the top shelves in the rear of the library. Before Dr. Sydney Smith told me about it in 1958, very few people had known of its existence; fewer still were aware of its historical significance. Its 2200-odd pieces

* For further details regarding the Darwin Reprint Collection, consult the Introduction to the *Reprint Catalogue,* copies of which are available from the University Library, Cambridge, England (where the collection is now housed).

contain over one hundred thousand words of marginal annotations made by Darwin. As a historical link between Darwin and his contemporaries, its value is obviously almost inestimable. A glance at a few selected samples from the collection was enough to confirm to me its importance as research material.

Other original sources consulted have been letters of Darwin and his contemporaries in the collections of the University Library, Cambridge; the American Philosophical Society Library, Philadelphia; the New York Public Library; and the British Museum. A number of previously unpublished extracts from each of these sources have been included in this book.

Special acknowledgment must be made of Professor Morse Peckham's formidable variorum edition of the *Origin of Species* (1959), which saved me the labor of collating the several editions of the *Origin*.

Finally, I must extend sincere thanks to Dr. Michael Hoskin and to Dr. H. L. Whitehouse for reading early proofs and offering suggestion, criticism, and encouragement; to Dr. Sydney Smith, not only for drawing my attention to the presence of the reprint collection, but for serving as my advisor and ever-willing sounding board for ideas; to Professor Robert C. Stauffer for allowing me to read his typescript of Darwin's original (1854–58) chapters of the *Origin,* and to both him and Professor B. J. Loewenberg for guiding me to, and helping me decipher, various scraps of Darwiniana; to Dr. Alun Steer and Miss Pamela Prior for invaluable aid in checking my German translations; to Peter Gautrey and the staff of the Anderson Room of the University Library, Cambridge, for helpful assistance; to Lady Nora Barlow for permission to use and print quotations from some of the unpublished sources; and—most important of all—to my friends and family without whose aid, indirect as it may have seemed to them, I could not have written this book.

Philadelphia
April 1970   Peter J. Vorzimmer

Introduction

A close examination of the last edition of the Origin
*reveals that in attempting on scattered pages to meet
the objections being launched against his theory the
much-laboured-upon volume had become contradictory.
. . . The last repairs to the* Origin *reveal . . . how very
shaky Darwin's theoretical structure had become.
His gracious ability to compromise had produced some
striking inconsistencies.*

—*Loren Eiseley,* Darwin's Century

*At the time of Darwin's death, Wallace was the only
one who believed that natural selection was the sole
causal agent in the evolution of species.*

—*Phillip Fothergill,* Historical Aspects
of Organic Evolution

*T*he sixth and final edition of the *Origin of Species* in 1872
was the last full-scale revision of Charles Darwin's thoughts
concerning the mechanism of the evolutionary process. Having
emerged from twelve years of unrelenting criticism extremely
shaken in his confidence over the demonstrable capacities of his
theory, Darwin effectively retired at this point from further
participation in debate concerning the theory of evolution. The
value of his contribution would stand or fall, he felt, on this
final and much-modified edition.

Many interpretations of his action have been suggested.

2. Charles Darwin: The years of controversy

Such contemporaries of Darwin as St. George Mivart and Samuel Butler saw it as an ineffective retreat in the face of the indisputable validity of criticisms made of his theory. Others, among them such eminent Darwinians as Thomas Henry Huxley and A. R. Wallace, while still maintaining their faith in the theory of natural selection, saw this retreat as the result of Darwin's personal inability to comprehend the exact nature of the position he was then in. In general his scientific contemporaries, of whatever personal or professional views, had come to look upon Darwin as adrift from the mainstream of thought about evolution. It was Darwin's personal conviction concerning the process of natural selection, a conviction maintained to his death, that kept him at this work.

These views, while substantially correct, tell only part of the story. In order really to comprehend Darwin's final position relative to the controversial aspects of the process of evolution both then and now, one must understand—through a detailed analysis of his work, his thought, and the influences upon them— how and why it became his particular and peculiar misfortune to find himself at the end of the life defending a position which he had become less and less able to demonstrate to the satisfaction of his peers.

1. The Darwinian mechanism

*T*he mechanism of evolution proposed by Charles Darwin was introduced to the world at large in the *Origin of Species* in 1859. This process he called "Natural Selection," and he viewed it as the agent in nature which preserves beneficially varying forms of existing species, while, through continued selection, it compounds some of them into new species.

Before attempting the necessary analysis of Darwin's theoretical mechanism and the assumptions on which it was based, a few preliminary remarks should be made.

THE BACKGROUND OF THE *Origin*

The publication of the *Origin,* marking the birth of modern thought concerning evolution, was the result of long gestation. Nearly twenty-three years had passed since Darwin returned from his voyage on the *Beagle* (December 1831–October 1836). On this journey Darwin was first led to feel that the adaptive nature of organic forms was the result of some form of selection. So busy was he on his return that it was July of 1837 before he began his first notebook on transmutation.

Nearly all the basic elements of his theory appear in the pages of these early notebooks.[1] Yet one element was still missing. Not until October 1838, when reading Malthus on population, had Darwin, in his own words, "at last got a theory by which to work."[2] Even though he had known that a natural form of selection was the operative basis of evolutionary change, he had been at a loss to provide it with some motive power. What natural force acted to push organic forms through the selective sieve? What gave natural selection the power to direct and compound change toward an adaptive end? Darwin found an answer in the force of population pressure and its resultant effects, as vividly described by Malthus. Malthus's words had wakened in Darwin the memory of his own past observations of this same phenomenon in the world of nature. The matter now seemed obvious; yet Darwin nevertheless "determined not for some time to write even the briefest sketch of it,"[3] until he could gather the necessary evidence to support his thesis. That time came in June of 1842 when, no longer able to contain himself, he wrote a thirty-five-page sketch containing the nucleus of his theory.[4] In 1844 Darwin wrote a longer (230-page) version, the *Essay of 1844*.[5] Both papers were prepared solely as exercises to focus his thoughts concerning the general theme; neither was intended for any form of publication. With much writing still to be done as the direct result of his voyage, Darwin devoted about a year to completing his study of the geology of South America.[6] That finished, another year was spent in preparing the second edition of his *Journal of Researches*.[7] After that, in October 1846, Darwin launched what became eight years of work on barnacles.[8] It was not until this was on the press (in September 1854) that he resumed work on the theory of evolution. For the next twenty months he gathered facts and corresponded with Sir Charles Lyell, Joseph Hooker, and Asa Gray on various aspects of evolution. It was Lyell who, in May 1856, first wrote to Darwin suggesting that he do a sketch of his theory of speciation for publication. Darwin, still somewhat loath to commit himself in writing, despite his own confidence, replied: "To give a fair sketch would be absolutely impossible, for every proposition requires such an array of facts. If I were to do anything, it could only refer to the main agency of change —selection—and perhaps point out a very few of the leading features which countenance such a view and some of the main difficulties."[9] Perhaps seeing the same merit in clarifying his ideas as in 1842 and 1844, however, he went ahead to attempt "a *very thin* and little volume," but by October he reported the project abandoned. "When I began I found it such unsatisfactory work that I have desisted, and am now drawing up my work as perfect as my materials of nineteen years' collecting suffice, but do not intend to stop to perfect any line of investigation beyond current work."[10] This procrastination may well have been due to the fact that Darwin was still having difficulty explaining the multiple divergence of species from a common stock.[11]

When, on June 18, 1858, Darwin received A. R. Wallace's own short essay on the mechanism of evolution,[12] he had eleven sizeable chapters completed in rough but readable form.[13] After the brief crisis over priority and his rush to write up his own paper for the Linnean Society, general publication of his theory in some form became an urgent necessity. Darwin spent the next eight months reducing those chapters to an abstract which became the *Origin of Species* of 1859.

Thus it might seem that the date of 1859, while it marked the beginning of the promulgation of his ideas, was for Darwin more a culmination than a starting point. Darwin looked upon the *Origin,* however, as a general introduction to a series of works. Although his ideas on evolution continued to develop after 1859, in a particular sense they cannot be viewed as merely the continuation of what had come earlier. For now he would theorize no longer in isolation from his contemporaries. His work had stimulated scientists to look back upon old and familiar phenomena from a distinctly new vantage point. He therefore not only initiated a wholly new concept of biological mechanism but, in so doing, provided insights whose lack had stalled progress in a host of related disciplines.

This book is directed toward a consideration of Darwin's mechanism of evolution and the broader theoretical assumptions on which that mechanism is based. It is concerned with those demonstrative aspects of the *Origin* and those of his later works only insofar as explanatory difficulties led him to alter his views with regard to this mechanism (as opposed to any change in interpretation of the facts). Thus, in considering the *Origin,* the main emphasis is placed on the first five chapters.*

THE MECHANISM OF NATURAL SELECTION

The Darwinian process of natural selection can be set down in the following logical pattern:

I. Inherent in the reproductive faculties of organic nature is a tendency to multiplication at a geometric rate of increase.

II. So fixed and finite are the interrelationships of organic nature that those elements which constitute the sustenance for yet other forms will not match this rate of increase.

A. (Conclusion from I and II) There is, among all living organisms, a struggle for existence.

III. In all organic forms† there appear a number of inheritable variations. Among these there occasionally appear some which prove advantageous to the individuals possessing them in the struggle for existence.

B. (Conclusion from A and III) Those organisms which possess advantageous variations will survive the struggle for existence.

* I. Variation under Domestication   II. Variation under Nature   III. Struggle for Existence   IV. Natural Selection   V. Laws of Variation

† The term "forms" is preferred here because of Darwin's own view that varieties and other intermediate subspecific forms were "incipient species."

C. (Conclusion from B and I) A permanent and adaptive change in the forms of organic nature will be effected (as, over time, the new forms replace the old).

In the above presentation, terms with modern scientific connotations have been purposely avoided. Instead, the terms and phrases used are nearly identical to those appearing in the pages of the *Origin*. With particular respect to the mechanism of selection itself, the *Origin* of 1859 is little different from either the *Sketch of 1842* or the *Essay of 1844*.*

THE LOGIC OF DARWIN'S DISCOVERY

The historical course of Darwin's discovery is not described in the narrative of his chapters, though they do give a rough indication of the logic of his discovery. During his travels, Darwin was struck at one and the same time by the similarities and differences appearing in the same species. The similarities were the species characteristics held in common, which identified individuals of a species as of the same general group. Most striking of all were the differences demarcating them not only as individuals but as varieties within the species. They all seemed adaptive in form. That is, each subspecific group possessed those particular variations which had rendered it more fit to cope with its particular set of environmental conditions. The notion of an adaptive "fit" between an organism and its peculiar set of environmental conditions suggested to Darwin that a "selection" had taken place. If this were the case, he reasoned, this set of peculiar regional conditions must constitute the selective standard for the organic beings to be contained in the region. Those not endowed with the requisite qualities would be rejected; those so endowed would be admitted. But

---

* In the *Origin*, however, it takes four rather long chapters to set forth the mechanism, rather more than ten times the length it took in both essays combined. As Sir Gavin de Beer has said in his introduction to the two essays, they may even be preferred over the *Origin* for their conciseness and clarity.

how is this gleaning to be achieved? Nature cannot reach out in her selection. How are the right forms to find their correct, adaptive place? If the conditions constitute the essential matrix, do the organisms themselves constitute the active agent? If so, what in turn drives them? Certainly not, for Darwin, any inner Lamarckian *sentiment intérieur*. No, whatever the source, it had to be external to the organisms themselves. But this power, this pressure, this force which would push the organic grist through the selective mill seemed to elude Darwin.

His next step in this search was to look to the state of domestication.* Perhaps here, in this artificial but parallel state, he would find a clue to the causes operating in nature. He quickly grasped the analogy between natural selection and the artificial selection practiced by man in domesticating animals and cultivating plants adapted to his particular ends. In both cases beneficial variations were preserved and compounded by selection to yield permanent, heritable improvement. The role and method of selection in both instances was the same; the selecting agent, however, was not. As previously mentioned, Darwin was to remain frustrated in his search until October 1838, when his reading of Malthus led him to realize where that power behind selection resided in nature. The vivid Malthusian picture of the pressure of natural overpopulation and the struggle for existence which ensued supplied the missing element. Where the end (and selective standard) of domestic selection has been adaptive fitness to man's end, in nature it was an adaptive fitness to the organism's own end—survival in the struggle for existence. The selective standard was the sum of the environmental conditions; the motivating agent which acted to match the organic elements against this standard was the ineluctable pressure of the struggle to survive.

---

* Darwin may well have been led to this by Lyell, for he had marked in his [1834] copy of Lyell's *Principles of Geology*, 2:354, the following passage: "The best authenticated examples of the extent to which species can be made to vary may be looked for in the history of domesticated animals and cultivated plants." (DL)

Darwin's continued stress on the analogy from domestication is of some significance. Darwin looked upon the state of domestication as a case of organisms living under and exposed to rather specialized conditions of life. He therefore believed that domestic selection could explain the broader process of natural selection through an example of a more specialized case. The conditions—such essential prerequisites for existence as light, heat, food, etc.—were the same; they varied merely in intensity or quantity. He was thus to continue to extrapolate from the domestic to the natural state on various aspects of evolutionary change. The fact that the results of man's efforts in plant and animal breeding were well documented and widely known to be successful in the improvement of species led Darwin to give increasing value to these analogies.

THE SELECTED MATERIAL: VARIATION

While the process of natural selection forms the operative core of Darwin's theory, it was necessarily contingent upon the natural organic tendency to variation. Darwin realized the importance of variation as the raw material on which selection operated. That *individuals* varied was, after all, a logically prior premise to the more general conclusion that *species* vary. Darwin's basic reasoning is not difficult to follow (see Figure 1.1). Nature produced variations, and selection used them in achieving speciation. Whatever the causes ("X"), the fact was established that individual organisms occasionally varied, many of these variations being inheritable. Of these, it would seem inevitable that a small number would prove advantageous to the individual in the struggle for existence. These were preserved through the survival of the individuals possessing them and were multiplied through the replication of the successful (and the concomitant extinction of the unsuccessful) unmodified forms. New variation was added to now-consolidated variation in following generations until true and complete (specific) divergence from the original parent-form was achieved.

Darwin's attitude toward variation was, in some respects, shortsighted. He saw variation as something peculiar to each individual organism possessing it. It was a phenomenon of the *individual* (see Figure 1.1, left of dotted line A). On the other hand, the process of selection, though starting from individual variation, was something that brought about new populations, new races, new varieties, and finally new species. The paths leading to individual variation were distinct from that one road which led to speciation. This point is noted again in discussion of the causes of variation.

The variation required by Darwin for the operation of his mechanism was minimal; the requirements as to the nature or extent of this variation were almost nil. However, in the *Origin* Darwin not only rejected all saltative* forms of variation, but *specifically* limited himself to those naturally occurring variations which he called *individual differences.*†

The process of natural selection therefore required only a minute difference between the individual and its parents. Any beneficial variation whatsoever, in any generation, over any period of time (so long as one accepts that a certain minimal amount of heritable variation does occur in nature) was evolutionary material. Even with variation at a required minimum, its occurrence had been well documented long before Darwin. From the viewpoint of functional dependence or of a strict logical economy, it would appear not necessary to deal with the causes producing variation. Darwin felt, as will be shown, that the efficacy of natural selection was in no way contingent upon the causes of variation. The assumption of only a modicum of variation as his basic premise rested on a safe empirical founda-

---

* Saltation = a leap or jump. For a discussion of this phenomenon see chapter 3, pages 46 to 69.

† "We have many slight differences which may be called individual differences, such as are known frequently to appear in the offspring from the same parents." (*Origin*. II:13) "These individual differences are highly important for us, as they afford materials for natural selection to accumulate." (*Origin*. II:15) "I believe mere individual differences suffice for the work." (*Origin*. IV:173) "Individual differences are amply sufficient." (*Origin*. I:293)

tion: they occur. Yet Darwin had felt it necessary, as early as 1854, to investigate such causes.

In his attitude toward "chance," "cause-and-effect," and scientific explanation in general, Darwin was a true child of the early nineteenth century.* He believed that there was no true knowledge of any fact or effect without knowledge of its cause. To say that variations were spontaneous or that they occurred "by chance" was either to confess ignorance, or to build a theory upon a foundation of mere chance.

> Mere chance, as we may call it, might cause one variety to differ in some character from its parents, and the off-spring of this variety again to differ from its parent in the very same character and in a greater degree; but this alone would never account for so habitual and large an amount of difference as that between varieties of the same species and species of the same genus.[14]

The variations upon which natural selection so completely depended are understood only when their true causes have been determined.

THE CAUSES OF VARIATION

In endeavoring to determine the many causes which produce variation, Darwin looked to the phenomenon of domestication. In the opening sentence of the *Origin of Species* Darwin started with the assumption that domesticated plants and animals "generally differ much more from each other, than do the individuals of any one species or variety in a state of nature."[15] This is an assumption found also in the two earlier essays. While some variation is common to both states, the fact that "Nature's variation [is] far less"[16] made it appear that "the most favourable conditions for variation seem to be when organic beings are bred for many generations under domestication."[17]

---

* Darwin was much influenced by his reading of Herschel and called himself "a true Baconian" in the search for causes.

Darwin next asked himself the question "In what does this power of domestication consist?"[18] to which he replied, "The power of domestication resolves itself into the accumulated effects of a change of all or some of the natural conditions of the life of the species."[19] Thus variation was not strictly a phenomenon of chance, a purely spontaneous accident, but something which had a direct cause: the conditions of life. Apparently an organism had to be stimulated into varying, for the hereditary process was extremely strong.

Darwin's reasoning in tracking down variation's causes can be clearly seen:

1. Variation from the normal type occurs both in nature and under domestication.
2. There is much greater variation under domestication than occurs under nature.
3. The state of domestication is a particular case of organisms living under particular conditions of life. While the conditions vary in intensity, the same basic requirements of existence are common to both states.
4. The general hereditary tendency of like producing like occurs throughout the organic world, modified only by the inherited effects of the conditions of life.

Proceeding from this, Darwin felt that it must be conditions (food, light, heat, etc.) common to both states that produce variation. These conditions are common to both states because variation itself is, also. They should differ only insofar as the amount and extent of variation between the two states differ. On the basis of this reasoning Darwin, in the *Origin* of 1859, pinpointed the following causes:

A. The Direct Effect of the Conditions of Life*
B. The Indirect Effect of the Conditions of Life
C. Habit, Use, and Disuse

* A more detailed analysis of each of these is given in chapter 4.

D. Correlation of Growth

E. Compensation or Balance

Although he included all these as relevant factors in the production of variation, Darwin had come to feel by 1859 that, even taken together, they accounted for only the slightest amount of variation. While he had attributed a considerable amount of variation to these causes in the essays of 1842 and 1844, he changed his mind in the interim before the *Origin.* * As Darwin himself summarized it at the end of the chapter "The Laws of Variation" in the *Origin:* "Whatever the cause may be of each slight difference in the offspring from their parents—and a cause for each must exist—it is the steady accumulation through natural selection . . . that gives rise to all the more important modifications of structure."[20] Despite the fact that Darwin was somewhat ingenuous when it came to the causal factors he recognized as valid in the works of his contemporaries, he always appended to his description of these his own remarks. In every case he noted that a particular cause was only "a possible explanation," that many organisms have structures "which cannot be explained by . . . one or another of these factors." At yet other times he stated: "There is not sufficient evidence" or "Such considerations as these incline me to lay very little weight. . . ." Thus Darwin limited any implied power that previous authors had given to such factors.

There is one further point regarding these causal factors: of the five factors recognized by Darwin, it is possible to make a distinction between what might be called *primary* and *secondary* causes of variation. The primary causes may be said to *initiate* variation in the first instance, while the secondary factors can bring about *further* variation only by acting upon

---

* As early as 1855 Darwin was making comparative weighings of the skeletons of wild and domestic non-flying ducks to determine the heritable effects of use and disuse. Between November 1856 and April 1857 (LL–II–86–91) Darwin searched the literature and performed experiments which led him to doubt the extent of such forms of variation.

variations produced through primary causes. Thus both the direct and indirect action of the conditions of life can be termed *primary* causes. Exposed to such influences, the organism is stimulated to generate variant forms. An organism, having once varied in some respect, is now subject to other factors which may bring about further change. For example, a change in one part may, under the principle of correlation, elicit a change in some other part; or, under the "law of balance," a change in one part of an organ system may elicit a *compensatory* change in another part of that same system. Additionally, the effects of habit, use, and disuse, being often inherited, can result in further permanent change. Although at this time Darwin did imply that these latter (secondary) factors merely amplify or extend existing characters, it was not until he went more deeply into the subject, from 1862 onward in preparing his *Variation of Animals and Plants under Domestication* (1868), that he clearly recognized the difference between such primary and secondary causes of variation.

NATURAL SELECTION AND THE CAUSES OF VARIATION

Darwin's inadvertent lumping together of all these causal factors in the first *Origin* was to result in considerable future difficulty. His shortsightedness in not seeing that some of these factors (the secondary) could do more than merely supply slight modifications was also to prevent him from seeing the internal difficulties he had unwittingly included in the first *Origin*. Darwin saw these causes (as in Figure 1.1) as merely providing simple variation to feed into the mechanism of natural selection. It was as if nature, through these particular causes, delivered up individual variation to yet another natural process by which the variants were made the basis for greater change—the basis of new populations, races, varieties, and ultimately species and beyond. In Darwin's view the compounding of (initial) variation into a distinct divergence from specific type was achieved

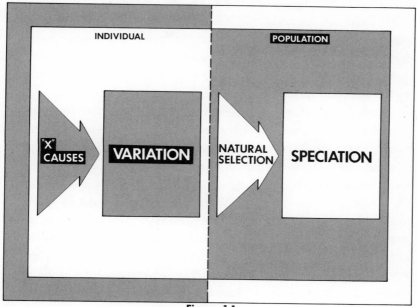

Figure 1.1

by a quite different and independent agent.* "My conclusion is that external conditions do extremely little, except in causing mere variability. This mere variability (causing the child *not* closely to resemble its parent) I look at as *very* different from the formation of a marked variety or new species. (No doubt the variability is governed by laws, some of which I am endeavouring very obscurely to trace.) The formation of a strong variety or species I look at as almost wholly due to the selection of what may be incorrectly called *chance* variations or variability."[21] This was in November 1856, and in the period before

* This holds true for either the Darwinian or the modern mechanism of speciation. For Lamarck, however, the compounding of initial variation did not require a separate or additional agent. "Conditions" not only initiated variation, but affected the whole population in the direction of change and could amplify this to the level of specific change. Additionally, the conditions or change in them (usually deleterious or uncomfortable) stimulated the organic spirit into an instinctive reaction which amplified these effects into greater permanent change. (See E. S. Russell, *Form and Function* [London: Murray, 1916], p. 219.)

the *Origin* the firm belief in the effects of these factors held by a considerable number of his contemporaries led Darwin to include them with separate sections of a whole chapter devoted to each.

REPLICATION, VARIATION, AND SELECTION

At the same time as he noted the necessity of inheritable variation, Darwin also saw the equal importance of the normal reproduction pattern of like producing like. These two phenomena, under the ever-present power of selection, provided the basis for the permanence of evolutionary change. (See Figure 1.2.) As the incipient species diverged (left to right in the diagram), moving at the same time through generations in time (top to bottom), so the change effected through the *tendency to variation* was rendered permanent through the *process of reproductive replication.* That selection was present is indicated by the fact that a straight line can be drawn from A to Z. Had the form "B" produced no variants, merely duplicating its original specific form (imagine the arrow between the Bs continued

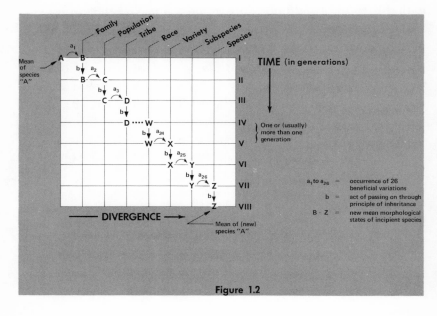

Figure 1.2

straight down the time axis), as no doubt it had, the species would not have remained adapted to the changing conditions of life. B may also have produced variations B_1, B_2, . . . , B_n, as well as C_1, . . . , C_n, or even, for that matter, D, E, or F. But only C had the requisite survival value under the given conditions (and was therefore selected). Thus, while these two natural phenomena (variation and replication) are prior to and necessary for the evolution of new specific forms, neither one alone is sufficient. The same applies to the process of natural selection. Only when the three are taken together can they effect specific change.

Darwin looked upon replication and variation as two separate phenomena. Both were universal processes occurring throughout organic nature, but producing nearly opposite effects. The process of replication was seen as moving relentlessly on, always duplicating exactly in one generation what had characterized the preceding one. Variation, on the other hand, was the natural tendency to depart, however slightly, from parental type. Variation was a phenomenon occurring in the body of an organism; replication was a peculiarity of the reproductive process. On the basis of this view, Darwin saw the two as clearly separate, arising from different and unrelated causes: variation prompted by forces external to the organism, replication from within. Of the two, replication was the more constant, for it would operate whether there was variation present or not, whereas variation was always subject to reproduction. Thus the general tendency in Figure 1.2 is for the species to move from A straight down the left-hand axis, reproducing itself accurately in each generation. This tendency is modified by the tendency toward the occasional production of inheritable variation. Were the variations not inheritable they would be represented as fluctuations to the right and left of the mean along the horizontal line marking that generation (as in normal somatic phenotypic variation), but the next generation would always follow the original specific type.

In summarizing the shortcomings of the first edition of the *Origin* it will be necessary to distinguish between, first, the assumptions of fact made by Darwin (or made by his contemporaries and recognized as fact by Darwin), and, second, the conclusions to which he was led from them. First the assumptions:

1. That there is much greater variability under domestication than in nature.
2. That the conditions of life can *indirectly* (by way of the reproductive elements) produce inheritable change in living organisms.
3. That the conditions of life can *directly* produce inheritable change in living organisms.
4. That habits continued over a number of generations (stimulated by some necessity arising out of change in conditions) can become permanent and inheritable.
5. That an organism can increase or enlarge any part through utilization of that part (or decrease it through disuse) and that such advances (or retrogressions) in the state of that part are inheritable.
6. That, on the Principle of Correlation of Growth, change or variation in one part can produce correlated change in other parts of the same organism and that the modified state is inheritable.
7. That on the Principle of Compensation (or Law of Balance) a change in one part of the organic substance necessitates a physical change in some other part of the same organism.
8. That saltative variations are extremely rare and nearly always detrimental to the individuals possessing them, besides being generally uninheritable.
9. That if organisms "be allowed freely to cross, any small tendency in them to vary will be constantly counter-

acted"[22] or present variations "would tend to blend together"[23] with the normal forms.

These are but the more important and fundamental examples
of like assumptions (many of rather doubtful validity) made by
Darwin throughout the *Origin*. They are of importance here
mainly for the conclusions to which they led Darwin with respect to the theory of natural selection:

1. That the determinants involved in the inheritability of
   any observed variation are simply a matter of the individual constitution.
2. That of the two basic phenomena in nature — the process
   of reproductive duplication of the parental features in
   the offspring, and the inheritable effects of external conditions — the latter could modify the course of the
   former.
3. That the only type of variation on which the process of
   natural selection need depend are the infinitesimally
   small inherited modifications known as individual differences.
4. That naturally fortuitous instances of physical separation
   or isolation are not necessary conditions for the operation
   of natural selection.
5. That there is no relation between the secondary causes
   of variation and the cause (or causes) which bring about
   eventual speciation.

All these conclusions will be seen, throughout the following
chapters, to have been of paramount importance in the development of Darwin's ideas about the processes of evolution. The
first, in particular, precluded Darwin's making any distinction
between purely somatic or phenotypic change and the more
profound germinal or genotypic change. Assuredly, there was
at the root of all this a fundamental ignorance of the true
mechanism of inheritance. But Darwin's conclusions drawn

as a result of his investigations into the causes of variation were to have the greatest effect in undermining his own idea of natural selection. When he recognized so many external factors as producing permanent inheritable effects, he opened a veritable Pandora's box of chimeras, most of which he was not to face until long after the *Origin*'s appearance—all this despite his avowal: "Over all these causes I am convinced that the accumulative action of Selection is by far the predominant Power."[24] Nevertheless, the other causes were there, and after 1859 it was to be a different story. The increases in size and number of page changes that would take place in the *Origin of Species* between 1859 and 1872 give some indication of what happened. Nearly every important change bearing on natural selection or its foundations was to arise out of criticisms pointing to weaknesses originating in the first edition. The story of Darwin's handling of his theory of natural selection after 1859 is one of documented qualification and nagging doubt.

2. *The Study of Inheritance*

*Darwin's attack on the problem of heredity was almost
as irresolute and confused as Mendel's had been bold and
perspicacious. He had accepted the lore and hearsay of
fanciers nearly as confidently as he had his own careful
observations. . . . Darwin apparently could not, even
for purposes of temporary study, make a clear-cut
separation in his mind between variations and natural
selection, as he could not make a separation between the
problem of heredity itself and his old preconceptions
regarding the influence of environment and of
use and disuse.*

—William Irvine, Apes, Angels, and Victorians

The subject of inheritance was confined to but a single
chapter in the first edition of the *Origin of Species.* That
new variations as well as extant characters were, for the most
part, inheritable was Darwin's sole concern in regard to genetic
theory at that time. His main intention had been to demonstrate
natural selection as the effective cause of speciation. Even his
discussion of the variations on which his theory depended
occupied but two chapters. All this was due to the necessary
abstracting that had arisen out of his rush into print. Having
had nearly three times as much material on each of the two
subjects in his notebook chapters, Darwin looked forward, on
completing the *Origin,* to devoting an entire work to the study

of variation and its causes. It was not until starting on the causes of variation during the preparation of his next work (*The Variation of Animals and Plants under Domestication*) that Darwin felt called upon to treat the subject of inheritance in some detail.

One can therefore distinguish two main periods in Darwin's thought on inheritance: that period from his earliest readings in the literature in 1837 to his beginning the chapter on inheritance for the *Variation* in 1862; and that from 1862 until 1865 when he completed his own hypothesis, "Pangenesis." The first was a formative period during which Darwin absorbed much of contemporary information on inheritance, incorporating it into his theory. The second was a period in which he actively pursued his own secondary investigations into the phenomena of inheritance. This chapter is concerned primarily with the first period, for the ideas gleaned then became not only an implicit part of the *Origin,* but formed as well the basis of Darwin's later research.

THE BACKGROUND STUDIES OF HEREDITY

The earliest of those hundreds of papers which Darwin read during his preparation of the *Origin* was that of Thomas Andrew Knight, written in 1799.[1] This first paper by Knight for the Royal Society was something of a landmark in the history of genetics. It not only gave a detailed description of dominance and reversion in the genus *Pisum* (Mendel's fruitful subjects), but was the first of a new tradition attempting to study such phenomena for their own sake as well as for their relationship to underlying principles of genetics. There were, at that time, hundreds of plant and animal breeders throughout Europe and their literature abounded with papers describing the anomalies resulting from breeding experiments. But these observations were purely descriptive, going no further than to record particular results from certain crossings. There were no speculations about more general principles, no attempts to uncover "laws" of inheritance. The writings reflected the prevailing notion that the only general law of inheritance was that like always generates like, with observed exceptions viewed merely as nature's own unpredictable irregularities.

The science of genetics as a discipline arose not out of any single biological science, but from many. The study of inheritance and related phenomena in the nineteenth century, as now, overflowed into several areas of knowledge; continuing advances in each increased the need for pure genetic research. While it was not until the last quarter of the nineteenth century that genetics came into its own as an independent discipline, it had been taken up as a study in itself as early as 1761 by Joseph Kolreuter in Germany and in 1799 by Knight in England. During the pre-*Origin* period the number of investigators in each area increased greatly, thereby offering numerous disparate sources of fresh observation and data.

The oldest fields providing information on genetics were those of plant and animal breeding. In terms of practical necessity it had become important for breeders to formulate empirical generalizations, from which predictions could be made on the results of certain matings. These guiding maxims accumulated gradually, as a sort of lore, and the closing decades of the eighteenth century saw the advent of a new group of naturalist experts: breeding specialists. Discoveries and techniques in fertilizing, grafting, hybridizing, etc., had all added to the accumulation of knowledge in the field. The need for such specialists stemmed therefore not only from the many problems it was felt they could solve, but from the growing advances and new discoveries whose significance it was their function to interpret, and from the conclusions they could pass on to the working breeder. A number of worthwhile and optimistic endeavors in the science of breeding had marked the beginning of the nineteenth century. In animal breeding these were exemplified by projects attempting (a) to increase the yield of best meat; (b) to increase both amount and types of wool; (c) to produce better work animals; (d) to breed better and faster race horses; and (e) to breed new and better kinds of domestic animals (dogs, cats, pigeons, etc.). In the cultivation of plants, attempts were directed toward (a) increasing size and yield of vegetable crops; (b) producing new plants and herbs for medicinal purposes; (c) producing new plants for dyeing purposes; and (d) cultivating new types of ornamental flowers. Thus the needs and problems of breeder and cultivator alike pointed to the desirability of discovering the basic principles governing heredity. Breeding itself, as an empirical craft, had to wait upon the new science of genetics for the knowledge that would raise it, too, to a science. With historical hindsight we can now see that the attempt to work from the empirical facts of breeding toward a comprehensive theory of heredity, without any real form of scientific method, would prove an impossible task. Yet without the great mass of accumulated data and descriptions from breeders and cultivators, later analysts and theoreticians (Darwin above all) could not have begun their work.

Another area which contributed genetic information and which was closely allied to biological science (whose more important practitioners were indeed academicians) was that of the hybridologists. The father of hybrid science was Joseph Kolreuter (1733–1806), whose introduction of scientific method into the study of breeding laid the cornerstone of genetic studies. His early and middle years had been taken up with other botanical research; it was his work on fertilization that led him to study inheritance. He kept lengthy and detailed records of all his experiments. Wherever possible, he quantified his descriptions of organic characters: measuring, weighing, and counting every individual in each generation. His conception of scientific method led to controlled experiments involving back-crosses as a test of genetic purity. Kolreuter's experiments revealed much on reversion, blending, dominance, and sterility. Continuing this work was his pupil, Karl Friedrich Gärtner (1771–1850). Gärtner performed some ten thousand crosses and produced 350 different hybrids. It was from the studies of these two men that Darwin was to draw most heavily. "The conclusions of such accurate observers as Gärtner and Kolreuter are of far higher worth than those made without scientific aim by breeders."[2] Kolreuter and Gärtner were the first in a long line of hybridologists, among whom Charles Naudin and Karl von Nägeli were outstanding. From them, too, Darwin later gathered helpful information.

Still further impetus was given to the study of heredity by those physiologists and physicians whose specialty was the reproductive system and the phenomenon of generation. Advances in basic physiology (including cell theory) spurred them into investigating the gap between the facts of inheritance and the laws of physiology.

Shortly after 1800 there arose from within the budding science of embryology a new field, teratology. Established by the elder St. Hilaire (Isidore Geoffroy), teratology was the study of the production of highly anomalous, monstrous forms. Its practitioners were both embryologists and morphologists, part of whose endeavor it was to seek the origins of such variations and the means by which they were produced. These unusual deviations from common types seemed to exemplify faulty heredity, yet St. Hilaire and his disciples (notably A. Moquin-Tandon and Camille Dareste) noticed that many of these abnormalities arose not through reproduction but during development and thus, they felt, were not of hereditary origin. Their observations and conclusions, absorbed by researchers on inheritance (Darwin among them), added to, and became part of, established scientific thought.

Further interest in genetic studies was aroused by medical practitioners who, like the breeders, felt a practical interest in the basic facts of heredity. There was no end to the number of diseases and pathological conditions thought to be inheritable. Ranging from syphilis, tuberculosis, and epilepsy to such conditions as hemophilia, albinism, birthmarks, etc., the list of such phenomena extended to include broader problems, for example, insanity, alcoholism, criminality, and moral degeneration. Among these same interested men were a number of statistically and genealogically conscious researchers. Their particular studies of sex ratios and longevity, as well as of more detailed phenomena, provided the factual raw material on which theories could be constructed and suggested regularities which these same theories would have to explain.

Finally, the work of taxonomists and field naturalists aided development of genetic study. From the beginning of the century the problems of description and classification pointed toward the necessity of understanding the causes and principles of organic variation. The rash of descriptive material covering thousands of newly described species recorded in the encyclopedic volumes of the previous century had resulted in ever-increasing difficulties in placing new species in relationship to old. Gaps between species had become so small and gradations so fine within many genera that taxonomic decisions seemed increasingly arbitrary. It was naturalists of the same type as Darwin (men like William Henry Herbert, Edward Blyth, Thomas Wollaston, and Wallace) who took up this problem. They came to feel that one must find a dynamic causal basis for taxonomy—a decision made at roughly the same time by a number of morphologists. Variations must, they felt, be studied as a class of phenomena, with their causal laws worked out. Wollaston's work of 1856, *On the Variation of Species,* must have been read with some trepidation by Darwin. It dealt, however, solely with variations and their precipitating causes and in fact it was of great help to Darwin, as his frequent citations show. It remained for Darwin and Wallace, investigating the same problems, to link speciation, variation, and inheritance in one study.

DARWIN'S VIEW OF INHERITANCE

Since our concern with studies on heredity lies in their relation to Darwin's thought, it will be best first to give a résumé of his general outlook, then to trace it to its sources.

Darwin's first concern was with variation. He was eager to show that variation (or some significant proportion of it) was inheritable. It was from this starting point (or rather with this goal in mind) that Darwin undertook his study of inheritance. His first question was: "Is a given character (or variation) inheritable?" Darwin had spoken of "the wide difference between the inheritance of a character and the power of transmitting it to crossed offspring."[3] He saw that the inheritability of a character was a different matter from its actual, effective transmission. For, as he himself had revealed,[4] an inheritable character was, in certain cases, not transmitted at all. Thus it would first be necessary to ascertain whether a particular character or variation was inheritable. Here, in the form of an axiom, Darwin offered a single answer: . . . "We are led to look at inheritance as the rule, and non-inheritance as the anomaly."[5] This, he felt, applied to new variations as well as to existing features. He noted "how strongly new characters of the most diversified nature, whether normal or abnormal, injurious or beneficial, whether affecting organs of the highest or most trifling importance, are inherited."[6]

If inheritance was the rule, Darwin speculated about the cause of its infrequent alternative, non-inheritance:

> A large number of cases of non-inheritance are intelligible on the principle, that a strong tendency to inheritance does exist, but that it is overborn by hostile or unfavourable conditions of life. . . .
>
> Many cases of non-inheritance apparently result from the conditions of life continually inducing fresh variability.[7]

For purely *a priori* reasons Darwin believed that the funda-

mental principle of inheritance was not unlike the first Newtonian law: that a character, once heritable, continues to be
inherited (exactly) through an infinitude of succeeding generations, unless acted upon by some external force. But, as
was true of the Newtonian laws, this described an ideal situation, whereas in nature there were always external influences
that could modify such a situation. The question of transmissibility came first, but after that, duplication would follow
on the grounds of this first genetic principle. Non-inheritance,
like non-transmissibility, presented no problems; it occurred
very rarely and it was "obvious that a variation which is not
inherited throws no light on the derivation of species."[8] Non-
duplication was a more important phenomenon; its causes were
to exact replication as the forces of friction were to Newton's
first law. A change in conditions, acting upon the normal
genetic motion of constant duplication, caused a change in
that action which resulted in variations in character. Without
such change, reproduction proceeded normally, and offspring
were identical to their parents.

Identity with parents, however, became difficult to interpret since the parents may differ between themselves in a
single character. In such cases, how would the offspring be
characterized? Where the parents were alike, the answer was
simple: under normal conditions, their offspring would be
identical to them. (See Figure 2.1.) Where the parents differed,
the principal result was that the offspring would be a blend
of the two.* There were, however, two not infrequently observed classes of exceptions recognized by Darwin. The first
was that of *dominance* (called by Darwin "prepotency"), a
condition in which one of the two parental characters for the
same feature totally masked the other. The second was *reversion,* to which Darwin assigned several causes. Blending or

---

* That the offspring could be at the same time both a blend of parental
characters, yet differ among themselves, was attributed to an uneven mixture
of the two parental characters.

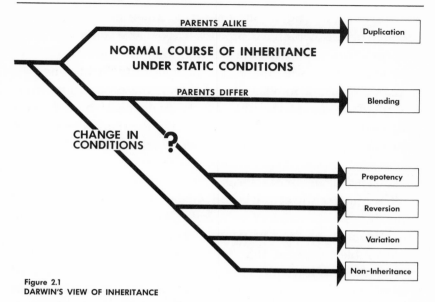

Figure 2.1
DARWIN'S VIEW OF INHERITANCE

duplication were the normal results of inheritance; they were altered only by the exceptions resulting from prepotency and reversion.

When the conditions of life changed, however, the reproductive system, so eminently sensitive and susceptible to such changes, was often rendered incapable of duplicating the characters of the preceding generation. One result was that the system quite often completely failed to pass on a variation or modification that had appeared in the previous generation.* Deviations fell into two categories. First, there were reversions. Brought on not only through the mating of parents of differing constitutions, they could equally be precipitated, Darwin felt, by the effect of changed conditions. Second were true variations, by far the largest class of deviations from normal inheritance due to changed conditions. Being unique—unlike any characteristic past or present—true variations were

* Darwin's belief here that non-inheritance (of acquired characters) was an infrequent exception to normal processes is a good indication of the strong place that inheritance of acquired characters, as a normal process, held in his theory.

the paramount result of abnormal inheritance. No other *product* of the hereditary process was of any import to Darwin, for none could be considered "true" variation. Yet the *action* of inheritance under certain conditions held some extremely important implications of which the process of blending stood foremost. For this (as is made clear here and in chapter 6) was felt by Darwin to be the normal result of inheritance; other results were merely exceptions.

SOURCES OF DARWIN'S IDEAS

The nineteenth century had opened with a strong legacy from the past: the almost universally held belief that offspring are a blended mixture of parental characteristics. Despite the considerable advances that had been made, both in outlook and in the sheer weight of accumulated information (toward a more complex understanding of the results of mating), that view remained current during the first half of the century. Darwin's belief in blending inheritance was certainly, therefore, in keeping with his times.

As has always been true, one finds within existing dogma the expression of quite contradictory views. It was on the eve of the new century, in 1799, that Knight reported his study of dominance. At that time, blending and dominance appeared to alternate in nature, with blending as the rule and dominance as its common exception. Why one parental character completely overmastered another in the offspring remained a mystery. The same feature in a different species, or a different feature in the same organism, was just as often a blend between the two parental characters. Dominance had merely been an empirical fact without any causal explanation.

Knight had crossed gray with white peas with the result that only gray progeny were produced. This was an obvious example of dominance, for he had performed numerous reciprocal crosses of families of gray peas with those of white and, in every case, there were only gray-pead progeny. However, when he crossed second-generation (hybrid) grays with white, white peas were produced. On the surface of things, he had been able to produce white as well as gray peas from gray-white matings. The presence of grays amid the white progeny (in the hybrid crossings) precluded the possibility that white may have merely alternated with gray as the prepotent character. The fact remained that the only time Knight obtained white peas from a gray-white cross was when the gray was a hybrid. His logical conclusion was that the gray hybrid must hold within it the power to produce white-pead offspring (ordinary gray-white crosses producing only gray) and that this power must therefore have come from the gray hybrid's white parent. It was not then a case of white becoming dominant, merely a case of gray not dominating under these conditions. In a much later paper,[9] Knight remarked that no matter how many times he crossed gray with white, crossing the resultant (hybrid) gray with white again, and so on, there never appeared any blend between the two: simply gray and white. Thus, as in his earlier experiments, he demonstrated the dominant power of gray over white seed color, at the same time showing that non-dominance need in no way imply blending. The appearance of characters latent in one of the parents had been the *only* observed alternative in gray-white crosses.*

It was not until 1822 that investigations similar to those of Knight were carried on. In that year Alexander Seton[10] and John Goss,[11] also working within the genus *Pisum*, reported non-dominance (due to segregation) in the second hybrid generation, preceded by dominance in the first. Goss had gone

---

* Darwin cited Knight's first paper several times in the *Variation* and, while noting his results concerning dominance and reversion, appears to have seen little bearing on the problem of blending. Outside of one paper by Knight in 1809, Darwin cited none of his other works, nor any of Seton or Goss, and none are found in the reprint collection. In the case of Knight, however (as Professor Conway Zirkle has indicated to the author), this is probably because Knight believed in superfoetation, the ability of a child to have more than a single biological father. Hence he misinterpreted the hereditary segregation that he described.

further than either Seton or Knight (up to that time), noting that while matings among white peas produced only white, all-blue matings yielded both blue and white, and continued blue-white matings produced always blue or white, never any intermediates. Knight's second paper on the subject, appearing in the following year, commented on the work of Seton and Goss, remarked on further experiments performed himself, and elaborated on his earlier findings.

From similar experiments with fruit, involving not one but five sets of characters, Augustin Sageret, in a memoir of 1826,[12] postulated that the first hybrid generation represented not a fusion of the genetic elements but a coexisting unblended combination. For him, the reappearance of non-hybrid parental types was proof of this simple unblended combination followed by segregation. Though he adopted a number of Sageret's detailed findings, Darwin had not been impressed with Sageret's speculations.

Despite the implication of these experiments that blending never seemed to enter into—much less overtake or obliterate—the results of numerous distinct crosses, the general belief in blending continued. This was no doubt to a great extent due to the fact that these papers were part, not of a genetic, but of a horticultural tradition. Thus the above works lost much of their wider significance due to their inclusion among a mass of strictly botanical works. This lack of a special genetically oriented literature—itself a reflection of the absence of a common, unified field of endeavor—greatly inhibited the promulgation of hereditary information (the same difficulty which Mendel's work of 1865 faced). Hence there was much duplication and little advancement among independent workers during the first half of the century. Nevertheless, investigations continued—particularly those which sought some regularity, some pattern to the character of dominance. The search was frustrated by innumerable complexities. From one feature to another within the same organism, from the same feature within species of the same genus, one could not predict when prepotency would occur. No one could say without prior empirical knowledge whether a given character in any single species would predominate or not. The researchers' lack of success was partly attributable to the nature of their approach, which arose out of their more general view of prepotency in its empirical context.* They looked upon blending and dominance less as isolated generative phenomena than as events thoroughly enmeshed on an observational level, hopefully related to other observable regularities. They hoped to demonstrate, within such large biological groups as classes, etc., that particular characters, and *sets* of characters,† were usually or always dominant, oftentimes related to sex. Thus, they sought uniformities and correlations which unfortunately did not exist.

These workers had started out on this most optimistic of levels—not with single, reasonably well-defined characters, but with whole sets and systems—partly because biological lore, that voluminous legacy from the past, pointed in that direction. Linnaeus himself believed that the external characters of the male predominated over those of the female. It was in searching for such rules as this, which transcended any limitations of race, species, or even of classes, that the various groups of researchers began their attack on heredity.

There were, however, some investigators who approached the problem within a single species hoping that by lowering their aim they would thus achieve a stricter, and therefore a predictable, regularity. One of these was John Lawrence, a horse breeder, who, in a work of 1829,[13] tried to pinpoint prepotency of features in the horse according to sex. In his attempt he did find many regularities whose application yielded some useful and practical information. But far more common were work-

* And partly because even today it is impossible, without prior experimental knowledge, to know whether a given feature is dominant over its genetic alternative.

† That is, in terms of systems (reproductive, digestive), or in terms of areas of the body (external vs. internal characters, etc.).

ers like Alexander Walker, who, in his book *Intermarriage* (1838),[14] assigned dominance according to sex to whole organ systems, body areas, etc., that would hold for the entire class of mammals, including man. Others following in the same tradition—such as J. Orton in his *Physiology of Breeding* (1854)[15]— although starting with the correct basic idea that "there is no casual blending of the parts and qualities of the two parents, but that each parent contributes to the formation of certain structures," nevertheless went off in quite unfruitful directions. Orton saw each feature as an "either-or" choice between those of the two parents; and, unlike nearly all his predecessors, Orton stated the basis for his presumptions.[16] Noting that various parts and various systems originated from distinct sources in the embryonic state (from each of the three main germ layers), he stated his feeling that this was the connection between whole sets of characters, each germ layer having been contributed by one of the two parents. That the different germ layers had separate sexual origins, he felt, was the reason that dominance seemed to follow sexual lines.

But already by the late 1840s the usefulness of all these endeavors was being seriously called into question. In 1847 Dr. Prosper Lucas' massive two-volume treatise[17] covering nearly every aspect of the research on problems of heredity pointed out the severe limitations and masses of exceptions facing nearly every so-called rule that had thus far been postulated with regard to animals. In 1849, Gärtner, in his equally extensive botanical work,[18] echoed similar feelings with regard to plants. From his extensive readings of the latter works, Darwin could see by 1862 that little had been established in the way of general rules governing prepotency. It seemed as unpredictable and irregular as ever.

REVERSION AND PREPOTENCY

As indicated, Darwin believed blending to be the normal result of inheritance, although at the same time he recognized both reversion and prepotency as common exceptions.

When two breeds are crossed their characters usually become intimately fused together; but some characters refuse to blend, and are transmitted in an unmodified state either from both parents or from one.[19]

Darwin described three forms of reversion. First, there was "Reversion to lost Characters by pure or uncrossed Forms."[20] That is, the parents as well as the immediate progenitors were alike, but the offspring differed from them in presenting a character possessed at one time by a long-removed ancestor.

Second, there was "Reversion to Characters derived from a Cross."[21] In Darwin's own words: "When two races or species are crossed there is the strongest tendency to the reappearance in the offspring of long-lost characters, possessed by neither parent nor immediate progenitor."[22] Thus far, reversion involved the reappearance of a *long-lost* character; the two cases above differed only in that in one case the reversion appeared from within a "pure" strain, while in the other it appeared among a first hybrid generation. In the former case Darwin assigned as cause a change in conditions; in the latter he thought it due to the trauma of having two widely differing constitutions thrown together in a single individual.

Darwin went on to describe a third form of reversion:

Another form of reversion is far commoner, indeed is almost universal with the offspring from a cross, namely, to the characters proper to either pure parent-form. As a general rule, crossed offspring in the first generation are nearly intermediate between their parents, but the grandchildren and succeeding generations continually revert, in a greater or lesser degree, to one or both of their progenitors.[23]

Prepotency, therefore, meant the persistence of one parental character in the *following* generation; reversion, its persistence when separated by one or more generations. That prepotency was, in fact, the tendency to revert, thereby overcoming the normal and ever-present tendency to blend, is illustrated by the following comment:

> When two distinct races are crossed, it is notorious that the tendency in the offspring to revert to one or both parent-forms is strong, and endures for many generations.[24]

In addition to his historical researches on prepotency and reversion, Darwin performed a number of his own crosses involving the two phenomena. The earliest of these were his crossings of several varieties of pigeon in 1855–56. In these crossings, he simply established an order of prepotency in a number of feather types and similar markings. As a result of this and his readings of other cases, sometime between 1856 and 1862, Darwin formulated his "rule of prepotency": "that a character which is present in one form and latent in the other is generally transmitted with prepotent force when the two forms are crossed."[25] In an experiment which he thought might confirm this rule, Darwin undertook, between 1863 and 1865, to breed *Antirrhinum*. From his own botanical knowledge (and supported by Moquin-Tandon earlier), Darwin believed that "plants bearing peloric or regular flowers have a strong latent tendency to reproduce their normally irregular flowers."[26] Following, then, from his "rule," he bred the peloric with the normal, zygomorphic form. Of the ninety hybrid offspring, all had irregular flowers, none were peloric. His crosses having been reciprocal, he concluded that irregular flower structure was prepotent over peloric—a demonstration of the applicability of his rule. Yet, when he bred the hybrid non-peloric *Antirrhinum* (through self-fertilization) one-fourth of the resultant offspring were peloric! His conclusion was that "the tendency to pelorism appeared to gain strength by the intermission of a generation," and that prepotency was a subject of such extreme intricacy that it was "not surprising that every one hitherto has been baffled in drawing up general rules on the subject."[27]

Prepotency and reversion, while recognized as exceptions to

the more general phenomenon of blending, were nevertheless felt by Darwin to be transient in their effects. Throughout his writings prepotency is represented as a quality, a quality of power or force. It had, in Darwin's view, a kind of genetic momentum which he felt would gradually decay in following generations. The result would be a uniformity of character due to the inevitable tendency to blend. As reversion was the manifestation of prepotency, it too (in most of its forms) would eventually cease. In his summation on prepotency and reversion, Darwin discussed the eventual extinction of these forces.

> No one supposes that less than three generations suffices, and most breeders think that six, seven or eight are necessary, and some go to still greater lengths. But neither in the case of a breed which has been contaminated by a single cross, nor when, in the attempt to form an intermediate breed, half-bred animals have been matched together during several generations, can any rule be laid down how soon the tendency to reversion will be obliterated. It depends on the difference in the strength or prepotency of transmission in the two parent-forms, on their actual amount of difference, and on the nature of the conditions of life to which the crossed offspring are exposed.[28]

While blending may not have been the sole or necessary result of the crossing of distinctly different individuals *in any single generation,* it certainly seemed to Darwin to be the eventual result of continued reproduction. Though the prepotent power of a character may overbear that of blending in the first or any other single generation, the latter was the more general, more common result of reproduction. Blending was the ever-present force while prepotency was a power which gradually and eventually decayed.

Darwin had seen this for himself, at first hand, in his breeding of *Antirrhinum.* The first hybrid generation showed 100 per cent prepotency. The second (exhibiting dominant monohybrid segregation) showed that the prepotent power of zygomorphism had diminished to approximately 75 per cent.* Darwin admitted that it was anybody's guess as to how long it would take to achieve complete obliteration of the prepotency in question. This was because he felt that the power of prepotency could have its motive force revived through new crossings or changes in conditions. But its eventual decay was certain. A uniform blend of the original parental characters remained a foregone conclusion: the decay of prepotency and the supremacy of blending were both equally inevitable.

TRUE VARIATION

Though the nature of variation will be discussed in chapter 3, and its causes in chapter 4, something can be said here of the sources of Darwin's belief in the several causes of variation.

In the broadest sense, variation was the result of all but the normal processes of heredity. That is to say, the forces of blending, prepotency, and reversion all resulted in producing dissimilarity between offspring and parent, as well as among the offspring themselves. Such dissimilarity could, in this sense, be considered "variation." The phenomenon of variation in its more limited sense was, however, entirely different. The former effects in no way represented the appearance of real novelty save in the very limited sense of contrasting one generation with a preceding one. True variation was unique in its appearance. In the matter of understanding of the overall phenomenon of variation, none of the other factors (blending, etc.) supplied any knowledge of the real causes of difference; to account for dissimilarities by such mechanisms meant, for Darwin, that "we thus only push the difficulty further back in time, for what made the parents or their progenitors different?"[29] It was plain

---

*From a first hybrid generation of 90 plants, Darwin obtained, through self-fertilization, 127 offspring among which were 88 zygomorphic, 2 intermediate, and 37 peloric forms. Darwin had not started these experiments until after November 1862 (ML–I–212) and it is doubtful that he could have finished until 1864–65.

that the study of real variation and its causes was of far greater importance to Darwin than the general study of inheritance and the other, secondary sources of genetic dissimilarity. It is historical fact that Darwin's researches into inheritance came only after he had felt the need to set variation into its proper genetic context, a task which he felt he could perform in the second volume of the *Variation.*

As mentioned in the first chapter, Darwin recognized five causes of variation in 1859: Direct Effect of Conditions; Indirect Effect of Conditions; Habit, Use, and Disuse; Correlation; Compensation. None of these were original with Darwin nor were they original in the sources from which he derived them.

Direct Effect: The fact that certain environmental factors could directly produce change in the individuals living under them had been described in great detail throughout the pages of both Knight and Prosper Lucas, two of Darwin's most quoted sources. Both works went into such details as the nature of food, food excess, qualities of sunlight, temperature, soil—with the resultant changes in each case ascribed to the direct effects of these conditions. The heritability of such changes had been assumed by those authors as well as by Darwin. Lucas, however, had prefaced his work with a belief that all variation arose spontaneously, yet his encyclopedic work listed so many instances of the factors producing variation that Darwin exclaimed marginally: "He gives so much on following pages to external conditions that I know not what is left for his spontaneity!"[30]

Indirect Effect: It was the teratologists, specifically St. Hilaire (1832)[31] and Moquin-Tandon (1841)[32] who stressed variation as the indirect result of environmental conditions. They had been struck by the non-specific responses of variation to such conditions, a fact which indicated to them that these conditions acted upon the reproductive and developmental faculties to produce variation. They, as well as Darwin, saw this not as an alternative, but as an addition to the direct effects.

Habit, Use, and Disuse: The origins of a belief in the inherited effects of use and disuse extend too far back in time to trace specifically.[33] The first author to whom Darwin referred on this subject was Isidore Geoffroy St. Hilaire,[34] but the unavowed influence of Lamarck on the same subject was no doubt of considerable significance.* Nearly every author to whom Darwin had access accepted without much reservation the fact that such effects were inheritable.

Correlation and Compensation: In the same way, neither the principle of correlation nor that of compensation was original with Darwin. Darwin directly attributed the principle of correlation to Cuvier's principle of connections: "All the organs of an animal form a single system, the parts of which hang together and act and re-act upon one another; and no modifications can appear in one part without bringing about corresponding modifications in all the rest."[35]

Darwin first attributed the law of compensation to St. Hilaire, later pointing out the latter's debt to Goethe, who first stipulated: "To no part can anything be added without something being taken away from another part, and vice versa."[36]

Every one of the causes of variation recognized by Darwin had had its empirical validity upheld for nearly half a century by the time he included them in the first *Origin.*

Darwin's views on inheritance at the time of the first *Origin* reflected those of his contemporaries. Indeed, his were primarily an amalgamation of theirs; there was little contribution of his own. Those principles which he incorporated into his own beliefs were nearly all accepted on the testimony and evidence of some researcher.

---

* Darwin had read Lamarck a number of times, and reports in his autobiography that in his student days he had been much struck by Lamarck, having been introduced to his views by Dr. Robert Grant. Though he rejected much of Lamarck as nonsense (i.e. the *sentiment intérieur*), he did accept the inheritance of acquired characters (while not original with Lamarck) through Lamarck's works.

Darwin's recognition of prepotency and reversion as alternatives to blending in any single generation, together with his rejection of the effects of both as ultimately transient, left blending still a force whose effects ran counter to selection. His acceptance of such causes of variation as the direct effect of conditions, habit, use, disuse, correlation, and compensation influenced his view of heredity. Variations acquired during the lifetime of an organism seemed to have originated through processes quite independent of those of inheritance. For Darwin looked upon inheritance as the act of transmission, the perpetuation through duplication of whatever had come before. His interest lay, therefore, not so much in the processes of inheritance as in their resultant products. Even among these, he was concerned only with such as represented true deviations from type, as opposed to those differences which represented merely reversion to former types, predominations of a single type, or varying blends of parental types. In short, his concern was with variations from specific form, not with the differences exhibited between individuals of one generation from those of another. It was these latter dissimilarities that appeared to be more closely associated with the process of inheritance and the factors whose operation modified it. By restricting his interest to true variation he had, in a sense, drawn away from inheritance proper. Having shown the normal outcome of inheritance, including the fact that his required type of variation was inheritable, he went on to construct his own hypothesis (pangenesis) by which he hoped to account not only for those aspects of genetic phenomena operative in his theory, but for all known genetic phenomena. In adopting this procedure, Darwin was, for the moment, forgetting that blending was a process through which his variations would have to pass.

As will be pointed out again in a later chapter, Darwin's growing belief that the greater part of evolutionary variation originated through the indirect effects of external conditions on the reproductive system was to bring him closer to the problem of blending. For in the years following the publication of his work on variation, as he came less to accept the theory of directly acquired change in favor of that indirectly acquired, so he came to see the process of change as intimately involved with that of inheritance. Blending was the normal result (as he himself had pointed out) of that process. Chapter 6 is concerned with inheritance and the problem of blending after 1862.

3. The Nature of Variation

Darwin side-stepped this problem. He simply accepted without explanation the observed fact that organisms do vary one from another. He did not distinguish between inheritable and non-inheritable variations. Darwin's problem was the action of Natural Selection in the formation of new species, given a variable progenitor.

—*Edward O. Dodson,* Evolution: Process and Product

A brief glance at the first five chapters of the *Origin* reveals that the advantageous variations in natural organisms constituted for Darwin the raw material for the process of natural selection. Since the creation of a new species is achieved by means of accumulative selection of these variations, an understanding of the nature of such changes, and of the forces which produce them, is of paramount importance in gaining a clear understanding of the process of natural selection itself.

Because we are aware today of the distinction between the germinal (or genotypic) and the somatic (or phenotypic) cellular divisions of every living organism, these two types of organic variability can be readily distinguished.

Germinal variations, first of all, are those which occur in the actual genetic constitution (genotype). Since the genotype determines the direction of individual development, variations within the genotype reveal themselves in the observable physical constitution (phenotype) of the organism.

Somatic variations are those which occur in the phenotype. The greatest number of variations in the phenotype are strictly somatic in their origin, having been acquired by the organism during its lifetime. Since it is only the genotype that is passed on in the act of reproduction, these phenotypic variations are transient: they die with the individual. A number of phenotypic variations, however, have their origins in underlying genotypic change.

From the modern vantage point it can thus be seen that the category of phenotypic variation includes two distinct forms of change: variation of strictly somatic origin and variation emanating from genotypic change.

In the modern view, the principle of natural selection operates upon all variation manifest in an organism's structure or function. Thus selection operates on the phenotype. Whether selection can, over time, compound these changes into the total divergence implied in speciation depends upon the inheritability of these changes. Since only the genotype is transmitted, natural selection can be effective for speciation only when it is rooted in genotypic change.

The formulation of the distinctions noted above had not been made in Darwin's lifetime. On the other hand numerous biologists were beginning, as the result of individual researches, to make similar distinctions.

DARWIN'S VIEW OF VARIATION

To understand Darwin's attitude regarding the nature of variation one must begin with his general views on the principles of variation and the phenomena of inheritance. To begin with, *inheritance* meant to Darwin merely the transmission of parental characters to the next generation. Inheritance implied *transmissibility*—a mysterious attribute[1] associated with each character, but without any correlation between this capacity and the nature of the character itself. On the basis of this some-what unfortunate distinction, most characters were inherit-able.[2] This meant that every character either was transmis-sible or it was not: there was no alternative. For Darwin's theory declared: " . . . any variation which is not inherited [transmissible] is unimportant."[3] The process of variation was never associated with inaccurate or imperfect transmission.

At the purely empirical level on which he gathered his facts and drew his conclusions (and guided by his particular view of inheritance), Darwin recognized two classes of variation: indi-vidual differences and saltations.*

Individual differences, which in normal reproduction dis-tinguish offspring from parent as well as from each other, were viewed by Darwin as merely *modifications.* That is to say, from certain causes† the parental character becomes slightly modi-fied in the offspring. In such cases the difference between orig-inal character and variant is slight. This lack of disparity between the two is what Darwin meant by these being "con-tinuous" variations. They were variations upon a theme rather than an outright change in theme (character) itself. The term is perhaps more clearly understood when contrasted with those "discontinuous" variations, saltations. The latter were seen as complete breaks in character between parent and offspring. Here was something new—a sudden and distinct *change*—not a modification. Thus, in Darwin's view, just as the phenomenon of inheritance revolved around the question of transmission, so the principle of variation was a matter of continuity or discontinuity in form.

Though Darwin employed at least ten terms in referring to organic variation, he distinguished between only two basic

---

* Darwin was not always consistent in his use of the term *variation.* In some places he refers to all deviations from normal as *variations;* in others he distin-guishes between *variation* and *saltation.* In the latter instances it is clear that he is referring to "slight" vs. "great" forms of variation.

† Darwin listed the causes following his chapters on variation, and these are treated in the next chapter.

types. These were *continuous* variations, which he most often called "individual differences," and *discontinuous* variations, to which he most often applied the term "saltations." In each category, however, he frequently used a number of synonyms:

continuous	*discontinuous*
difference	saltation
modification	monstrosity
deviation	jump
change	sport
anomaly	

The synonymous terms in the class of continuous variation were often qualified by such adjectives as "slight," "small," "infinitesimal," and "individual"—all indicating their continuity with parental features. In the same sense, the term "discontinuous" meant for Darwin a variation totally unlike anything characterizing parent or progenitor. In all cases, they were jumps of a highly anomalous nature.*

With historical hindsight it can now be seen that Darwin's view of organic variation was based on his observation of phenotypes. We know now that such a limitation obscures any distinction between two fundamentally different types of variation.

What Darwin had before him was the full spectrum of natural variation. The mutations recognized today as forming the material basis for the theory of natural selection would have been indistinguishably sprinkled over one area of that spectrum. Because of the inherent limitations of the empirical view, the terms Darwin did use to categorize this variation bore only a marginal relationship to the more fundamental source of genetic change.

Since the efficacy of natural selection so manifestly depends upon the variation it compounds, a vital part of Darwin's post-*Origin* thought revolves around this issue.

Darwin rarely mentioned saltations in the *Origin*. This was not solely because he had been able to demonstrate speciation

* See chapter 1, page 10.

by the selection of individual differences alone, but because he had tried saltation as a possible source of evolutionary change and had found it wanting.

At first Darwin felt that all variation, so long as it was inheritable, was suitable material for selection and therefore for speciation. He soon came to see the difficulties inherent in the selection of monstrous forms. Apparently inheritability itself was no guarantee that any such variation could be employed for speciation.

Darwin began by treating "monstrosity" as a term nearly synonymous with "saltation." Consistency was of little concern since both were "discontinuous," and Darwin used all three interchangeably. The main point was that they were sudden, abrupt, highly anomalous breaks in the chain of organic continuity. Darwin was to build his theoretical edifice on what he felt were firmer foundations. Later, after the *Origin* appeared, he would be pressed by his critics into a greater elaboration of his reasons for rejecting saltations.

First, he believed monstrosities (or saltations) were generally sterile. Second, if not sterile, they were usually traumatic in their effects and rarely advantageous. Third, while not uncommon to the domestic state, they were extremely rare in nature. Fourth, existing adaptation and organic complexities were not explicable by saltation. Finally, there were no cases in which a monstrosity or saltation appearing in one form resembled a normal structure in an allied form.

Thus the *Origin* was written from a firm base of opposition to saltation or any other form of discontinuous variation as suitable material for the natural selection process, but with an equally firm commitment to the natural selection of individual differences.

THE INITIAL ATTACKS ON DARWIN'S VIEW

Criticism of Darwin's stand on variation came before the *Origin* had appeared. After his first reading of an advance copy, Huxley, with his usual perspicacity, said: "You have loaded yourself with an unnecessary difficulty in adopting *natura non facit saltum* so unreservedly."[4] He was warning his friend not only that the statement itself contradicted fact but, more important, that here was an additional source by which to explain the evolutionary process, so that he need not so restrict himself. Huxley was puzzled to know why, if inheritable saltation did exist, Darwin's selection theory shouldn't make use of it. He continued by reasoning that if one believes in the general effectiveness of selection, then advantages of any kind (whether saltative in origin or not) would be selected. Furthermore, the net advances of large or small jumps would be to accelerate a process which would otherwise take much longer if limited to *only* very slight modifications. On such grounds as these Huxley felt that one could not pass over saltations. Since most of Huxley's letter was given to praise and expressions of admiration, his remark on saltation appeared more a warning than a criticism. Whatever Darwin's interpretation, he ignored Huxley's comment, making no reply to the question in his return letter. This aloofness may itself have had some effect on Huxley, since he was never one to let pass what he personally felt to be an important oversight. He was, after all, the "bulldog of Darwinism," a vociferous and energetic combatant of public criticism. His own reservations must therefore go on record and so, in his own review of the *Origin* that April, Huxley stated:

> Mr. Darwin's position might, we think, have been even stronger than it is if he had not embarrassed himself with the aphorism, "Natura non facit saltum" which turns up so often in his pages. We believe, as we have said above, that Nature does make jumps now and then, and a recognition of the fact is of no small importance in disposing of many minor objections to the doctrine of transmutation.[5]

The rest of the review was eminently fair and favorable. Huxley was acutely aware of the still larger task of convincing many people of the general efficacy of the theory of natural selection to explain evolutionary process. His unity with Darwin far outweighed this minor disparity of viewpoint, so that his few critical comments seemed lost amid his outpouring of enthusiastic support.

Comment in the closing months of 1859 and throughout most of 1860 was concerned principally with the matter of overall acceptance of the *Origin of Species*. Nearly all the non-scientific arguments were based on a rather logically backward approach to the problem. These critics started by drawing out the various social, anthropological, and theological implications of Darwin's theory; then, finding these subjective extrapolations tantamount to sacrilege wherever they touched upon accepted ideas, they rejected the Darwinian theory on the grounds that nothing was possible if it contradicted known truths. Nothing could be true if it implied such things as man's kinship to apes and other "soulless" animals, creation without God, or a justification of a merciless competitive struggle for existence. Such a doctrine could never be true if it ran counter to so many established truths, whose validity, they felt, had been demonstrated by centuries of acceptance.

The immediate scientific arguments were also of an equally broad and general nature, which, in the case of many individual scientists, merged deeply and almost imperceptibly into a religious context.[6] The strictly scientific grounds adduced against the theory dealt mainly with evidence from the geological and paleontological record and the subsidiary question of the amount of time involved.

Yet even among the good-sized core of scientists who inclined toward a belief in Darwin's theory, there seemed to be, in 1860, some nagging questions concerning the nature and size of variations, doubts which would soon be paralleled among the anti-Darwinians.

Although Darwin had apparently passed over Huxley's admonition, there appeared on February 18 in *Gardener's Chronicle* an article so strongly worded and going so far in behalf of speciation by way of monstrous variation that Darwin could no longer ignore the issue. The author of the article was Professor William Henry Harvey, whom Darwin had included among his earliest adherents.

Harvey stated in no uncertain terms that speciation could be effected by jumps or saltations. Further, he said, these jumps were so extremely large and divergent that speciation could be effected in a single leap! He cited a case of monstrous *Begonia* sufficiently unlike its normal counterpart to be classified a separate species. Two other cases were given, accompanied by a claim that more could be cited.

To a certain extent, Darwin was vulnerable from the start. Having dismissed the idea of *speciation* "per saltum," Darwin had also neglected to give some recognition to the fact that many *individual forms* do arise in this manner. Any remark about saltations that he made usually referred only to their possible utility in speciation. Those monstrous forms to which he did allude, he said, were "frequent under domestication but extremely rare under nature."[7] This is clearly a rejection, not an oversight, of the role of monstrous forms in natural speciation. Many of Darwin's readers, whose reading comprehension was no doubt inhibited by their anxiety to join the "free-for-all" against Darwinism, could not accept this.

Harvey's criticism, however, went beyond this obvious and superficial level. He had said not only that speciation took place by means of monstrosities, but that it could be effected equally by means of jumps or saltations of less divergent nature. He was, in fact, making the distinction which Darwin had not made. But the cogency of his criticism was lessened by two factors.

First, in his use of examples Harvey overstressed speciation in a single jump, and (like Darwin) he did not place sufficient emphasis upon the less divergent saltations.

Second, J. D. Hooker's reply in the following number of the *Chronicle*[8] rendered most of Harvey's remarks beside the point.

He attacked Harvey on two grounds: first, that the *Begonia* case in particular was doubtful if it intended to demonstrate the creation of a new *species*. He doubted if any of the cases would be so classified and concluded (rather wittily) by pointing out that a monstrous *Begonia* "would still, no doubt in all details, be a *Begonia*."⁹ His second ground, though not itself entirely to the point, was that speciation "per saltum," even if admitted, in no way denied a theory of natural selection. It was a gross misconception on Harvey's part, said Hooker, to assume, if speciation *could* occur through saltation, that through some form of exclusion it could not occur by natural selection of smaller differences.

Darwin may have been impressed, but he remained unshaken.

> As the *Origin* now stands, Harvey's is a good hit against my talking so much of the insensibly fine gradations; and certainly it has astonished me that I should be pelted with the fact that I had not allowed abrupt and great enough variations under nature. It would take a good deal more evidence to make me admit that forms have often changed by *saltum*.¹⁰ *

He had missed Harvey's point (though Harvey's own exposition was partly to blame) and continued using the terms "monstrosities" and "saltations" interchangeably. He thought enough of Harvey's remarks, however, to send a copy to Lyell.

> I send by this post an attack in the *Gardener's Chronicle*, by Harvey (a first-rate Botanist, as you probably know). It seems to me rather strange; he assumes the permanence of monsters, whereas, monsters are generally sterile, and not often inheritable. But grant his case, it comes that I have

---

* Having been thoroughly aware of the difficulties of saltation and having foreseen an attack if he dared to include them in his process of speciation, Darwin had carefully avoided them altogether. Little wonder he was so shocked to find himself reproved for not having included them!

been too cautious in not admitting great and sudden variations. Here again comes in the mischief of my abstract.[11]

The extent of Darwin's admission here would not be entirely
clear if judged on the basis of this letter alone. Together with
his stand throughout the year, however, it indicates his realization that if he had devoted more space to the appearance of
monstrous forms in *individual* cases, while yet denying the possibility of their employment in the process of speciation, he
would have saved himself some tiresome explanation.

The effect of Hooker's reply was to stiffen Darwin's previous
attitude. In view of Hooker's support from the field of botany,
Darwin was less than ever convinced by the arguments for
saltation as agent of speciation. Here was scientific support, not
merely arguing speculatively as to whether or not saltation
could be selected, but declaring that saltation was not of itself
sufficient cause for the production of a new species. In any case,
Darwin remained unswerving in his view regarding saltations
and monstrosities simply from the fact that he was never aware
of any distinction between the two; Hooker's reply did nothing,
moreover, to convince Darwin of his misunderstanding.

The problem of speciation by saltation was to arise again
in only a few weeks' time—in America. On March 8, the American botanist Asa Gray read to the Boston Scientific Club a paper
on the axiom "Natura non agit saltatem."[12] Gray's botanical
training and vast firsthand knowledge of variation led him to
see the difficulties attached to speciation based on either monstrosities or individual differences. He was rather skeptical about
the practical accumulability of individual differences. As he said
in his review of the *Origin:* "These variations are supposed to be
mere oscillations from a normal state, and in Nature to be limited if not transitory."[13] He was equally skeptical about speciation by saltation for reasons somewhat similar to those of
Darwin. Whereas Darwin relied entirely upon individual differences as the basis of speciation, Gray's rejection of such differ-

ences led him to search for a middle ground, an alternate source of variation. Thus, while generally believing that "Natura non agit saltatem," he said he did not "suppose that Nature makes no distinct steps at all, but only *short steps—*not *infinitely fine gradation!*" Gray was the only man at this time who saw distinctions among individual differences, saltations, and monstrosities. Like a number of other field naturalists of the period, he knew from a sort of "intuitive-induction" two fine but important points: first, that far more often than not, real changes in species were step-like changes: small, perhaps, but nevertheless distinct and discontinuous; second, that there exists a definite, though in many cases indistinctly known, limit to "individual" variations in any single direction. Although this paper was never published, it was to be partly responsible for precipitating a series of debates in the foremost scientific circle in America, the Academy of Science. It is also an indication that Gray, Darwin's foremost American adherent (in a role similar to that of Huxley), had equally similar reservations regarding the nature of variation. But Gray, again like Huxley, was a defender of the evolutionary faith and although he had doubts on many points, he found himself closely allied to the Darwinians. This may be attributed not only to his general scientific accord with evolution, but also to his stand in opposition to Professor Agassiz.[14]

Agassiz's position as the foremost zoologist at Harvard, together with his great national popularity, made him, more than any other single man, the voice of science in America. Harvard, the dominant scientific institution in America, was to be the scene of the great debate on evolution. Agassiz had been leveling strongly worded attacks against Darwinism since the *Origin* appeared. For decades before the *Origin* he had been an aggressive anti-mutationist in the matter of the creation of species. While a number of other reputable scientists allied themselves with him, there was nevertheless a small core of highly reputable but less ostentatious naturalists (among them Gray) whose belief in Darwinism led them to oppose Agassiz. In these circumstances, Agassiz's attacks, long unanswered in the public arena, finally brought on a formal, but open, debate. A special meeting of the American Academy of Sciences had been called (in Boston) for March 27. No one had to wait those three weeks, however, for on March 13, five days after Gray's paper, Agassiz broke out in a further polemic against Darwin on the nature of variation.[15]

Agassiz's own axe which he had been grinding (both before, and now even more agitatedly since, the appearance of the *Origin*) was his view regarding the general permanence of species, with the occasional introduction, at different epochs, of new ones. As a geologist, Agassiz was, like many others of his generation, a catastrophist.[16] The earth, in this view, had undergone a series of great and abrupt changes. These cataclysms, so amply evidenced in the earth's strata, often destroyed all (or nearly all) the living forms; after each destruction, in single acts of creation, new species were introduced by the Creator. Both geological and paleontological records were brought forward to support this view. To Agassiz, species surviving such catastrophes continued to reproduce their kind without any fundamental modifications *in the form of the species itself.* Thus "species" to him was a clearly discernible concept; it was a true and unvarying form.

> Whatever views are correct concerning the origin of species, one thing is certain, that as long as they exist, they continue to produce, generation after generation, individuals which differ from one another only in such peculiarities as relate to their individuality. The great defect in Darwin's treatment of the subject of species lies in the total absence of any statement respecting the features that constitute individuality. Surely, if individuals may vary within the limits assumed by Darwin, he was bound first to show that individuality does not consist of a sum of hereditary character-

istics, combined with variable elements, not necessarily transmitted, in their integrity, but only of variable elements. Whatever minor differences may exist between the products of this succession of generations all are *individual peculiarities,* in no way connected with the essential features of the species, and therefore as transient as the individuals; while the specific characters are forever fixed. These individual differences, with all the monstrosities that may have occurred, during these countless generations, have passed away with the individuals, as individual peculiarities, and the specific characteristics alone have been preserved.[17]

Darwin read this in the early autumn of 1860 and dismissed it with the marginal comment: "All mere assertion." Perhaps Darwin may have been too immersed in his own theory to view it differently. But Gray, through more objective eyes, saw that Darwin's arguments to the contrary were equally mere assertion. Said Gray: "Apparently every capital fact in one view is a capital fact in the other."[18]

But Agassiz was dwelling upon an important weak point in the *Origin* and in Darwin's attitude: his failure to distinguish between "real changes" and "individual differences"; or, in Agassiz's terms, between what "might be" inheritable and what was not. Agassiz thus combined two attacks with a single assertion. He attacked the selectability of individual differences while also attacking the effect of monstrosities on the process of selection.

Agassiz's declaration of the uninheritability of natural variation emphasized the impossibility of the cumulative selection of individual differences. Yet this criticism was not so much directed specifically against the *nature* or *kind* of variation as it was against the permanence or heritability of *all* variation. In Agassiz's view, no variation of any kind could provide the basis for permanent change in the specific character of a given species. Thus Agassiz rejected all types of variation (monstrosities, saltations, and individual differences) insofar as he rejected the process of evolution itself. It is perhaps for this reason that Darwin dismissed his criticisms. Nevertheless, Agassiz made an important distinction between the transient nature of monstrosities and individual differences.

When the special meeting convened, it was not Agassiz (whose opinions had already been widely promulgated) but his friends and supporters who spoke. The first was Dr. Francis Bowen, a professor of philosophy at Harvard. His position was, for the most part, identical to that of Agassiz, from whom it is likely he obtained the requisite scientific briefing. Bowen cited the major obstacles facing the process of natural selection, particularly with reference to the manner in which it could produce real change, given the variations which arise under nature.

> Variations, if slight, do not injure or improve the animal's chance of life, are seldom transmitted by inheritance, and so cannot act by accumulation, and cannot therefore affect permanency of type. . . . On the other hand, variations, if great, either die out by sterility as monsters, or are rapidly effaced by crossing the breed.[19]

Again, speciation was impossible because of the permanency of type; naturalists like Darwin were looked upon merely as hypnotized by cases of individual variation. Impermanent individual ramifications of the species-character could not be the foundation of new species. On went the attacks of the anti-Darwinians (rather more anti-evolution than anti-Darwin) until April 10, when Professor Theophilus Parsons made the final speech. His view was not unlike that of Huxley for he too felt that Darwin had unnecessarily and unwarrantedly limited himself to slow and minute modifications, and he could not see why the process of natural selection should fail to take advantage of large jumps as well as small gradations. But Parsons, with the shrewd logic of the able lawyer he was, went further than this and attempted to demonstrate that the two nearly antithetical

theories of Darwin and Agassiz were thoroughly reconcilable. He attempted to retain the theory of Darwinian selection on the one hand while still clinging to the notion of speciation effected by sudden production of new species through large
saltations. He described this method of speciation as operating
"by some influence of variation acting upon the ovum before
or at conception or during its uterine nutriment" and, in the
case of a wolf, fox, or hyena, with the result that "the brood
will come forth puppies and grow up dogs and produce dogs."[20]

As one might have expected, Darwin was not impressed by
any of these remarks. He wrote to Lyell that Agassiz's criticism
was "not good at all, denies variations and rests on the perfection of Geological evidence. Professor Parsons has published
in the same 'Silliman' a speculative paper correcting my notions,
worth nothing."[21] In a letter to Gray written the same day, he
was a little more specific: "The whole article seems to me poor;
it seems to me hardly worth a detailed answer. If you see Professor Parsons, please tell him I reflected much on the chance
of favourable monstrosities (i.e. great and sudden variation)
arising. I have, of course, no objection to this, indeed, it would
be a great aid, but I did not allude to the subject, for, after
much labour, I could find nothing which satisfied me of the
probability of such occurrences."[22]* Darwin continued, citing
the three classes of arguments which led him to his decision
against saltations: (1) the difficulties attached to the nature
and number of such anomalies;† (2) his demonstration of the
complete sufficiency of individual differences; and (3) the fact
that species exhibit too much beauty, too much complexity in
their adaptations to their environment to permit belief that they
were produced by sudden jumps.

* Merely having monstrosities perpetuated and accumulated under the influence of selection was not enough. Selection itself, as the ultimate force of speciation, was seen as operating on individual differences. Reconciling saltations with
selection was not enough. Slight variations were as much a part of evolution as
selection, and saltations were not reconcilable with them.

† Sterility, liability to accidental loss, numerical inferiority, etc., etc.

Each time Darwin argued this issue, he felt he had the final, conclusive word. Yet it seemed he could not escape the problem, for always there were more and seemingly cogent arguments presented.

While American scientists were debating about variations there appeared an article by the teratologist Dr. Maxwell T. Masters, an English expert on the subject of variation. Masters' article and letter to Darwin (of the same date) show that at least he (Masters) had no theoretical axe of his own to grind. His paper began by making some important distinctions. Whereas a "variety" does not impair function, is constant, permanent, and reproducible, a "monstrosity" interferes with function, is less constant, less permanent, and is rarely reproduced. With some insight, Masters added that while the amount of slight or individual change can be quite large in any one direction, it is never observed to pass beyond the "species boundary." Although he agreed with Darwin that speciation does not take place through any form of monstrosity, he reminded him that his assumption of variation (in any single direction) as limitless was still just a conjecture. Darwin concluded: "It is of the highest importance to ascertain whether this be so or not."[23]

While Masters' article offered little help and much caution, his letter provided an example which must have immediately recalled to Darwin Harvey's earlier remarks:

> From the observation that in our *Thesium* the newly sprouted twigs again produce flowers, but which, as shown, approach the Juffruticose Thesiae and individual flowers of Leptomeriae, it is to be supposed, that if such perverted specimens should chance to survive the winter and . . . be continued in . . . changed conditions, in time the abnormal state might easily become habitual. . . . In this way we obtain a plant which, were it found in a wild state, [would] be considered as specifically, or even generically distinct. Nature here appears to give us an indication how she may

have created many species and genera out of existing types. I will not go too far into this question, lest I be reproached for hypothetical views. . . .[24]

As it had been with Harvey, Darwin did not seem impressed by the example and tended to believe more in Masters' opening statements regarding the high improbability of monstrous saltations being employed in speciation. "I have great doubts," he wrote back to Masters, "whether species in a state of nature ever become modified by such sudden jumps."[25] Nature provided a tougher environment than that of domestication. Weaknesses protected in the domestic state, Darwin felt, might bring sudden death in the natural state. Masters' phrase "were it found in a wild state" seemed the crux of the problem for Darwin. There appeared to be little more to say on the matter.

In August, Karl von Nägeli, one of the last reviewers of the *Origin,* came out against the theory of monstrosities. But, unlike most of the others, in doing so he did not eliminate the possibility of other types of saltations.

> This development of races takes place at one time by gradual, at another by sudden transition, but never by considerable leaps; for if the latter were possible, something of the kind must have been observed before this, in the course of numerous attempts at cultivation, which are constantly being made. Until such leaps are known to us by experience, we ought not to go beyond variation as sought by the development of races.[26]

Although Darwin noted Nägeli's comment, his silence on this belief that selection took advantage of "sudden transition but never considerable leaps" leaves little doubt that he hoped to account for natural speciation within the scope of individual variation. Within just a few weeks, however, Darwin would be presented for the first time with a clear exposition of the necessity and the place of small saltations in the evolutionary scheme.

Prompted by Hooker (with whom he corresponded) to send on some of his ideas on variability, Harvey dispatched to Darwin a fifteen-page closely written letter:

> I cannot as yet (probably never shall) receive the theory of natural selection as a satisfying explanation of the origin of species—but I am willing to admit that it explains several facts which are not otherwise easily to be accounted for. Until, however, something more is known of the inciting causes of the Variations and Correlations of Organs, I can only regard Natural Selection as one agent out of several.[27]

He went on to note that while there exists a tendency of forms to vary, distinct species have nevertheless many points in common, and are thus often difficult to distinguish from one another. "These," he said, "are difficult to the believer in separate acts of creation and are perhaps the strongest evidence in favour of a doctrine of mutation. But it does not therefore necessarily follow that the mutation has been effected through Natural Selection alone."[28] Harvey was slowly coming around to the old point that the origin of species means nothing until one explains the origin of variations. He went on, referring to

> unknown *Laws of Variation,* those namely which cause an organism *"to sport"* or diversify itself *unexpectedly.* Natural Selection is no doubt ready to take advantage of such contingent variations, but cannot be said either to *explain* or to *originate* them. If therefore these are *necessary* as starting to set Natural Selection in motion, we are surely calling up a wholly different agency to any set forth in your theory.[29]

At this point it would seem that Harvey was leading up to a familiar argument—a demand for the "true" causes of variation. With Darwin, variation had been for the most part a basic assumption—an observable phenomenon on the basis of which his theoretical mechanism began the process of speciation. But it is here that Harvey made an important turn. He saw the relevancy of discussing the origins of variation. In doing so, he felt, one would be better able to differentiate between heritable and uninheritable variation. One might also be able to determine whether or not there was some definite limit to the extent to which individual differences could be accumulated. In closing, Harvey reminded Darwin that the theory of natural selection becomes superfluous if one accepts the inheritability of the effects of habit and use. There is little doubt that he was making it difficult for Darwin to fall back on any subsidiary mechanisms to strengthen the power of selection.

> When you suppose one species to pass, by insensible degrees into another, so many facts of variation support your view that it does not seem very improbable; but where a generic limit has to be passed, bearing in mind how *persistent* generic differences are, I think we require a *saltus* (it may be a small one) or a real break in the chain, namely, a sudden divarication.[30]

Here then was the crux, in one clear sentence. Harvey had patiently outlined the difficulties of selection of only individual differences; he had recognized all the problems attached to the more monstrous forms of saltations; he saw clearly the double-edged difficulty of the "species barrier" (that at one and the same time it accounted for the constancy and permanency of a species and inhibited the formation of new species). Yet through all this he had clearly in mind a way out of the difficulty. He continued:

> I know you account for genera by the dropping out of supposed intermediate infinitesimals. But we know also that *sudden* divarications do sometimes occur in nature; and it is *possible* that they may be even necessary consequences of repeated and long-continuing infinite change.[31]

Clearest of all for the understanding of his idea was Harvey's own example of a kaleidoscope:

> Starting with any pattern of figure, by very slow turning of the tube you may get successively a great many modifications of the figure without any radical change in the pattern, thus illustrating several species of the same genus. But when you have turned the tube so far as to cause such a displacement of the fragments of glass as makes them topple over, a perfectly new pattern will *suddenly* start up and may then by further slow turning be modified till it in turn shall topple over. Of course this is merely a possible illustration of the gradual succession of species and genera, if they arise by smaller *and greater* divarications.[32]

Not only did Harvey feel that this seemed to explain away many problems facing Darwin in the light of his original stand, but he added two further arguments why jumps have probably been employed in speciation. First, he pointed to the phenomenon of inter-specific sterility,* a difficulty explained if jumps had occurred. Second, he argued that "by admitting the possibility of *sudden* divarications we get rid of those perfectly innumerable forms of life which your hypothesis requires us to believe in, but of whose existence there is so little evidence either in existing nature or among fossils."[33]

Throughout his reading of the entire fifteen-page letter Darwin made copious (but largely illegible) notes, then labeled the entire collection "Keep"; yet, despite any momentary impression that it might have made, Harvey's commentary did little to change Darwin's mind. In his letter of reply (some two thousand words) Darwin had this to say:

About sudden jumps: I have no objection to them—they

---

* Inter-specific sterility had been a stumbling block for Darwin even in the first *Origin*. He had been at a loss to account for the gradual acquisition of sterility, despite its obvious usefulness in keeping distinct forms from mixing. (See chapter 8.)

would aid me in some cases. All I can say is, that I went into the subject, and found no evidence to make me believe in jumps; and a good deal pointing in the other direction.[34]

Darwin had not budged an inch since the beginning, and if anything, he seemed to have closed his mind on the subject. But, like Huxley when he found Darwin unmoved, Harvey felt obliged to put his view before the public. On October 8, he sent Darwin a reprint of a speech that he had given before the Dublin University Zoological Association on February 17. On the cover was written "with the writer's *repentance,* October, 1860" and in it Harvey said:

It strikes me that there is a fallacy at the very base of Mr. Darwin's argument; and that his whole superstructure rests on the *assumption* that Variability acts indefinitely and continuously, without check or hindrance.[35]

Alongside this paragraph Darwin noted: "Good to admit that continued variation is an assumption." Together with this reprint, Harvey included another long letter—still hoping to drive home his point.

The first impression of your book on my mind was that it too boldly assumed *unlimited* variability as the cornerstone of the argument; and this was the first stumbling block in my way, for I am strongly impressed with the notion (perhaps wholly wrong) that there is no law of organic or inorganic nature unlimited in its operation. And so, however widely species may vary, I suspect an oscillation in every case.[36]

Harvey continued, pointing out once more the necessity of saltations.

We must, I think, draw a broad line between varieties arising from altered conditions of life, from use and disuse, and those variations that introduce new stages of being.[37]

Harvey concluded:

> . . . *saltations* for which I have all along been contending—
> the non-recognition of which in the theory of natural selec-
> tion appears to me like leaving out the keystone of the
> arch.[38]

But sensing that Darwin would never change his mind, or could
not see his point, he added resignedly: "but it is useless to
carry on the discussion." Never again did he refer to anything
but non-theoretical matters with Darwin.

Until this time, Darwin had never seen, nor had it ever been
pointed out to him, that there was an important distinction to
be made regarding saltations. Here, however, was a man who
(like Darwin) rejected monstrosities as agents of selectivity, yet
at the same time attacked the efficacy of the natural selection
process of individual differences. In rejecting monstrosities
while nevertheless calling for a form of saltation, Harvey was
indicating the role of an intermediate form—something larger
than a slight difference, yet not of a monstrous nature. Unfortunately, Darwin saw only the difference between "continuous"
and "discontinuous" variation and, since Harvey's form was saltative nonetheless, he rejected the idea.

By the end of November (1860), Darwin had started the
third edition of the *Origin*. Feeling it now necessary to make
his views on monstrosities explicit, Darwin added a few remarks at the opening of his second chapter ("Variation under
Nature").

> It may perhaps be doubted whether monstrosities, or such
> sudden and great deviations of structure . . . are ever per-
> manently propagated in a state of nature. . . .[39]

He went on to list three reasons for this. First, they were
generally sterile. Second, adaptation and complexity could not
be accounted for in a single, sudden jump. Third, he had not
been able to discover any case where a structure found nor-

mally in one form appeared as a sudden monstrous character in an allied form. Since their appearance was the only way to determine the possible origins of an existing structure, their absence, Darwin felt, indicated that useful or advantageous modifications do not appear in such a manner. Yet Harvey, and Darwin's other critics during that year, did produce some effect. The third edition abounds with very slight—often single-word— alterations indicating that he was no longer rejecting saltations so exclusively as earlier, but only in their role in speciation. Where he had previously referred to "that old canon, 'Natura non facit saltum,' " he now spoke of it as "that old but somewhat exaggerated canon."[40] Darwin also modified his references to individual differences. "Infinitesimally small inherited modifica- tions"—the backbone of his theory—became only "small."[41] Where he had said: "I believe a large amount of inheritable and diversified variability is favourable, but I believe mere in- dividual differences suffice for the work," he now said: "Mere individual differences probably suffice." Though the change is slight, the further modification in the fifth edition showed the trend of his thought, for there he stated:

> A large amount of variability, under which term individual differences are always included, will evidently be favour- able.[42]

Elsewhere he changed such phrases as "she [Nature] can never take a leap, but must advance by the shortest and slowest steps" to "advance by short and slow steps,"[43] indicating a de- sire to emphasize the step-like nature of the variation while at the same time toning down the implication of extreme slight- ness that had been present before.

CRITICISMS AFTER 1860

The subject of saltative variation was dropped while Darwin spent most of 1861 working on orchids. When Darwin took up *The Variation of Animals and Plants under Domestication* in the autumn of 1862, the problem of saltative changes came up again. In documenting thousands of cases of domestic variation, Darwin had seen numerous cases of monstrosities and agreed in the conclusion that "all those who have studied monstrosities believe that they are far commoner with domesticated than with wild animals and plants."[44] This coincided with what he had long felt about variation in general, and for a similar reason: that the peculiar and unnatural conditions of domestication had a marked effect upon the organism, producing all kinds of variation, monstrosities included. Above all, his increased knowledge of the subject brought him to the significant conclusion that "monstrosities graduate so insensibly into mere variations that it is impossible to separate them."[45]

It was just after having concluded all but minor corrections in the *Variation* in the spring of 1866 that Darwin started on the fourth edition of the *Origin.* His investigations into the phenomena of prepotency, reversion, and blending concluded with the view that the latter was the ultimate and predominant effect of crossing. At about this same time there appeared the English translation of the book, *Plurality of the Human Race* by G. Pouchet.[46] This work represented a long polemic against the *Origin,* its most remarkable feature being its almost total lack of comprehension of the *Origin.* Having been somehow led to believe that Darwin assumed species to undergo great and abrupt changes, Pouchet leveled the criticism that free crossing of saltations with unmodified forms would obliterate the former through the process of blending. Darwin replied (after first pointing out his gross misinterpretation of the nature of the evolutionary variations) by giving his usual answer to the problem (see chapter 5, p. 115); yet he stated elsewhere in the same edition:

> If monstrous forms of this kind ever do appear in a state of nature and are capable of propagation (which is not always the case), as they occur rarely and singly, they must be transmitted in a modified state.

If perpetuated in this crossed state, their preservation will be almost necessarily due to the modification being in some way beneficial to the animal under its then existing conditions of life; so that, even in this case, natural selection will come into play.[47]

Since monstrosities would be blended in the very next generation, some form of selection would be necessary for their preservation. In only a few generations the monstrosity would be reduced to the level of a slight modification. Diluted as it was and shared by each of the offspring at each generation, it would, by the fourth generation, be reduced to one-sixteenth of the original form. Yet, in terms of number, if each generation starting from the original two parents doubled in number, there would, in this fourth generation, be 256 individuals thus characterized! It would therefore be only when monstrous deviations assumed both the quality and quantity of individual differences that they would have any value in effecting evolutionary change. Their diminution to the level of individual difference as the result of their multiplication seemed only to prove the primary importance of both selection and the smaller, ever-present individual difference. While still maintaining little confidence in the theory of modification by saltation, Darwin had become by this time, as the above quotation indicates, somewhat less than total in his rejection of saltations. This was still not to be the last word on the subject, but it was final until Fleeming Jenkin's review of 1867.

The lack of any discussion on the subject of saltative variation, together with Darwin's frequent quotation "Natura non facit saltum,"[48] prompted a number of his contemporaries to take up the cause of speciation by saltation. Some, like Agassiz, did so as another means of espousing a theory of separate, distinct creations involving the total extinction of previous forms. Others did so, not as a counterproposal to selection, but as an alternative to the selection of individual differences. Still others, like Huxley, felt that saltations would supplement individual differences as an additional source of evolutionary variation. Whatever the critical source, the following points emerged: first, that saltations do occur, often permanently modifying an individual organism and a number of its descendants; second, that in terms of gross change, saltations cover in one leap what is represented in the accumulation of innumerable individual differences (and all in the same direction); third (said Huxley), that if beneficial saltations do occur they will, on Darwin's own utilitarian principle, be selected; fourth, that most individual differences are transient, appearing as variations on a theme, with the theme itself unchanged; and following from this, that individual differences cannot be selected so as to modify and extend beyond existing specific characters. (See chapter 5 on the limits of variation.) It was felt, by these people, that saltations could effect specific change. In the fifth place, it was claimed that saltations account for (a) the absence of intermediate forms and (b) inter-specific sterility. Finally, there was a belief which was an implicit part of a number of these criticisms: that not all saltations are monstrous, but that there are in fact small jumps—a type of variation lying somewhere between the commonly occurring individual variations and the grosser forms of anomaly.

Despite the apparent cogency of nearly all these remarks to a modern reader, there are nonetheless quite understandable reasons why Darwin persisted in his rejection of all saltations. It is not simply that, for the most part, he saw them as nearly all monstrous, but that they were all *discontinuous* in nature. True, he did not recognize a slight or middle-sized saltation, but this would have been due not so much to an oversight as to a contradiction in terms. There was for him no middle ground of variation, for the simple reason that variations were either continuous or not. Within these categories, he quite clearly saw some gradation. For example, he never looked upon bud variations or "sports" as being so grossly anomalous as a number of other real botanical monstrosities (e.g. *Begonia*). Yet both were saltations and, in a sense relative to continuous forms of variation, still monstrous in their degree of difference between variant and parent. So, despite all these comments, the difficulties regarding sterility, rarity, trauma, functional advantage, adaptive complexity, and general demonstrability as evolutionary source material remained, in Darwin's thought, firmly associated with the entire class of saltations.

4. The Causes of Variability

> *To me it seems that the "Origin of Variations" provides the real story of the "Origin of Species"—in not showing us how the individual differences first occur, [Mr. Darwin] is really leaving us absolutely in the dark as to the cause of all modification—giving us an "Origin of Species" with the "Origin" cut out.*
>
> —Samuel Butler, Life and Habit *(1878)* and Evolution, Old and New *(1879)*

Despite its size and the vast range of material which it contained, the *Origin of Species* remained, in Darwin's view, only an abstract. When Wallace's paper came into his hands he had already amassed several volumes of material. The urgency of the situation, together with the sheer mass of over twenty years' work to be condensed, led Darwin to view the *Origin* as only a meager beginning. For him it served as a stop-gap to establish his priority on the idea until such time as he could prepare the complete account of his theory.

Each of the several manuscript volumes he had on hand was reduced to a mere chapter in this abstract. Originally, each was to be a separate work, one volume of a set which, in its entirety, would provide the complete account, all evidence included, of the origin and evolution of species. Little wonder that, from the moment the proof sheets of the *Origin* left his hands, his only thought was to press on with this more detailed work. Any thoughts of a work of several volumes, however, were soon precluded by his involvement in the controversy over the *Origin*. By the opening months of 1860 he had contented himself with the possibility of three volumes. The first of this projected set was to cover variation in domestication, the second to deal with variation in nature, and the third to demonstrate the process of natural selection. It was not until April 10 that Darwin was able to begin on *The Variation of Animals and Plants under Domestication*. Even at that, work soon came to a halt when he fell ill in June. Despite weeks of Victorian "water cure" at a spa, his ill health continued after his return home. What little time the condition of his health permitted him for work was taken up with ever-mounting correspondence on the great controversy. By the time he concluded a further nine weeks' rest in mid-November, Darwin had spent less than two months of 1860 on his work.

THE THIRD *Origin*

If Darwin had looked forward on his return to resuming work at last, his hopes were short-lived. For, less than a week later, he received a note from John Murray, his friend and publisher, urging him to prepare a new edition of the *Origin* "at once."[1] The *Variation* was put aside again.

From the point of view of his public, this would have been a most appropriate time for Darwin to reconsider some of the problems of the *Origin*. The critical comment of the past year seemed to cry out for reply.[2] Yet, for a number of reasons, Darwin refrained from any extended discussion.[3] In the first place, he felt acutely aware of all the trouble Murray had gone to in bringing out the first two editions. Though comment and criticism were plentiful, sales were nonetheless low. Wishing therefore to spare his friend cost and inconvenience, Darwin limited himself solely to deletions and minor corrections. Second, Darwin had been left quite unimpressed by the comments of most of his critics. He felt the majority had made muddled interpretations of his idea and that, consequently, nearly all their comments were worthless. Thus there are few changes of any significance in the third *Origin*. Of these, only those made in reply to one perceptive critic, Bronn, will be mentioned here.[4]

Early in October, while convalescing at Eastbourne, Darwin received a manuscript from Professor H. G. Bronn, the German paleontologist. Bronn was doing the German translation of the *Origin* and had written a chapter of criticism which he intended to append to the German edition. In this additional chapter he listed those phenomena which he felt remained unexplained in the *Origin*. Darwin was impressed: "There are some good hits," he confessed to Lyell. "He makes an apparently, and in part truly, telling case against me."[5] Murray's request would be at least an opportunity to answer Bronn.

Among Bronn's remarks four important points stood out. The first called upon Darwin to explain concerning his theory the existence of a number of seemingly inexplicable associations of characters. These were such constant conjunctions of features as blue eyes and deafness in cats, hairlessness and imperfect teeth in dogs, and less anomalous relations such as Cuvier had pointed out between horn, hooves, and dentition in mammals. These were seemingly difficult enough to explain on purely morphological grounds and appeared to be wholly impervious to explanation in terms of an evolutionary process.

The second objection was the existence and perpetuation of superficial and/or useless variation. If the process of natural selection operates only when variations are beneficial, why do useless structures persist?

Third, the occurrence of a variation in one part of an organism would seem to require other, simultaneous changes in order to accommodate it. A good number of allied changes would be necessary, and each must be structurally and functionally related both to the new variation and to one another. Without such allied change, not only would any new variation be incapable of assuming its beneficial (and therefore, selective) role, but it might, by its singular nature, prove deleterious to the otherwise normal individual. How could Darwin explain this?

Finally, Bronn saw in the production of variation as the result of "the direct action of the conditions of life," the implication that all the members of a population would be undergoing change at the same time. Asked Bronn: "How is it that all the forms of life do not present a fluctuating and inextricably confused body?"[6]

Each of Bronn's queries required an explanation involving the cause of variation. Because Darwin had not at this time delved far into either the nature or the causes of variation, he was forced merely to repeat and reemphasize points already made in the first editions of the *Origin*.

In reply to the first two queries, he saw that there was a common explanation: the principle of correlation.* Unusual associations of features and the existence of useless variations were seen as the secondary results, the by-products, of correlation. Selection had operated on the adaptive changes with which these secondary features were correlatively linked. As selection assured the perpetuation of the former, so it automatically entailed the selection of the latter, whether useful or not.

As for Bronn's third query, Darwin could see but dimly the possibility of correlation as an explanation. This was primarily because he felt he could account for what appeared to be simultaneous change by the sequential acquisition of allied changes through the process of natural selection. Besides, too little was known at this time about the dynamic aspects of correlation for Darwin to consider it as an alternative.[7]

Bronn's final objection, wherein he saw that, under the direct action of the conditions of life, all members of the population would become modified, evoked a completely divergent reply:

* See chapter 1, p. 13, and this chapter, pp. 84–85.

"It is sufficient for us if some few forms at any one time are variable, and few will dispute that this is the case."[8] This point, which, whether intentionally or not, Darwin had overlooked, would be forced to his attention later.

RESEARCH ON ORCHIDS

With the new edition off to the printer, Darwin immediately resumed work on the *Variation*. Up to that time he had completed only two chapters, but the amount of material already accumulated would require two volumes. The first was to be an encyclopedic compilation of variation in domesticated animals and plants. The phenomenon of variability itself, including its causes, was a subject Darwin now felt more and more the need to discuss. This would occupy the second volume. Since it was this latter aspect that now completely filled his mind and interest, he was more than ever eager to press on. The mere recording of morphological descriptions he found increasingly laborious, so that the work appeared to stretch endlessly before him. He longed to give up writing for field work.[9] After three months of describing variation in fowls, he could labor no longer. He shelved the *Variation* once again. This time the digression was of his own choice, for he had found a subject of fascinating attraction: orchids. He had become interested in orchids through his convalescent constitutionals at Down. There were a number of species native to Down whose delicate complexities and intricacies of sexual structure had fascinated the inquisitive botanist. No doubt he still remembered Bronn's objection that his theory could not account for such apparently useless, merely ornamental characters. Here were outstanding examples of what seemed to be purely decorative variation whose existence, according to his own theory, must have been the result of the process of natural selection. This became a challenge, and an appropriately refreshing one. Darwin set to work immediately, writing off to all his botanical correspondents (chiefly Hooker) for information, seeds, and specimens. The avid and exhaustive collector of facts was off on new research,* and for nine months, without a trace of ill health, he occupied himself exclusively with these complex flowers.

The result of these months of work was a modestly small quarto volume in which in brilliant and convincing style he showed that the beauty and complexity of the family Orchidaceae was in fact highly utilitarian. By demonstrating the consistency of these findings with the operational criteria for the process of natural selection, he had proved, within the framework of a highly specialized study, the far-reaching value of his theory. He was now ready to take up the neglected *Variations* once again. By November 1862 he had completed the tedious recording of variations that filled the first volume, and had started his study of variability.

THE CAUSES OF VARIATION

As already noted in chapter 1, Darwin recognized the following causes of variation:

1. The indirect effect of the conditions of life
2. The direct effect of the conditions of life
3. Habit, use, and disuse
4. Correlation
5. Compensation, or balance

While acknowledging all these, the influence he attributed to each varied considerably. A detailed examination reveals the extent to which Darwin found each responsible for the production of variation.

The indirect effect of the conditions of life Darwin considered to be the most prominent cause of evolutionary variation.

---

* "He was soon as irrevocably dedicated to orchids as he had formerly been to barnacles. It was a briefer and perhaps a more fortunate dedication, though he had waxed nearly as lyrical over structural beauty in the sliminess and smelliness of the barnacle as he now did over that in the bright colour and exotic form of the orchid." See William Irvine, *Apes, Angels, and Victorians* (New York: McGraw-Hill, 1955), p. 153.

I am strongly inclined to suspect that the most frequent cause of variability may be attributed to the male and female reproductive elements having been affected prior to the act of conception.[10]

That the reproductive system is eminently susceptible to changes in the conditions of life; and to this system being functionally disturbed in the parents, I chiefly attribute the varying or plastic conditions of the offspring.[11]

In the case of indirect action the specific nature of the affecting condition(s) mattered not, for the changing environmental conditions merely sufficed to trigger a highly sensitive and complex system into malfunctioning,

So that this system, when not rendered impotent, fails to reproduce offspring exactly like the parent form.[12]

There still remained a large amount of variation unexplainable as the effect of conditions of the reproductive elements. In situations where a variation had already become evident during the lifetime of the organism under the new conditions, it was obvious that such elements could not have come into play. Variation in the somatic structure *preceding* reproduction ruled out the reproductive system as the site and source of such variation. In such cases, the sexual elements appeared to serve only as vehicles for the transmission of changes.

It is certain that variability may be transmitted through either sexual element, whether or not originally excited in them.[13]

As further evidence against a reproductive origin for all variation there were such asexual phenomena as grafts and bud variations. Darwin was therefore led to conclude:

Thus direct action of changed conditions perhaps comes into play much more frequently than can be proved, and it is at least clear that in all cases of bud-variation the action cannot have been through the reproductive system.[14]

The direct effect of the conditions of life was the cause that was to give Darwin the greatest trouble and the influence he took the most pains to determine.

According to Darwin, a variation due to "direct action" was an effect—a specific organic response—of a particular environmental stimulus. In the opening chapter of the *Origin,* he noted:

> Some slight amount of change may, I think, be attributed to the direct action of the conditions of life—as in some cases, increased size from amount of food, colour from particular kinds of food, and from light, and perhaps the thickness of fur from climate.[15]

While recognizing that conditions could stimulate variation by their direct action, Darwin remained "extremely doubtful" about *how much* change could be effected in this manner. He had good reasons for his doubt. In the first place,

> Instances could be given of the same variety being produced under conditions of life as different as can well be conceived; and, on the other hand, of different varieties being produced from the same species under the same conditions.[16]

Second, in the gathering of evidence to support direct action, nature seemed more paradoxically inconsistent.

> As we see innumerable individuals exposed to nearly the same conditions, and one alone is affected, we may conclude that the constitution of the individual is of far higher importance than the conditions to which it has been exposed.[17]

Yet,

> In some few instances, a marked effect has been produced quickly on all, or nearly all the individuals which have been

exposed to some considerable change of climate, food, or other circumstance.[18]

Here, then, was the same point that Bronn had made earlier. Furthermore, there was the historical problem that

> when a variation is of the slightest use to a being, we cannot tell how much of it to attribute to the accumulative action of natural selection and how much to the conditions of life.[19]

Darwin concluded:

> Such considerations as these incline me to lay very little weight on the direct action of the conditions of life.[20]

Yet he found it necessary to remind his readers:

> We should remember that climate, food, etc., probably have some little direct influence on the organisation.[21] . . . My impression is, that with animals such agencies have produced very little direct effect, though apparently more in the case of plants.[22]

Thus, in the first *Origin*, while recognizing both modes of environmental action, he inclined toward indirect action as the most frequent cause of the two. But he could not help feeling that he had not sufficiently investigated the subject to warrant any final conclusions. The matter was set aside as one of the first problems to be taken up in the *Variation*. When he did get to the subject, the facts still did not at first appear to change his views:

> My greatest trouble is not being able to weigh the direct effects of the long-continued action of changed conditions of life without any selection, with the action of selection on mere accidental (so to speak) variability. I oscillate much on this head, but generally return to my belief that the direct action of the conditions of life has not been great.

At least this direct action can have played an extremely small part in producing all the numberless and beautiful adaptations in every living creature.[23]

The work of completing the first volume still lay before him at this time and the subject did not come up again until almost a year later when, in March 1862, Hooker wrote:

I am greatly puzzled just now in my mind by a very prevalent difference between animals and vegetables: inasmuch as the individual animal is certainly changed materially by external conditions, the latter (I think) never except in such a coarse way as stunting or enlarging. . . . Be all this as it may, in neither plant or animal would the induced character be of necessity inherited by the offspring by the seed of the individual, to any greater extent than if it had not been changed—at least so far as the animal is concerned; though with regard to the plant it might be. . . . Thus a wild complication is introduced into the whole subject that perplexes me greatly.

I cannot conceive what you say, that climate could have effected even such a single character as a hooked seed. You know I have a morbid terror of two laws in nature for obtaining the same end; hence I incline to attribute the smallest variation to the inherent tendency to vary; a principle wholly independent of physical conditions—but whose effects on the race are absolutely dependent on physical conditions for their conservation.[24]

In the light of existing confusion about the effects of conditions, Darwin could readily understand Hooker's "wild complication." But that he should go further (than dismissing the effects of direct action) and dismiss the conditions of life completely, was unthinkable to Darwin.

You speak of "an inherent tendency to vary wholly independent of physical conditions"! This is a very simple way of putting the case; but two great classes of facts make me think that all variability is due to change in the conditions of life: firstly, that there is more variability and more monstrosities (and these graduate into each other) under unnatural domestic conditions than under nature; and secondly, that changed conditions affect in an especial manner the reproductive system. But why one seedling out of thousands presents some new character transcends the wildest powers of conjecture. It was in this sense that I spoke of "climate" etc., possibly producing without selection a hooked seed, or any not great variation.

I have for years and years been fighting with myself not to attribute too much to Natural Selection—to attribute something to direct action of conditions; and perhaps I have too much conquered my tendency to lay hardly any stress on conditions of life.[25]

For Hooker it had been a question of choosing spontaneous variability over the direct action of conditions, whereas Darwin had made quite a different distinction. Darwin saw the apparently spontaneous variations produced through the reproductive system as one aspect (the indirect effects) of the conditions, while the other aspect represented the direct effects. All variations were elicited by some change in conditions; the difficulty for him lay in how much to attribute to each.

Though it now appeared that he believed himself to have *over*stressed the direct action of conditions, only a week later he wrote:

Nevertheless I am pleased to attribute little to conditions, and I wish I had done what you suggest—started on the fundamental principle of variation being an innate principle, and afterwards made a few remarks showing that hereafter, perhaps, this principle would be explicable.[26]

Seven months later, having the entire first volume of the *Variation* behind him, Darwin sent another progress report to Hooker:

> I hardly know why I am a little sorry, but my present work is leading me to believe rather more in the direct action of physical condition. I presume I regret it, because it lessens the glory of Natural Selection, and is so confoundedly doubtful. Perhaps I shall change again when I get all my facts under one point of view, and a pretty hard job this will be.[27]

The summer of 1863 saw him begin the two chapters dealing with the conditions of life. Before going into any detail, Darwin carefully defined his terms. The terms "direct and indirect action" referred to the manner in which conditions acted. Direct action meant that the modified organism(s) had been in direct contact with the conditions producing the variations. Under indirect action, the modified organism was affected not directly but through the reproductive system of its parent. Darwin added two more terms, referring this time to the nature of the effects produced. By "definite" effects he meant those that appeared as a specific response to a particular condition. These were common to all or to nearly all members of the population. "Indefinite" effects were purely random, fluctuating variations, unrelated to the conditions evoking them. Therefore, whether it was the direct or indirect action of conditions (and there was ample evidence to support the influence of both), the effects were nearly always "indefinite,"

> the kind of variation which ensues depending in a far higher degree on the nature or constitution of the being, than on the nature of the changed conditions.[28]

But documented cases of the direct and definite effects of conditions there were, and, in concluding the section devoted to such phenomena, he remarked:

It is possible that great and definite modifications of structures may result from altered conditions acting during a long series of generations. In some few instances a marked effect has been produced quickly on all, or nearly all, the individuals which have been exposed to some considerable change of climate, food, or other circumstance.[29]

Recognition that such a cause did sometimes operate in nature was not to assert that it was as likely a cause of variation as the effects of indirect action,

Hence, although it must be admitted that new conditions of life do sometimes definitely affect organic beings, it may be doubted whether well-marked races have often been produced by the direct action of changed condition *without the aid of selection* either by man or nature.[30]

Here Darwin's position was at least consistent. Each cause of variation was *just* a cause of variation and as such was subject to the process of natural selection, which alone could effect transformation.

Use, habit, and disuse were the next set of variation-producing factors which Darwin considered. These three factors differed from other causes in one important respect. Under the effects of environmental conditions the organism is merely passive—responding to external stimuli. In the cases involving habit, use, and disuse, *the organism itself becomes the operative agent in bringing about variation.** This is an important distinction and one of which Darwin gives no indication that he was aware.

For Darwin, "habit" was a term of wider meaning than that of today. In the case of plants, he meant by "habit" such phenomena as period of flowering, photo-period, and times of ripen-

---

* While it is true that a change in certain environmental conditions will bring about a change in behavior, it is still the change in use brought on through change in behavior that is the immediate cause of variation.

ing of pollen and ovules. With animals, the term referred to such obvious and overt habits as hibernation and shedding. In general, with plants he meant by the term the periodic and functional aspects rather than the purely morphological—whereas with animals he was referring to distinct patterns of behavior, such as are grouped under the heading of *instincts*. For Darwin, instincts were the inherited effects of previously acquired habits.[31]

Darwin's belief that the effects of increased use were inheritable accounted for yet another cause of evolutionary variation. An existing structure could undergo change either through its increased or excessive use, or if put to a distinctly new use. In this way, use could be closely linked to habit, for new habits can result in the employment or increased use of certain structures. Thus change in habit produced a change in use and this ultimately produced a structural alteration.[32]

Variation through disuse was naturally the converse of alteration through use. In such cases, lack of use resulted in an atrophy or diminution of a structure and was believed inheritable.

> On the whole, I think we may conclude that habit, use and disuse, have, in some cases, played a considerable part in the modification of the constitution, and of the structure of various organs, but that the effects of use and disuse have often been combined with, and *sometimes* overmastered by, the natural selection of innate differences.[33]

Darwin then discussed *correlation* as the next cause of variation.[34]

> I mean by this expression that the whole organisation is so tied together during its growth and development, that when slight variations in any one part occur, and are accumulated through natural selection, other parts become modified.[35]

This was, in fact, the Cuvierian "Principle of Connections," which had taken on a more dynamic, functional view.[36]

> I know of no case better adapted to show the importance of the laws of correlation in modifying important structures, *independently of utility, and therefore, of natural selection,* than that of the difference between the outer and inner flowers in some Compositous and Umbelliferous plants.[37]

Here, by "important structures" Darwin meant those of strictly taxonomic, rather than of adaptive importance. At this time, he recognized correlation in the limited sense of an explanation of the seemingly unrelated combinations of characters arising as the result of the evolutionary process. Variation of an *adaptive* nature appearing to be correlated could be explained as the result of the natural selection process.

> We may often falsely attribute to correlation of growth structures . . . which in truth are simply due to inheritance; for an ancient progenitor may have acquired through natural selection some one modification in structure and, after thousands of generations, some other and independent modification; and these two modifications, having been transmitted to a whole group of descendants, would naturally be thought to be correlated in some necessary manner. So again, I do not doubt that some apparent correlations, occurring throughout whole orders, are entirely due to the manner alone in which natural selection can act.[38]

As noted, Darwin's view of correlation did not change as the result of Bronn's remarks of 1860. He had done little further work on the subject at that time and Bronn had offered no explanation. However, by the time Darwin started writing his chapter on the subject for the *Variation*, he had learned much more. Correlation was to become more than a phenomenon linking one variation to a preceding one.[39]

The work which most influenced Darwin during the interim

between the *Origin* and the *Variation* was Herbert Spencer's *Principles of Biology*.[40] On the subject of correlation, Spencer's views considerably extended those of Darwin. Where the latter had, up to that time, viewed correlation primarily as a mysterious cause-and-effect sequence between one variation and another, Spencer had gone deeper and beyond Darwin's empirically oriented investigations. By attempting to base the principles of biology on a physico-chemical foundation, Spencer viewed such phenomena as correlation from a level far below (speaking intra-systemically) that of Darwin. He described correlation and correlative change as the result of the basic organic drive to maintain physiological equilibrium.[41] Darwin's amended view of the principle of correlation, indeed his very method of presentation in the *Variation*, was directly due to Spencer's influence.

Darwin first discussed the causes of variability. Having decided that these consisted primarily of the direct and indirect effects of the conditions of life, he went on to discuss in the following chapter the manner in which the two acted. At the start of that chapter (chapter 24, the first of three on the same general subject), he stated that he was now going to discuss "the several laws which govern variability." Thus he implied that, having dealt with the causal origins of variability, he would now deal with the various factors which, in turn, *work upon* this variability. Chapter 25 started with correlation, a subject on which Spencer's influence was apparent from the beginning.

Darwin began by adopting the principle of the regulative, coordinating, and reparative power "common in a higher or lower degree, to all organic beings, and which was formerly designated by physiologists as the nisus formativus."[42] In nearly three pages of fine print Darwin described the internal organic forces which are continually at work to maintain physiologic harmony, concluding:

This subject has been here noticed, because we may infer that, when any part or organ is either greatly increased in size or wholly suppressed through variation and continued selection, the co-ordinating power of the organisation will continually tend to bring all the parts again into harmony with each other.[43]

It was from this force maintaining internal equilibrium, together with those external factors producing variation (and therefore disruption) in the system, that Darwin's enlarged view of correlated variability emerged. Correlative change was now seen as a response of the organism in order to readjust itself to the change which had taken place within it. At the same time as the organism was *accommodating itself to the change,* it was, in fact, *accommodating the change to it.* However, Darwin went into little detail over the actual process, for he was understandably more concerned with the variations produced than with the process producing them. In fact, E. S. Russell was in the main correct when he said that Darwin "took it for granted that the 'correlated variations' would be adapted to the original variation."[44] Since Darwin neglected to discuss the correlative process in any detail, it is only through his previous discussion of the *nisus formativus* and his descriptions of particular cases that we can glimpse his impression of the nature of the force at work.

Modifications in whatever manner caused, will be to a certain extent regulated by that co-ordinating power or *nisus formativus.*[45]

Implicit between the lines of his examples was the notion that many times the correlative process *did* adaptively assimilate new variation. In other words, a variation which may have proved deleterious when taken by itself was effectively assimilated through correlation.

Darwin further implied that correlation need not be preceded by an initial *structural* change.

> Changed habits in any organic being, especially when living a free life, would often lead to the augmented or diminished use of various organs, and consequently to their modification.[46]

He offered the following example:

> The increased or diminished length of intestines, which apparently results from changed diet, is a more remarkable case, because it is characteristic of certain animals in their domesticated conditions and therefore must be inherited. The complex absorbent system, the blood-vessels, nerves and muscles, are necessarily all modified together with the intestines.[47]

While the whole subject of variation appears to have taken on an added complexity with recognition of a whole new class of secondary variation, Darwin was not aware that any of these new factors involved additional difficulties as far as the theory of natural selection was concerned. He had made a sharp distinction separating the causes of variation from those factors which transformed such variation and effected a specific change. His intention here had been merely to assign the various causes of variation, and this he had done. The results of correlation— including its interaction with habit and use—were viewed only as additional variation on which the principle of natural selection could and did act. This accounts for the fact that Darwin's reply to Bronn in the third *Origin* remained substantially unchanged. Though he had now recognized a natural process whereby simultaneous variation could be effected (without calling natural selection into play) he still maintained that

> there is not the least necessity for believing that all the parts have been simultaneously modified; they may have been

gained one after the other, and from being transmitted together, they appear to us as if simultaneously formed.[48]

The line between correlation as merely another cause of variation and natural selection as the agent of evolutionary change
was still firmly drawn. However, in this edition Darwin now
cautiously and significantly added:

> Correlation, however, will account for various parts chang-
> ing, when any one part changes.[49]

Yet this was by no means to be the last word on the subject.
Later critics, reading from his works, were to force Darwin's
attention back to correlation and what they felt to be an important unresolved difficulty surrounding it.

Balance or compensation was the last source of variation
cited by Darwin in the *Origin*. He described this as "the actual
withdrawal of nutriment from one part owing to the excess of
growth in another and adjoining part."[50] This was almost
identical to St. Hilaire's "Law of Balance,"[51] and Darwin saw it
as not unrelated to correlation. Indeed, in the *Variation* it is
viewed as a subsidiary process, almost a corollary, to that of
correlation.

In the *Variation*, although Darwin did list a number of additional sources of variation, he assigned little importance to any
causes other than those already mentioned, and it was principally these same causes that were to result in future difficulties.

In concluding this chapter it will prove helpful to specify
the implications that lay in Darwin's acceptance of many of
these causal processes—particularly as they were at the root of
Darwin's great difficulty in effectively countering his later
critics. Though he was aware of a number of these implications,
the significance of others eluded him. Here is a listing of four
of the more important of these:

1. The recognition by Darwin of heritable variations as

brought about through the direct action of conditions, through use, habit, and disuse, and through correlation and/or compensation. This reflected a belief in the inheritance of acquired characters.

2. Darwin's view that variation as the direct effect of conditions, as well as variation due to correlation, was *passively* acquired—the organism being *acted upon* in the one case and involuntarily changed from within in the other. With variation effected through use, habit, or disuse, however, it was *the organism itself* that was the *active* operative agent in the production of such variation. Though Darwin did not seem aware of this distinction,* in the eyes of many of his critics this was an unthinkable process by which to account for evolutionary change.

3. Darwin's feeling that if the environment could directly effect variation in the organism, then, from the fact that members of the same population are nearly identical, all such members should vary in the same way. This was one implication of which Darwin seemed aware:

> In some few instances [of direct influence of conditions], a marked effect has been produced quickly on all, or nearly all, the individuals which have been exposed.[52]

> When many individuals of the same variety are exposed during several generations to any change in their conditions of life, all, or nearly all the individuals, are modified in the same manner. *A new sub-variety would thus be produced without the aid of selection.*[53]

Yet, despite this recognition, Darwin felt that direct action

---

* This point, in which the organism is seen as the agent of change, is highly reminiscent of Lamarck's Second Law (see E. S. Russell, *Form and Function*, pp. 221–225), and, together with the first point, on the inheritance of acquired characters, shows remarkable similarity to Lamarck's postulated means of evolutionary change—despite the fact that Darwin saw these only as causes of variation.

presented no difficulties for selection. He based this opinion on the following reasoning: first of all, such action could not result in adaptive variation. Though its effects were often definite, they were not necessarily beneficial or adaptive in nature. It would require a process of selection (negative to eliminate the unadaptive; positive to perpetuate those that were beneficial) to achieve any real change. Only natural selection was capable of compounding variation (for whatever cause) and of actually bringing about an adaptive transformation. Further, selection was unavoidable for it amounted to nature's ever-vigilant eye; it was, felt Darwin, always in operation.

Variation as the result of the conditions of life was fundamentally different from those changes which are brought about through correlation and compensation. In the former case Darwin was dealing with the general variability of organisms —the tendency to depart, however slightly, from type. Under the action of the latter, the changes produced are correlative with previous variation. Thus there was *primary* variation on the one hand, and a *secondary* change or variation on the other, depending on the first for its initiation. It was in the *Variation* that Darwin first made the distinction himself,[54] yet he saw no more to this than that there were two distinguishable methods by which variation was produced, the second having a dependence on the first.

It was not only correlation and compensation that produced this secondary variation; there was also the implication in the *Variation* that use or disuse, prompted by a change in structure, could produce further change. As things stood in the *Origin*, the effects of use and disuse were seen as primary variation, but from this later study it could be seen that these same factors could act equally upon newly formed characters as well. In this manner, habit through use could bring about further, secondary change. Of such a possibility, Darwin supplied only an occasional glimpse. In describing how the Irish elk acquired its

gigantic antlers, Darwin listed the many other changes necessary (starting from the appearance of extremely enlarged
horns) to accommodate such a structure. He concluded:

> Although natural selection would thus tend to give to the
> male elk its present structure, yet it is probable that the
> inherited influence of use has played an equal or more im-
> portant part.[55]

If use could amplify and/or strengthen an existing character,
then it could certainly work the same modifications on a variation just arisen and so obviate the many additional slight
variations on the same feature required in subsequent generations by the process of selection. Again Darwin felt the same
as with direct action and correlation—the great and prevalent
adaptive complexities of nature could not be explained by the
operation of such factors.

4. The fact that the distinction between primary and secondary variation was greater and more important than Darwin
imagined. For secondary variation—if we can continue to call it
that—is often more than mere additional variation. In many
cases it increases the adaptiveness of the preceding variation
which induced it. As Darwin himself noted, correlation as a
form of internal self-adjustment was the mechanism of accommodation—within the individual and, in an important respect,
between the individual and his environment.* Together with
compensation and use, he saw such causes as producing *definite
evolutionary change*, not merely just *further variability*. Here
was the great distinction. These secondary factors *acted upon*
variation or variability, "governed it," as Darwin said, and in so
doing were legitimate counterparts to natural selection.

In order to make this more understandable, it is perhaps

---

* Only by readjusting itself internally through correlation could an organism
maintain a proper adaptive relationship to its environment. While this has no relationship whatever to the production of change adapted to a particular environment, it is a necessary step if the change is to be of a beneficial nature.

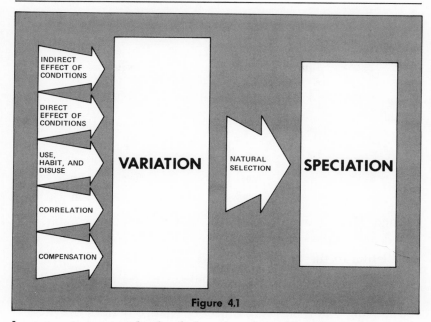

INDIRECT EFFECT OF CONDITIONS

DIRECT EFFECT OF CONDITIONS

USE, HABIT, AND DISUSE

VARIATION

CORRELATION

COMPENSATION

NATURAL SELECTION

SPECIATION

Figure 4.1

best to review with the help of a few illustrations Darwin's overall attitude to the whole problem. See Figure 1.1 (chapter 1), which represents Darwin's basic view of the manner in which variation leads to speciation. Here Darwin's clear-cut distinction between variation and its causes on the one hand, and speciation and its causes on the other, can be seen. Also as noted in chapter 1, Darwin's principal aim, after the *Origin,* was to investigate the causes of variation. Having done so, and thereby having secured a firm causal foundation for his raw material,* he could then treat of speciation and its causes. Figure 4.1 illustrates the break- down of these causes as given in the first *Origin.* By the time the *Variation* was under way, the complexities of variation-pro- duction had caused Darwin to create some further distinctions. Figure 4.2 shows this enlarged view. Correlation (compensa- tion, too) was now correctly seen, not as an initiator of variation, but as a factor which worked upon variation, yielding further

---

* And thus answering the plaint of many critics that he had built his species out of pure chance, on the foundation of spontaneous, uncaused variation.

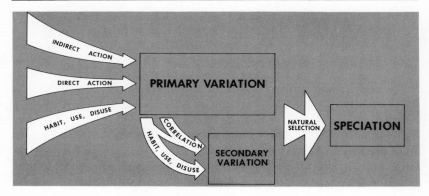

Figure 4.2

change. Here it was also implied that the effects of habit, use, and disuse were modified by and "inextricably commingled" with correlation in the production of secondary change. Yet with all this, Darwin still adhered to his original view separating the cause of variation from the cause of evolutionary change, thus never recognizing that there were causes of change besides the process of natural selection. It is easy to point to his insistence in upholding this distinction as having prevented him from seeing the process of change as continuous. But this would be only a superficial explanation of the matter, for the distinction itself was grounded in a number of firm beliefs:

First, there was Darwin's deeply rooted belief that organic nature contained no force within it which tended toward its own perfection or evolution.* It was the particular and peculiar conditions of existence that prescribed the form of organic life. Adaptation to environment was the first condition of existence, and selection from among nature's varying products was the way in which such a requirement was met.

Second, ruling out any vitalistic drive as able to produce the great mass of adaptive complexity observed in nature, it was

---

* In this belief, Darwin felt himself diametrically opposed to Lamarck. The latter's *sentiment intérieur*, that vitalistic drive toward biological improvement from within the organism, Darwin abhorred. Thus it is somewhat strange, despite the evidence and interpretation of contemporaries, that Darwin should maintain that habit, use, and disuse could produce inheritable change.

unthinkable that such complexity should have come about purely by accident. Only a force external to organic life, and acting upon it, could effect such change. This, of course, was the process of selection.

Finally, the mere continued existence of an organism (the perpetuation of the adaptively fit, and the destruction of the unfit) amounts to an act of selection. This process is constantly operative, taking precedence over any other process of nature.

Yet the implications outlined above remained. Darwin's later critics would not feel so bound to observe his rather fine distinction. For it was this distinction (between the causes of variation and speciation) and the beliefs on which it was based that separated the several assignable causes of one type of change and prevented any clash with the theory of natural selection.

A great part of Darwin's future difficulty stemmed from his failure to deal with the many implications arising from his study of the causes of variation. This appears all the more unfortunate because he looked upon the *Variation* as resolving many of the doubts and problems arising from the *Origin*. As it turned out, the *Variation* tended more to add to them than to resolve them. The barrage of critical attacks that began in the early 1870s was, for the greater part, based on those oversights. Darwin's failure in later years to demonstrate the primacy of natural selection, though precipitated from without, stemmed from his own pages. His implications and inconsistencies could not long remain buried within his tortuous, often indecisive writings, or protected by his own faith that the theory of natural selection could surmount any future difficulties.

5. Blending Inheritance

Jenkin had put his finger on a critically weak point in Darwinian theory—its dependence on a mistaken theory of heredity. The unanswerableness of the criticisms led Darwin to make one of the strangest about-faces in the progress of science. Darwin, a long-time anti-Lamarckian, became an unwilling and unavowed convert.

—*Garrett Hardin,* Nature and Man's Fate

The state of Biology at the time not only made a complete analysis impossible but also led [Darwin] to certain errors in the application of his central idea. He had to accept the pre-Mendelian view that the heredity of the offspring is an organic blend of the heredities of the parents. He therefore came to believe that Natural Selection operated at least to some extent through variations caused by the environment. That theory involved accepting the Lamarckian inheritance of acquired characters because a character can play no part in evolution unless it is inherited. He was uneasy about being forced into this position.

—*W. P. Thompson, "The Cause and Mode of Evolution"* in Evolution: Its Science and Doctrine

A number of writers in searching for a "turning point" in Darwin's evolutionary thought—a point at which he was forced to revert to once-rejected Lamarckian mechanisms—have fastened upon the attack made by Fleeming Jenkin in 1867.[1]

One reason for this appears to lie in the fact that Jenkin's name alone stands out in the available published material as a critic employing against the idea of natural selection the effect of a blending in inheritance. Furthermore, the appearance of Jenkin's review immediately before Darwin undertook the great revisions appearing in the fifth *Origin*[2] also suggested some causal connection. These facts seemed to be corroborated by evidence from Darwin himself that "Fleeming Jenkin has given me much trouble . . . Fleeming Jenkin's arguments have convinced me. . . ,"[3] and together these presented a convincing case for establishing Jenkin as the major cause for the change that followed. In arriving at this conclusion, these writers have by implication asserted a great deal of misinformation regarding both genetic and evolutionary thought at this time. Contained in their view are the following assumptions:

1. That, while not the first writer to note the swamping implications of blending inheritance, Fleeming Jenkin was the first to bring this to bear against the theory of natural selection.
2. That Jenkin's essay was the first employing this criticism to be acknowledged by Darwin and was one which he (Darwin) felt posed some serious problems.
3. That the effect on Darwin of Jenkin's review was to bring about a great reassessment in his thought, the result of which was a staggering reduction of the implied power of natural selection.
4. That the impact of Jenkin's criticism was due to the fact that Darwin had previously overlooked the problem of blending.
5. That the criticism forced Darwin to create a Lamarckian theory of inheritance—his "pangenesis" of 1868.

Thus it is on the basis of these assumptions that the story of Charles Darwin and of his struggle with the implications of blending inheritance appears to achieve a focus in the criticism of Fleeming Jenkin. When one observes in Jenkin's writing such originality and validity (enhanced by Darwin's own oversights), one is led to feel in it an urgency which Darwin never felt.

But, on studying the post-*Origin* period, one sees that these assumptions are incorrect; for all these historical deductions hinge upon a mistaken impression of the nature of Darwin's post-*Origin* "change." There is no "turning point" in Darwin's evolutionary thought. What unrolls before us in the twenty-three years after the *Origin* is a gradual but progressive modification.* As for Jenkin and the place of his critical attack, this chapter attempts to indicate their importance and to describe from the beginning the place of the concept of blending inheritance in the development of Darwin's thought.

BLENDING INHERITANCE

The term *blending inheritance* refers to the view (erroneous, as it turned out) of inheritance as a fusion of both paternal and maternal elements in the offspring in an inseparable mixture which results in external features appearing to be midway between the two. Such a view is merely a description of what can be observed on a purely superficial level in most crosses; it is so common as to be considered universal. In fact to many nineteenth-century naturalists it was the general rule—with a few rather unimportant exceptions.

The modern view, on the other hand, while it recognizes the integrity of the fundamental nucleic units which are believed to constitute the "genes," nevertheless recognizes also both the interaction and the blending of their biochemical products. It is in precisely this region that the distinction between genotype and phenotype—between the profound and the superficial changes—has become considerably obscured.

The *swamping effect* occurs in blending inheritance if one or a few aberrant organisms arise within the normal population.

* Darwin started to modify the *Origin* before the first edition had gone on sale. The seeds of nearly all the significant changes can be seen in the first edition.

Since these rare variant forms must breed back into the general population, the new and unusual characters will be "swamped" by being absorbed into and blended with a vast pool of normal characters.

The concept of blending inheritance as a natural process, together with all its implications, has also been called "the paint-pot theory of heredity."[4] The analogy is that of the normal population as a bucket of white paint with the variant forms a few drops of black. The result of mixing the two paints is analogous to the effect of free inter-crossing in nature. Just as it is impossible to separate two once-distinct fluids after mixing, so it is also impossible, because of the heritage of blending, for small changes to be accumulated in the process of natural selection.

BLENDING INHERITANCE BEFORE JENKIN (1867)

As has already been pointed out, blending inheritance is not so much an hypothesis as an empirical generalization. A blending of two distinct kinds is readily observed throughout organic nature (in the process of sexual reproduction). The first such blend is marked by the fact that the offspring appears to consist of a conglomerate mixture of *features* from both parents.* The second or "true blending" occurs when the offspring can be seen to represent, in terms of a *single feature,* an equal blend of the two distinct parental characteristics for that feature. The latter of these two kinds of mixing forms the basis for the "swamping effect."

Both these types of hereditary mixing had been observed for centuries before the time of Darwin and Jenkin. By the time the study of hereditary phenomena became a scientific discipline in the last quarter of the eighteenth century, blending in inheritance had become accepted as axiomatic. Yet, at about this time, two related phenomena were also recognized, both

---

* That is, that the offspring as a whole represents a blend between the two parents, although each feature comes either from one parent or the other.

obvious exceptions to blending as an all-inclusive or even predominant factor. One was the phenomenon of *dominance* or
"prepotency" and the other was that of *reversion.** In addition,
the development of the science of teratology (study of monstrosities) from the field of embryology put emphasis on "sports"
and other monstrous forms which were also seen as unpredictable results of intercrossing. All this had been widely covered in the new literature of genetics during the 1790–1820
period, some twenty-five years before Darwin wrote his first
essay on the theory of evolution. In short, not only had blending
inheritance been widely described as an hereditary process,
but, in addition, numerous exceptions to it had also been widely
documented and acknowledged. The content of Darwin's ex-
tensively annotated reprint collection shows that he had made
himself acquainted with a great part of this literature.

BLENDING INHERITANCE IN DARWIN'S WRITINGS BEFORE 1860

The Transmutation Notebooks *of 1837–39:* Explicit references to any "problem" attached to a notion of blending inheritance are not to be found in the *Notebooks*. But it must be
remembered that these notebooks served the primary purpose
of recording useful extracts from contemporary sources on subjects bearing on the transmutation of species. On the whole,
they amounted to a collation of mainly empirical evidence supporting one or another aspect of Darwin's theory. Nevertheless,
in a significant number of places Darwin added some broader,
theoretical speculations. A number of these definitely indicate
Darwin's awareness of the blending that seemed implied in the
free crossing of wild forms. These began in the sections on geographical distribution and on the analogy from domestication.

When two very close species inhabit the same country are
not habits different[?] . . . but when close species inhabit

* Reversion here means a throwback, over more than one generation, to a
characteristic possessed by an ancestor.

different countries habits similar? Law? probable $\therefore$ if habits & structure similar would have blended together.[5]

The implication is clearly there; yet nowhere was it brought home more forcefully than when Darwin pursued the analogy between species in the domestic state and those in the wild. The same parallel which led him to look for the selecting agent in nature analogous to artificial selection by man presented him with the problem of finding some natural means to prevent the crossing which, in the domestic state, was effected through the breeder's vigilance.

> Varieties are made in two ways—local varieties when whole mass of species are subject to same influence, & this would take place from changing country; but grey-hound & poulter pidgeon have not been thus produced, but by training, & crossing & keeping breed pure—& so in plants *effectually* the offspring are picked out & not allowed to cross.—Has nature any process analogous[?]—if so she can produce great ends —But how[?]—even if placed on Isl[d.] if &c, &c. . . .[6]

There the problem was to remain until he next took up the subject a few years later.

The Sketch of 1842: When preparing this first outline of the process of evolution, Darwin returned to the implications of blending. This short essay, never intended for publication, represented merely his current speculations, together with a desire to put things down in logical order. In so doing, he set down before him all the relevant facts and laws of organic nature—all the phenomena—for which his hypothesis must account. Even more important in this discussion were the conditions *under which* his theoretical mechanism was thought to operate. Thus, when he recognized that, with blending,

> if varieties be allowed freely to cross, such varieties will be constantly demolished . . . any small tendency in them to vary will be constantly counteracted,[7]

he was at the same time showing his increasing awareness of a problem which must be resolved if the process of natural selection were to remain effective. In the case of animals and plants under domestication the answer to the problem was not difficult: it was artificial selection by man. When it came to the all-important section "On variation in a State of Nature and on the Natural means of Selection" however, he made only a single comment, in the form of a query:

> But is there any means of selecting those offspring which vary in the same manner, crossing them and keeping their offspring separate and thus producing selected races: otherwise as the wild animals freely cross, so must such small heterogeneous varieties be constantly counterbalanced and lost, and a uniformity of character preserved.[8]

To find his answer, Darwin looked back over the known facts and laws by which he could overcome this formidable natural tendency. He toyed momentarily with "the direct and definite effects of conditions"[9] but he dismissed this as insufficient for a process which must create beautiful and complex adaptations. At this point in the narrative he changed the subject and the query passed unanswered. Yet in this essay Darwin did acknowledge the phenomenon of *reversion*. He saw it, however, as a return to an original type — a counter to variation rather than a means of overcoming blending.[10] Despite this awareness of some non-blending inheritance, Darwin did not put forward at this time any possible solution, any answers, to his own query as to how natural selection is to work against the constant blending through inter-crossing.

The Essay of 1844: In his second essay of 1844 Darwin did not forget this unresolved problem. At the very beginning he raised it again:

> Even in the rare instances of sports, with the hereditary tendency very strongly implanted, crossing must be prevented

with other breeds, or if not prevented the best characterized of the half-bred offspring must be carefully selected.[11]

I conclude then, that races of most animals and plants, when unconfined in the same country would tend to blend together.[12]

In this considerably larger draft he responded by pointing out the necessity—as he had hinted in 1842—for some natural form of isolation. With such a supporting phenomenon, Darwin felt he could face the swamping effect with a single variant.

If (as is probable) it and its offspring crossed with the unvaried parent form, yet the number of the individuals being not very great,* there would be a chance of the new and more serviceable form being nevertheless in some slight degree preserved.[13]

With this type of isolation he was not selectively removing the variant from the normal population (for there is only one variant), but was instead pocketing off a small segment of the parent population *with* the variant. Throughout the essay he gave examples—since he was now acutely aware of the difficulties in free crossing—of situations in which opportunity for speciation was best afforded by natural geographic isolation.[14] Although aware of the difficulties in having only a rare and single variant, Darwin saw in this particular form of isolation a way out of having to increase the number of simultaneous variants beyond his original intentions. At this time, Darwin felt that very few beneficial variations actually occurred in nature.[15] If the breeder had only one variant, Darwin said:

the effect of this one peculiar "sport" would be quite lost before he could obtain a second original "sport" of the same kind. If, however, he could separate a small number of cattle,

* In this case he was talking about an island with a small and static population.

including the offspring of the desirable "sport," he might hope, like the man on the island, to effect his end.[16]

Thus isolation into small groups would lower the ratio of variant to normal individuals.

Though acknowledging the phenomenon of reversion, Darwin did not employ it as an argument (as he had done with isolation) to counter the supposed effects of a blending inheritance. In this second essay, however, Darwin seemed to ignore, for the moment, the tendency to blend, stating: "at whatever period of life any peculiarity (capable of being inherited) appears . . . it tends to reappear in the offspring at the corresponding period of life.[17] An interpretation of this statement, in context, seems to show that Darwin felt there was some prepotent power in the variation to manifest itself despite an initial appearance in blended form. Though his thinking along this line was more implied than directly stated, such a view corresponded with another idea of his; for he also recognized a form of what might be called *genetic impetus*. He believed that the more generations through which a peculiarity has passed, the more firmly and the longer it will continue—despite any tendency to blend.[18]

Darwin's concept of the role of isolation as aid to the process of natural selection was still limited. It was restricted to cases where nature had by chance created (through some change in conditions) isolating barriers in the forms of islands, mountains, rivers, etc. Even within these isolated groups, Darwin had not eliminated blending inheritance: he had only circumvented its swamping tendencies by reducing the relative numbers of the unmodified organisms.

In looking at these essays of 1842 and 1844, one gets the impression that Darwin was principally engaged in straightening out the more positive aspects of his mechanism—in describing how it operated and pointing out evidence showing it to have been effective in its task. He also wished to reconcile many hitherto inexplicable phenomena within his process, thereby establishing a form of corroboration. The fact that he was not at this time greatly concerned as to what natural processes must be held accountable for his mechanism is borne out by the very limited space he devoted to such an important point as *blending*. Between 1844 and 1856, he was to change on many points; for instance, he recognized his treatment of blending as both unsatisfactory and insufficient.

The First Origin: In the spring of 1856, Lyell, then Hooker, urged Darwin to write up the results of his nearly eighteen years of research. In August of that year Darwin finally began his projected work, *Natural Selection,* with a chapter on geographical distribution. The following November he was working on the subject of variation. Before long, he began to see that variations of a significant size (as opposed to slight modifications) were rare in nature—a conclusion whose truth he had suspected in 1844. It was in 1856 that Darwin first rejected all saltative forms of variation (monstrosities, sports, etc.) while emphasizing "mere variability" or "individual differences" as the major source of evolutionary variation. These changes appeared in the chapters he wrote on variation from November 1856 to July 1857 (not yet published as of this writing).[19] Thus saltations had proved difficult on two counts: first, that the amount of such "variations be exceedingly small in most organic beings in a state of nature and probably most wanting in the majority of cases,"[20] and second, that they were usually sterile or presented other difficulties related to their peculiar condition in perpetuating themselves.[21] For Darwin, their obvious and essential discontinuity with existing forms relegated them to the category of "freaks"—too unusual and too rare. On the other hand, he said: "every one admits that there are at least individual differences in species under nature."[22] Darwin was more than pleased to exchange rare, freakish, and mostly uninheritable jumps for universal and inheritable individual modifications.

In this same period, Darwin became dissatisfied with the way he had dealt in his earlier draft with swamping. He had seen the inadequacies of the theory of swamping, both in the sense that it would not work so well as he had thought, and in the sense that it seemed too dependent on fortuitous instances of isolation.

The main technical difficulty was that if the number of variants was not to exceed one (in each population per generation), then these isolated populations would have to be small.* From this fact there arose further difficulties. If the groups were so limited in number "this will greatly retard the production of new species through natural selection, by decreasing the chance of the appearance of favorable variations."[23] Further, if the population was small there would be much less survival pressure and/or negative selection. In other words, with room for all to survive, there would be no necessary elimination of older, less adapted forms. Darwin felt that he had been multiplying his probabilities: that of the chance opportunity of isolation times that of a favorable variation appearing within such a small population.

Because of the peculiar necessity to condense so much material under the pressure of time with which he prepared the first *Origin,* Darwin saw his primary task as that of setting forth and explaining his mechanism of evolution—showing how it could construct new from existing species. Equally important as supporting evidence (and comprising the second half of the work) were the chapters in which he demonstrated that the natural selection process could account for a multitude of biological and paleontological phenomena. Though there were two chapters devoted to difficulties encountered in his theory, these consisted mainly of *facts* then inexplicable under his hypothesis. In not one

* If there were fifty individuals, then only 15 per cent of the third-generation offspring would be ⅛th variant; if 100 individuals, then 1⁄12th variant, etc. Even this would be the case *only* if the variant merely outbred and doubled with each generation.

case did a difficulty seem to involve a *process* in nature.* It is thus possible to understand why the problem of blending inheritance was hardly mentioned, and, where mentioned, was not put forward as a form of counterprocess to that of natural selection. As will be seen, the main reason Darwin did not specifically pose blending as a difficulty in the *Origin* was simply that he had detailed the construction of his theory (between 1856 and 1859) with the problem of blending in mind. That the blending *phenomenon* was recognized in the *Origin* and its effect on selection acknowledged can be seen in many places:

> The process [natural selection] will often be greatly retarded by free intercrossing.

> Differences, however slight, between any two forms, if not blended by intermediate gradations, [are] sufficient to raise both forms to the rank of species.

> All the individuals, whatever their quality may be, will generally be allowed to breed, and this will effectually prevent selection.[24]†

These statements appear in the *Origin* mainly as implications of what would happen if the process of natural selection, under specified conditions, were not to function. Most of these citations, however, refer to problems of selection in the domestic state. They are warnings of what selection under nature must face, problems with which (it was assumed) the Darwinian process could successfully deal.

Darwin solved the blending difficulties along two separate

---

* A natural process or tendency, such as dominance, reversion, blending, etc., as processes of inheritance.

† It is interesting to note that at about this same time—when preparing the first *Origin*—Darwin was writing to Huxley: "I have lately been inclined to speculate, very crudely and indistinctly, that propagation by true fertilisation will turn out to be a sort of mixture, and not true fusion, of two distinct individuals, or rather of innumerable individuals, as each parent has its parents and ancestors. I can understand on no other view the way in which crossed forms go back to so large an extent to ancestral forms." (ML–I–103)

but important and related lines. First, by having now clearly delimited his meaning of "variation" to exclude anything except "individual differences," he had gained in terms of number and inheritability while eliminating the difficulties which pursued the concept of saltations. And second, by describing individual differences as common to all organisms, Darwin implied that, even excluding the disadvantageous and the merely neutral modifications, there would still remain for selection a *number* of advantageous variants.[25] Since very few were required, he therefore felt he had established a justifiable probability (with regard to likelihood of appearance and quantity) for his essential raw material.

Darwin's second important change was concerned with the negative side of selection. Whereas earlier emphasis had been largely on the positive aspects of selection,* Darwin in the *Origin* explored the full negative power of selection. He had given some clue in the 1844 essay when, noting that selection would preserve the more fleet predators, he added: "The less fleet ones would be rigidly destroyed."[26] It was this hint (for he had never explained how or why) of a form of rigid destruction that Darwin was to expand in the *Origin*.

Before the *Origin*, the theory of natural selection could be divided into two parts. First there was the *positive* side of selection: that organisms possessing variations favorable to the more efficient utilization of the environment are sustained and perpetuated. The *negative* aspect of selection in the earlier essays consisted (for the most part) merely of the fact that with a limited number of places in the polity of nature, there would be some inevitable elimination of organisms.

In the *Origin*, the process of negative selection took on more independent, less passive shades of meaning. Now, *under a change of conditions* those organisms which do not *maintain* a

---

* Positive in the sense that it referred more to those organisms selected; rejection was concerned only so far as it was the result of a struggle for a limited number of places.

minimal efficiency with respect to their environment are *eliminated*. And further, if the change in conditions is more than slight, then any segment (however large) of the population which cannot fulfill the minimal conditions of efficiency will be *destroyed*. The increase in the negative power of selection is apparent. It is no longer merely the static result of an excess number of organisms in a limited number of places. It is even more than the removal of organisms unadaptable to *new* conditions. It is the destruction of nearly all organisms save those which are minimally adapted. The net result is that more and more organisms are eliminated, with survival the privilege of only a small percentage of the population.

Here, within his description of the process, Darwin circumvented the swamping effect. On the one hand he increased the number of variants from a rare and single occurrence to a representative portion (the beneficially endowed) of differences commonly occurring in all organisms. At the same time, through a more destructive form of selection, he now eliminated large sections of the unmodified population.

To recall the paint-pot simile: Darwin was no longer adding a single drop of black to a large bucket of white paint. What he was now doing was to add a spoonful of black to a bucket of white paint from which, at the same time, he drained off from the bottom a sizeable amount of white. Since more black paint was added at intervals,* it would be only a short time before the paint would be greatly darkened. By adding more variants at the top, so to speak, while at the same time employing negative selection to eliminate many of the unmodified forms, a significant change could indeed be effected. In fact, blending was here an *ally*, for the still small amount of variants (or black paint) could not have an effect on a very large population (the white) were it not for the individual's capacity to blend.

Having mitigated the swamping effect from within the struc-

* Corresponding to the appearance of more individual differences in each generation.

ture of his mechanism, Darwin still required an amount of isolation (the role of the paint bucket in the analogy)—but he was
not nearly so dependent on it as before. Additionally, his notion
of isolation had become more refined, to include now the more
subtle types of ecological situations.* The difficulties attached to
such rare and fortuitous forms of isolation as he had invoked
before were now eliminated. Throughout all this, however,
Darwin had not so much eliminated blending as he had tacitly
assumed its presence within the scheme he set forth, and had
made it work *for* him. This incorporation of the natural force
of blending into the construction of his mechanism had not
forced Darwin to go out of his theoretical way. All he had done,
in fact, was to emphasize the more negative side of selection.
As for implicitly increasing the number of modified forms, this
was not so much a premeditated step to preclude blending problems as it was an automatic result of rejecting saltative forms
of change and committing himself to belief in the idea of individual differences—though it served the purpose excellently
against blending.

BLENDING INHERITANCE IN DARWIN'S CRITICS

Apparently feeling he had eliminated the effect of *swamping*
on his process of evolution, Darwin made no point of discussing
in the *Origin* the more general phenomenon of *blending*. Many
of his critics in the ensuing years were justifiably to interpret
this as a serious and damaging omission. One of the first of these
critics was Dr. Francis Bowen, Harvard professor of philosophy,
who opened the "blending" attacks only a few months after the
Origin appeared:

Variations, if slight, are seldom transmitted by inheritance
... variations, if great, either die out by sterility as monsters,
or are rapidly effaced by crossing the breed ... the very act
of crossing the varieties tends, by splitting the difference, to

* "Ecological niches" in present-day ecological terms.

diminish the distance between them. Under domestication, indeed, the varieties will be kept apart; but in the wild state, Nature has no means of preventing them from pairing. They will interbreed if not prevented and will thereby kill out instead of multiplying their variations.[27]

Considering his position (that at Harvard, as well as that as a philosopher) it seems probable that Bowen had been primed by his friend and intensely anti-Darwinian colleague, Agassiz.* This attack, coming as it did from a member of the highly prejudiced Agassiz circle, could have been passed over by Darwin and his followers.[28] But, coming from a believer it could hardly be dismissed; for even Asa Gray, Darwin's foremost American proponent, felt that blending produced considerable difficulties.[29] He believed, in much the same way as Bowen, that "variations are supposed to be mere oscillations from a normal state, and in Nature to be limited if not transitory" while larger variations "are found to blend in nature."[30] To Gray, what was an effective means of keeping an original species true was also a way of preventing divergence into new forms.

It was T. H. Huxley, Darwin's friend and champion of his theory in the public arena, who undertook to answer the critics of the blending theory and to reconcile the problem they posed regarding the process of natural selection. In his critique of the *Origin*,[31] Huxley noted that while blending is quite commonplace and many variations are swamped or at best diluted by its force, there are nevertheless an equal amount of instances where blending does not take place.

Once in existence, varieties obey the fundamental law of reproduction that like tends to produce like, and their offspring exemplify it by tending to exhibit the same deviation

* Agassiz had probably coached Bowen on his science in much the same way as Richard Owen was to aid Wilberforce, Bishop of Oxford, for the great English debate the next June. For Agassiz, see Edward Lurie, *Louis Agassiz: A Life in Science* (Chicago: University of Chicago Press, 1960), pp. 293–294.

from the parental stock as themselves. Indeed, there seems to be, in many instances, a prepotent influence about a newly-arisen variety which gives it what one may call an unfair advantage over the normal descendants from the same stock.[32]

In this approach, Huxley was not simply leading an objective battle on Darwin's behalf against the blending critics. He had in fact reproached Darwin, on related ground, for his rejection of saltative variations and consequent dependence on such minute modifications. His belief was that selection could and would act on any advantageous variation regardless of size or saltative origin.[33] Yet even Huxley accepted that individual differences would suffice:

> If a variation which approaches the nature of a monstrosity can strive thus forcibly to reproduce itself, it is not wonderful that less aberrant modifications should tend to be preserved even more strongly.[34]

Huxley had not only pointed out many instances of non-blending inheritance but had asserted an independent permanence and stability *in* the new variations. His views on the nature of evolutionary variation form the closest anticipation of present-day *mutation* in evolutionary thought up to that time. For while Darwin had himself pointed out some rare instances of non-blending, he had not in 1859 come out strongly with the notion of prepotency. It was Huxley who had elaborated on the *genetic* factors which overcame the natural mixing process of an otherwise blended heredity.[35]

Further arguments against blending could be found in the contemporary literature. Nearly all the practicing breeders and horticulturists of the time were acutely aware of the care that must be exercised to prevent the blending that resulted from intercrossing. W. C. Spooner, a horse breeder whose general tracts on cross-breeding Darwin read, was representative in his views. Despite the blending, he said, which is so often apparent in the first hybrid cross in animals, "the incongruities are perpetually breaking out . . . so that in the course of time, by the aid of selection, and careful weeding it is practicable to establish a new breed altogether."[36] This optimistic note from a practitioner of artificial selection semed to Darwin worth emphasizing. He had, after all, drawn his first idea of natural selection from analogy with domestic selection.[37]

Huxley's assurance that dominance (or non-blending inheritance) was widespread and strong enough to overcome blending, and Spooner's belief that selection could operate even in the face of blending, were no doubt reassuring to Darwin, but even so there had been, in the criticisms, nothing really new to him. He had anticipated most of what constituted the bases of these arguments.[38] Now he had not only his own functional solution, but a genetic justification for ignoring blending. As Huxley had pointed out, nature provides too many examples of non-blending for one to be overimpressed by the consequences of blending.

While Darwin had not felt it necessary to comment on the blending criticisms of his 1860 critics, he did remark in the fourth edition[39] of the *Origin* that there had appeared a book "by a French author, in opposition to the whole tenor of this volume."[40] The author was Dr. Georges Pouchet and the book: *The Plurality of the Human Race*.[41] This French physician pointed out that the all-important individual difference so restrictively relied upon and defended by Darwin as *the* evolutionary material "quickly disappears through cross-breeding at the tenth generation, if not at the first, in the midst of a population which does not possess it."[42] Pouchet's emphasis on this point produced a response from Darwin which he inserted as his reply in the fourth *Origin*. The reasons why Darwin waited until 1866 to comment against blending were more technical than theoretical. He was engaged on the second edition of the *Origin* the day the first edition appeared. The third edition, responding to criticisms of 1859–60, was devoted mainly to clarifying and expanding his concept of natural selection. It was after rejecting monstrosities and saltations as evolutionary material that Darwin became sensitive to blending—sensitive insofar as he at last found it necessary to point out how he had overcome the problem within the pages of previous editions. He started by repeating an admission he had made in the first *Origin:*

> No doubt the small changes or variations which do occur are incessantly checked and retarded by intercrossing, but . . .[43]

and he proceeded to give three reasons why the blending effects of inter-crossing could not counteract selection. Two of these were those that he had built into the conditions under which selection would operate. The third was the notion of a genetic impetus: that the individual offspring inherit from the parent the tendency to vary again in the same direction.[44] Even with these reasons, the ultimate justification for Darwin's belief that blending could not prevent selection was the observability of "the frequent existence of varieties in the same country with the parent species."[45] In other words, blending could not always have been effective. Darwin was only drawing attention here to what was apparent in the process of natural selection. At this juncture Darwin looked upon blending as a problem to trouble the minds of those who believed in large variations as the source of evolutionary change. For those like himself, whose material was the universal differences among all individuals, he had demonstrably circumvented the swamping effects of blending within the conditions he had set for natural selection. Having done this in the first *Origin* he did not expect to have to take up the subject again. Thus, at this time, Darwin had not only made explicit, but had resolved, his long-held views on blending some time before Jenkin appeared on the critical horizon.

BLENDING INHERITANCE IN DARWIN'S WRITINGS 1860–1867

The Variation: Almost as soon as the first *Origin* had been sent to the printers, Darwin began *The Variation of Animals and Plants under Domestication.* In writing the *Variation,* Darwin drew largely from contemporary sources. By the end of 1862 he had finished the first volume and was eagerly starting on the theoretical aspect of inheritance. It was his research into the various causes producing variation that had led Darwin into the more general study of inheritance.

As has been pointed out, Darwin believed blending to be the normal result of inheritance. He repeated this view in a letter to Hooker written just a few days before he started on the second volume: "This I believe is the common effect of crossing: viz., the obliteration of incipient varieties."[46] No sooner had he commenced work than he was considering those apparent exceptions to blending: prepotency and reversion. The earliest paper he read on the subject was that of Thomas Andrew Knight who, in 1799, described dominance and reversion in *Pisum.*[47] Suffice it to say, this was the first of a great mass of literature abounding in individual descriptions of both phenomena. Among these papers, however, were some which went beyond mere description to offer speculation about underlying causes. One of the first of these was written in 1830 by Augustin Sageret.[48] He felt that "the resemblance of hybrid to its predecessors consisted, not in an intimate fusion of the differing characters peculiar to each, but actually a combination."[49] And following from this, in breeding experiments involving fruit, Sageret reported segregation in not one, but five, sets of characters: a result which was, he felt, a vivid demonstration of his hypothesis.

Continuing in this tradition was Charles Naudin, whose views, as reported in two papers of 1858 and 1862,[50] seemed to denounce entirely the idea of a blending inheritance. Even when the hybrid appeared as a blend he felt it to be only a superficiality limited to the human eye. Instead, he looked upon the hybrid organism as a "living mosaic"—a composite mixture of distinct sets of parental characters. He went further, asserting that the two specific elements were often segregated in the following generations through the male and female sexual elements.

Naudin's view of the organism as a hybrid mosaic was interestingly dynamic. He looked upon the coexistence of the two different elements for each character as resulting in a discordant, unbalanced state. This discordance, he felt, accounted for many cases of hybrid sterility. At the same time, the tendency to return to one of the two equilibrated parental characters accounted for the reversions frequently observed. This tendency to return he saw as a conflict in which the stronger of the two characters prevailed. The extinction of the character of one resulted in the supremacy of the remaining one. This, said Naudin, could occur in any of the generations following crossing, but "among many of these second-generation hybrids, there were complete returns to one or the other of the two parent species."[51]

While accepting Naudin's view as accounting for prepotency and for reversion when limited to intervals of only one or two generations, Darwin felt that mere internal instability was insufficient to account for the reappearance of long-lost characters:

> Naudin's view is not applicable to the reappearance of characters lost long ago by variation; and it is hardly applicable to races or species which, after having been crossed at some former period with a distinct form, and having since lost all traces of the cross, nevertheless occasionally yield an individual which reverts to the crossing form.[52]

Commenting on an address given by George Bentham in which Naudin's hypothesis was criticized, Darwin remarked: "I am glad that he [Bentham] is cautious about Naudin's view, for I cannot think it will hold. The tendency of hybrids to revert to either parent is part of a wider law (which I am fully convinced that I can show experimentally), namely, that crossing races as well as species tends to bring back characters which existed in progenitors hundreds and thousands of generations ago."[53] His own view was "that every character is derived exclusively from the father or mother, but that many characters lie latent in both parents during a long succession of generations," reappearing as reversions through having been "either indirectly or directly induced by the change in their conditions of life."[54]

Naudin's hypothesis, accepted in part by Darwin, was well received by breeders as an explanation of many hitherto inexplicable facts. By 1865, a number of such men were incorporating this view within their own works. In his reading of W. C. Spooner's essay "On Cross-Breeding in Horses," Darwin must have seen Naudin all over again. For, in his discussion of the mixture of parental characters in a cross, Spooner noted:

> That this combination, which may be more of a mechanical than a chemical union, by no means implies such an equal division of influence, as the mingling of two fluids, in which case the offspring would be unlike either parent, but a *juste milieu* between the two, and there could be no handing down of type from one generation to another. It is rather such a fusion of two bodies into one that both defects and high qualifications are passed on from parent to offspring with a sort of regular irregularity, resembling the waves of the sea—each parent having the remarkable power of propagating ancestral peculiarities though latent in itself.[55]

Also in 1865, Madden and MacKnight in their *On the True Principles of Breeding* adopted a similar point of view, stating that blending was merely an external phenomenon that occurred only in the first hybrid generation. After that, offspring could break out in an endless possibility of variation, with a choice of variations for any single feature from among those possessed by its antecedents.[56]

Despite all these opinions and demonstrations that both prepotency and reversion could readily overcome the influence of blending,[57] Darwin looked upon these two exceptions as merely transient in their effects. Throughout his writings prepotency represented a quality, a quality of power or force. It was, in Darwin's view, a master of genetic momentum which he felt would gradually decay in subsequent generations. Thus uniformity of character, because of the inevitable tendency to blend, would prevail.

While blending may not have been the sole or necessary result of the crossing of differing individuals *in any single generation,* it certainly seemed to Darwin the eventual result of continued reproduction. Though the prepotent power of a character may overbear that of blending in the first or in any other single generation, blending was the more general, more common result of reproduction. Blending was the ever-present force, prepotency a force which gradually disappeared.

Darwin had seen this for himself at first hand, in his breeding of *Antirrhinum.*[58] The first hybrid generation showed 100 per cent prepotency of the zygomorphic over the peloric form. The second showed that the prepotent power of zygomorphism had diminished to 75 per cent. Darwin admitted that it was anybody's guess as to how long it would take to achieve complete obliteration of the prepotency in question. This was, he felt, because the power of prepotency could have its motive force revived through new crossings, changes in conditions, or any one of a number of factors. But its eventual decay was certain.[59] A uniform blend of the original parental characters remained a foregone conclusion: the decay of the prepotent power and the genetic tendency to blend were equally inevitable.

Certainly the case against blending inheritance had been

well documented in the literature before 1867, a fact of which Darwin was well aware. Ironically enough, it was Darwin himself who pointed out what he felt was the transient nature of such effects. By thus rejecting reversion and prepotency as alternatives to blending and thereby eliminating blending as a serious hindrance to the selection process, Darwin committed himself more firmly than ever to his earlier means of mitigating the blending force: isolation and large numbers of variants.

Darwin concluded the *Variation* by putting forward his own "Provisional Hypothesis of Pangenesis." It was in this theory of the hereditary mechanism that Darwin tried to account for all the observable facts and laws of inheritance—a considerable variety of phenomena to unite under a common theory. Anything which had been documented and accepted by a fellow scientist was included and assessed. From other sources and from his own work, Darwin included a number of Lamarckian factors as causes for variation.* The result of this was a considerably *ad hoc* hypothesis, with some physiological pretensions borrowed mainly from Herbert Spencer's recent *Principles of Biology.*† The most striking thing about this theory was that it was constructed to allow for the inheritance of changes or characteristics acquired by the parent organism during its lifetime. This strong core of Lamarckism in the *Variation,* in its appearance in 1868, has led two recent writers into some error regarding the chronology and relationship of Jenkin's criticism to the *Variation* (and "Pangenesis" contained in it).[60] Both these writers have been led to believe that "Pangenesis" was an effect, the cause of which was the inescapable force of Jenkin's criticism. Darwin, however, had finished the last chapter of the *Variation* on April 22, 1865, and had dispatched "Pangenesis"

---

* These were the inherited effects of environmental conditions, habit, use, and disuse.

† This was published in eight serial installments covering the two printed volumes. Darwin's interest lay in 1:289 *et seq.*, which appeared in the third installment during the summer of 1863. There is a remarkable similarity between Spencer's "physiological units" and Darwin's "pangenes."

to Huxley on May 27. The whole work had been sent to the printer on November 21, 1866,[61] and although Darwin did have some months in which to review the work and correct the galleys, he acknowledged that, having been specifically instructed by the printer not to make any but the most minor alterations, he did indeed make very few changes.[62] Since Jenkin's review did not appear until June 1867, there is extremely little possibility that this could have been a cause of any changes in the *Variation*.

FLEEMING JENKIN (1867)

Fleeming Jenkin's review was based essentially on the fourth edition, which had appeared the previous December. Though over forty pages in length and containing many individual criticisms, the main attack can be divided into two distinct halves. First, Jenkin dispatched individual differences by asserting that they could never be selectively accumulated to pass beyond the confines of a definite "sphere" of variation.[63] There was, he said, a point or "norm" around which individual types could vary. They could vary in every direction for this norm but not beyond a certain limit in any one direction; they were like oscillations about a fixed point. This fixed point represented an essentially specific character so that at best, dogs could be improved as dogs and rabbits as rabbits, but little else could be effected. Continued selection could avail nothing because the limit of this type of variation was reached well before even a new subspecies could be produced. In pointing this out, Jenkin felt he had shown the impossibility of employing individual differences as a source of evolutionary material. He then turned his attention to the obvious alternative, saltations.

To demonstrate the inadequacy of saltations in this, the second half of his attack, Jenkin employed two arguments. He began by citing all the usual difficulties encountered with saltations: they occurred rarely and singly, they were too freakish—too great a departure from the normal form—and were therefore usually sterile. Second, and on the supposition that there might occur some less drastically anomalous types of saltation, he invoked the swamping effect. Said Jenkin in no uncertain terms:

> It is impossible that any sport or accidental variation in a single individual, however favourable to life, should be preserved and transmitted by Natural Selection.[64]

He went on to describe blending and pointed out that in terms of whole populations "the advantage, whatever it may be, is utterly outbalanced by numerical inferiority"[65] and the variation would be swamped. "A highly-favoured white cannot blanch a nation of negroes."[66]

The most important thing to note in Jenkin's criticism is that he employed two separate arguments, one against individual differences, the other against saltations. Against mere differences he used the notion that there was a definite limit to variation. It was only against saltations that he employed the swamping argument. This was important, for, as we shall see, Darwin agreed with Jenkin's criticism regarding the swamping of saltations while at the same time failing to see that blending would apply equally to individual differences.

Busily engaged in preparing the fifth *Origin* early in 1869, Darwin wrote to Hooker:

> It is only about two years since last edition of *Origin* and I am fairly disgusted to find how much I have to modify, and how much I ought to add; but I have determined not to add much. Fleeming Jenkin has given me much trouble, but has been of more real use to me than any other essay or review.[67]

A few days later he wrote to Wallace. In describing how his work on the new *Origin* was going, he mentioned having improved on a number of points:

> I always thought individual differences more important than single variations, but now I have come to the conclusion

that they are of paramount importance, and in this I believe I agree with you. Fleeming Jenkin's arguments have convinced me.[68]

It is on the basis of these two statements, together with other circumstantial information, that previous writers have assessed Jenkin's influence on Darwin. Darwin's terminology and his confusing syntax make this a difficult sentence to understand. It seems not altogether clear whether "they" refers to "individual differences" or to "single variations." On top of that it is not entirely clear, especially to the modern reader, that there is any essential difference between the two terms. A "single variation" always meant for Darwin* a rare and discontinuous form of change, whereas "individual differences" never occurred singly, being universal to all organisms.

In replying to Darwin, Wallace, while correctly understanding the distinction between the terms, nevertheless misunderstood the syntax:

> Will you tell me where are Fleeming Jenkin's arguments on the importance of single variations? Because I at present hold most strongly the contrary opinion that it is the individual differences or *general variability* of species that enables them to become modified and adapted to new conditions.
>
> Variations or "sports" may be important in modifying an animal in one direction, as his colour for instance, but how it can possibly work in changes requiring coordination of many parts as in Orchids for example, I cannot conceive.[69]

In making this misinterpretation, Wallace had understood Darwin to mean that he had come to a conclusion opposite to that of his original view, having now been convinced of his

---

* As well as for most of his contemporaries (see Wallace's comment). The correct interpretation can be seen in a footnote in the beginning of the *Descent of Man* (Modern Library edition, p. 751).

error by Jenkin. Darwin tried to straighten him out by return mail:

> I must have expressed myself atrociously; I mean to say exactly the reverse of what you have understood. F. Jenkin argued in the *North British Review* against single variations ever being perpetuated, and has convinced me, though not in quite so broad a manner as here put. I always thought individual differences more important; but I was blind and thought that single variations might be preserved much oftener than I now see is possible or probable. I mentioned this in my former note merely because I believed that you had come to a similar conclusion, and I like much to be in accord with you. I believe I was mainly deceived by single variations offering such simple illustrations, as when man selects.[70]

Here again (though Wallace now understood) Darwin only furthered the confusion by placing the terms in such a way that they seemed synonymous. The syntax has been made more confusing for modern readers because these two terms appear synonymous. When Darwin said: "I always thought individual differences more important; but I was blind and thought that single variations might be preserved much oftener," he was in fact saying that while always suspecting that large single variations were uninheritable, he had been blind in not seeing the effect of swamping on them. It was Jenkin who convinced him that he was right in rejecting them. Jenkin had apparently not convinced Darwin to alter his view, but had instead convinced him that he had been right in his suspicions all along: large variations would be swamped by blending and were therefore useless for a study of natural selection.

As for the way Jenkin dealt with individual differences, Darwin did not agree. Since no one had yet demonstrated any limit to the accumulation of such differences, Darwin felt he was justified in rejecting Jenkin's statements to the contrary.

He also felt that if there were a limit to variation, it was large enough in extent to permit the formation of new species.

In one place in his review, however, Jenkin did remark that if large variations could never be preserved, then "still less can slight and imperceptible variations, occurring in single individuals, be garnered up and transmitted to continually increasing numbers."[71] The key phrase here for Darwin was "occurring in single individuals." It was in reading Jenkin that Darwin became fully aware of the good fortune he had had in basing his mechanism on universally occurring individual differences. For where there were some numbers of variant forms, swamping could be avoided. Jenkin had always talked in terms of the odd variant. Said Darwin in the fifth edition:

> I saw . . . that the preservation in a state of nature of any occasional deviation of structure, such as a monstrosity, would be a rare event; and that, if preserved, it would generally be lost by subsequent intercrossing with ordinary individuals. Nevertheless, until reading an able and valuable article in the *North British Review* (1867), I did not appreciate how rarely single variations whether slight or strongly-marked, could be perpetuated.[72]

Rare, single deviations were discontinuous. They appeared suddenly and out of nowhere. Whether large or small, in their sudden singularity they were all saltative to Darwin. So, after reading Jenkin, Darwin became even more firmly committed to the selection of mere individual differences. Although Jenkin's remarks were meant to apply equally to the swamping of even individual differences, Darwin did not attach any difficulties to them.

Yet Darwin had nevertheless seen that his theory required a significant number of the necessary variations—if not simultaneously, at least within a few generations. Already at hand, within his own theory as it then stood, were factors which fulfilled these requirements: the several factors which he had listed as "causes of variation"—Lamarckian factors upon whose operation the requisite variations would ensue.

As the result of Jenkin's impact, Darwin's view of the selection process in which blending was a necessary contingency showed three main changes: first, his implicit emphasis on isolation as containment,* together with an underlining of the power of *negative* selection; second, his reiterated belief that variant individuals pass on to their offspring the inherited tendency to vary again in the same direction;† third, his increasing attribution of variation to such Lamarckian factors as the direct action of environmental conditions[73] and the inherited effects of habit, use, and disuse. All these were factors to which he had previously paid passing recognition, but which at this time it became necessary to fall back upon with increasing emphasis in order to ensure the necessary conditions for the selective modification whose limitations were becoming more apparent.

In emphasizing doubtful genetic beliefs and Lamarckian factors whose role in the evolutionary process he had previously discounted, Darwin effectively opened up a Pandora's box of difficulties the results of which would, at a later date, bring about his total withdrawal from the scene of the debate about evolution. While it would remain for others to force Darwin's theoretical hand, it was Jenkin who, in committing Darwin to the views just described, brought about his inclusion of blending inheritance within his theoretical mechanism. Thus there was in 1867 no *turning* point, nor even any sense of emergency: it was more as if a door had closed quietly behind Darwin.

* A more detailed discussion on this subject will be found in chapter 7, particularly pages 160 and 163.

† A more detailed discussion on this subject will be found in chapter 6, particularly page 146.

6. The Limits of Variation

*If in every case we find that deviation from an average
individual can be rapidly effected at first, and that
the rate of deviation steadily diminishes till it reaches
an almost imperceptible amount, then we are as
much entitled to assume a limit to the possible
deviation as we are to the progress of a cannon-ball
from a knowledge of the law of diminution in its speed.*

—Fleeming Jenkin, "The Origin of Species" in
North British Review (1867)

*T*he first and most important condition for the effective
operation of the natural selection process was "a large
amount of inheritable and diversified variability."[1]

From the outset, Darwin had been aware of the necessity for
demonstrating five separate points regarding variation: (1)
that a requisite amount of natural variation did, in time, occur;
(2) that some portion of this would be advantageous to the
organisms possessing it; (3) that such variations appeared in
nearly every part of the organism; (4) that such variations were
inheritable; and (5) that these variations were of sufficient
diversity to allow their selective accumulation to form new
species.

Darwin discussed each of these points in the earlier essays

and they were later incorporated into the preliminary chapters on variation in the first *Origin*.

On the first point, Darwin began, in 1844, on a slightly pessimistic note: "Most organic beings in a state of nature vary exceedingly little. . . . Although the amount of variation be exceedingly small in most organic beings in a state of nature, and probably quite wanting (as far as our senses serve) in the majority of cases, yet, I think we may safely conclude that all organic beings with few exceptions, would vary."[2] The additional work done before the time of the first *Origin* yielded a more hopeful conclusion: "I am convinced that the most experienced naturalist would be surprised at the number of the cases of variability . . . which he could collect on good authority, as I have collected, during a course of years."[3]

On the second point, Darwin began with the statement that "every one admits that there are at least individual differences in species under nature"[4] to which he added that "if organic beings vary at all in the several parts of their organisation, . . . I think it would be a most extraordinary fact if no variation ever had occurred useful to each being's own welfare."[5]

On the third point, Darwin stated: "I think that there is sufficient evidence to show that every part occasionally varies in a slight degree."[6]

On the fourth point, Darwin foresaw little difficulty.

> If strange and rare deviations of structure are truly inherited, less strange and commoner deviations of structure may be freely admitted to be inheritable. Perhaps the correct way of viewing the whole subject, would be, to look at the inheritance of every character whatever as the rule and non-inheritance as the anomaly.[7]

The final point was more difficult to demonstrate regarding species in nature. Since it was a series of slight beneficial gradations that would be required over a very great period of time, all Darwin could assume was that if at present a great

diversity of variation could be seen, then, in time, the necessary diversity of form would occur. In his belief that
there was no apparent limit to the possible variation, Darwin realized he was in a minority. Here the influence of
Lyell was considerable. The first three chapters in the second
volume of the *Principles of Geology* were devoted to weighing
the arguments for and against the transmutation of species.[8]
The very first point in the chapter on arguments *against* transmutation was that of the widely held belief in a limit to variation. From the vantage point of actual observation, Lyell
pointed out the argument from domestication. Here he noted
the absence of a single authenticated example of true and
permanent change in the specific form. He went on to note
that, in fact, many domestic species which have undergone
some form of alteration have only reverted to their original type,
once freed from domesticating influences.[9] Some pages later,
Lyell recognized that changing conditions do produce modifications and that "the mutations thus superinduced are governed
by constant laws, and the capability of so varying forms part
of the permanent specific character"[10]—a recognition in which
Darwin must have found great support. Yet Darwin, perhaps
aware of Lyell's previously pessimistic reminder about the likelihood of an ultimate reversion to original type, felt compelled
to make the marginal addition "with no tendency to go back"—
a necessary assumption if selection was to pass permanently the
barrier implied in the notion of specific type.

Lyell concluded this chapter by listing the inferences he
had drawn from the evidence of his contemporaries. The fourth
of these is worth quoting in its entirety:

> The entire variation from the original type, which any given
> kind of change can produce, may usually be effected in a
> brief period of time, after which no farther deviation can
> be obtained by continuing to alter the circumstances, though
> ever so gradually,—indefinite divergence either in the way

of improvement or deterioration, being prevented, and the least possible excess beyond the defined limits being fatal to the existence of the individual.[11]

Here Darwin stopped, underscored "improvement or deterioration," and added "If this were *true,* adios *theory."* Nevertheless Darwin continued to swim upstream against the current of contemporary opinion.

That a limit to variation does exist in nature is assumed by most authors, though I am unable to discover a single fact on which this belief is granted.[12]

When discussing the view of some breeders that the supply of variations in domestic cattle had been exhausted, he commented:

I repeat that we know nothing of any limit to the possible amount of variation, and therefore to the number and differences of the races which might be produced by the natural means of selection.[13]

This assumption was carried forward into the *Origin* where he stated: "It cannot be asserted that organic beings in a state of nature are subject to no variation; it cannot be proved that the amount of variation in the course of long ages is a limited quantity."[14] This was to be but one of the ways in which Darwin bolstered his defensive position. Here he had moved into the realm of the unobservable where, for the present, his allies were the great amounts of time over which he could project this change, and the implication that extrapolations from the domestic to the wild state would be found invalid.

Still another way in which Darwin was to justify his position lay in his own definition of the concept of "species." If such a term amounted only to a set of characters peculiar to a group of organisms, and if any one or all of these characters them-

selves varied (however slightly), the door to permanent transmutation was open. In other words, by recognizing no permanent circumscribed organic entity, Darwin obviated any "species
barrier" that might impede a gradual transformation. His view
of varieties and other subspecific forms as "incipient species"[15]
reflected this notion.

We shall see below how both these views, though mentioned
in the first *Origin,* were later expanded by Darwin in response
to later critics.

VARIATION AND SELECTION: DARWIN'S VIEW

Since Darwin had said that "natural selection can act only
by the preservation and accumulation of infinitesimally small
inherited modifications"[16] he had to ask the following question:
"How, then, does the lesser difference between varieties become
augmented into the greater difference between species?"[17] First,
he said:

The variations are supposed to be extremely slight, but of
the most diversified nature; they are not supposed all to
appear simultaneously, but often after long intervals of time;
nor are they all supposed to endure for equal periods.[18]

The early differences would be very slight; in the course of
time, from the continued selection of swifter horses by some
breeders, and of stronger ones by others, the differences
would become greater, and would be noted as forming two
sub-breeds; finally, after the lapse of centuries, the sub-
breeds would become converted into two well-established
and distinct breeds. . . . As the differences slowly become
greater, the inferior animals with intermediate characters,
being neither very swift nor very strong, will have been
neglected and will have tended to disappear. Here, then,
we see in man's productions the action of what may be
called the principle of divergence, causing differences, at

first barely appreciable, steadily to increase, and the breeds to diverge in character both from each other and from their common parent.[19]

The following examples will, perhaps, make a number of points more clear:

Species (A, B, O, etc.) Produce Two Types of Variation:

(1) *Continuous Variations*   *(Individual Differences)*

$$A \longrightarrow A_a$$
$$B \longrightarrow B_a$$
$$O \longrightarrow O_a$$

(2) *Discontinuous Variations*   *(Saltations)*

$$A \longrightarrow A_g$$
$$A \longrightarrow A_e$$
$$O \longrightarrow O_e$$

Individual Variations occur in all Parts of the Organism:

(3)

in order to produce a new species, according to Darwin, variations must be slight, individual differences (i.e. continuous):

(4) $O \longrightarrow O_a,$ $A_a \longrightarrow A_b,$ $B_e \longrightarrow B_f,$
not $O \longrightarrow O_e,$ $A_a \longrightarrow A_f,$ or $B_e \longrightarrow B_k$

They must, of course, appear in the same structure,

(5) $O_{a_1} \longrightarrow O_{b_1},$ $A_{a_2} \longrightarrow A_{b_2},$
not $O_{a_1} \longrightarrow O_{b_2}$ or $A_{a_2} \longrightarrow A_{b_4}$

and they must increase or further the organism's adaptation to its conditions of life (i.e. continue toward the same adaptive end),

(6) $\quad O_{a_1} \longrightarrow O_{b_1}, \quad O_{m_1} \longrightarrow O_{n_1}, \quad O_{y_1} \longrightarrow O_{z_1}$
$$\text{not} \quad O_{f_1} \longrightarrow O_{e_1}$$

Thus, species "O" will produce a new related species "$\emptyset$" in the following steps:

(7) $\quad O \longrightarrow O_{a_1} \quad O_{b_1} \longrightarrow O_{c_1}, \quad O_{x_1} \longrightarrow O_{y_1} \quad O_{z_1} \longrightarrow \emptyset$

This, however, is a one-dimensional, orthogenetic description which belies the actual complexity of the process of natural selection. It does not, for example, illustrate the manifold variation from which the requisite advantageous forms are selected, nor does it show the time scale over which the process takes place.

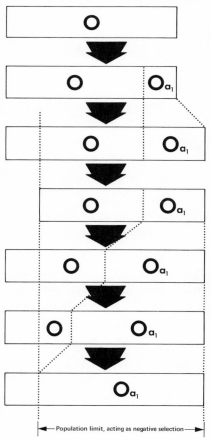

Population limit, acting as negative selection

In a population of species "O" there appear, from time to time over many generations, individual variations of the nature O_{a_1}.

Because of their beneficial nature, individuals possessing them have a selective advantage over the unmodified forms, which insures their perpetuation. Perpetuation due to selective advantage is the first part of the selective process.

A second part of the process which Darwin saw as occurring simultaneously with the first was that of elimination, or negative selection. This arose in two ways. Under relatively static conditions it was the result of the competition of a nearly limitless number of individuals for a limited number of places in nature. Under changing conditions it was the sheer removal of less adapted forms by the effect of new conditions.

Because of their advantage, individuals possessing beneficial variations tend to leave many more offspring. That is, many more of the offspring of these modified individuals live to maturity (and thereby reproduce another generation). They have either partly or completely inherited the beneficial characters of their parents. Thus, together with the introduction from time to time of more similarly modified forms (from the unmodified section of the population), the amount of O_{a_1} individuals in the population increases as the original forms decrease.* This is the part of the selective process in which the new forms multiply themselves.

Eventually, O_{a_1} will completely supplant the original form,† resulting in a new permanent form. It will be from within this new form that further modifications (O_b), some useful in the continuing process of adaptation (O_{b_1}), will occur.

Since only those new forms which further the adaptivity of the variety will be selected, a sense of direction can be noted in the selective process as a whole. Thus another aspect of the selective process, that of direction, can be recognized. Darwin saw each new form (O_{a_1}, O_{b_1}, O_{m_1}, O_{z_1}) as a permanent type, each representing some further improvement in the desired direction and each reproducing itself true to its type with the sole exception of ever-present individual differences.

It is clear that Darwinian natural selection involves, within the term, a number of discrete processes. There is the insured *perpetuation* of the modified forms due to their selective advantage in the struggle for existence. There is the concomitant *elimination* of the unmodified forms in this same struggle (or under a change of conditions favorable to the new forms).

* Since it is the newer types that have selective preference over the existing places in the natural economy.

†Or, the two forms will become separated into two isolated ecological communities—their new form separating the variants because of their pre-adaptivity to a different set of surrounding conditions.

There is the *multiplication* of the modified forms arising from their competitive advantage, and finally there is the *direction* imparted to the process of change through the selection of yet newer forms tending to further the adaptive change already initiated. A significant number of Darwin's critics were not to deny that the process of natural selection was capable of all four. Instead, they were to attack, not selection, but the type of variation selected—Darwin's "individual differences"—and this on the grounds of both non-inheritability and insufficient diversity.

Darwin felt he had not only demonstrated the sufficiency of individual differences as the material for speciation, but that he had gone further—actually to deny any such role to saltations. In so doing, he implied not only the necessity *and* sufficiency of slight variations, but also that they were the *only* means by which speciation could be effected. It was by so committing himself to individual differences, his critics felt, that Darwin had so severely limited himself as to prevent the natural selection process from working in the role to which it was otherwise quite suitable.

CRITICISMS (1860)

Darwin made a number of assumptions on the subject of variations in the *Origin,* but none of his critics was to challenge him on the *facts* of natural variation: that variations occurred, that some variations were advantageous, and that individual differences seemed to occur in every structure. As for the inheritability of such variations, or the assumption that there was no limit to the divergence that could be achieved through their cumulative selection, there were to be significant howls of protest from his contemporaries.

The first attacks came from America. A special meeting of the Academy of Sciences had been called in Boston for March 27 for the sole purpose of discussing the Darwinian theory of selection. The speakers included Agassiz, Bowen, Parsons, and

Asa Gray.[20] Each speaker including Gray (who, as an ardent Darwinian, was primarily defensive) attacked Darwin on the grounds that there was a limit to the selection of slight variations.

Agassiz was first:

> Let it not be objected that the individuals of successive generations have presented marked differences among themselves; for these differences, with all the monstrosities that may have occurred, during these countless generations, have passed away with the individuals, as individual peculiarities, and the specific characteristics alone have been preserved, together with all that distinguishes the genus, the family, the order, and the class and branch to which the individual belonged. Does this not prove that while individuals are perishable, they transmit, generation after generation, all that is specific or generic, or in one word, *typical* in them, to them, and that, therefore, while individuals alone have a material existence, species, genera, families, orders, classes and branches of the animal kingdom exist only as categories of thought in the supreme Intelligence, but as such have as truly an independent existence and are as unvarying as thought itself after it has once been expressed.
>
> Whatever minor differences may exist between the products of this succession of generations, all are *individual peculiarities,* in no way connected with the essential features of the species, and therefore as transient as the individuals; while the specific characters are forever fixed.[21]

Darwin's sole marginal comment on the above was that it was "all mere assertion" but, in a following letter to Gray, he gave this opinion:

> I am surprised that Agassiz did not succeed in writing something better. How absurd that logical quibble—"If species do not exist, how can they vary?" As if any one doubted

their temporary existence. How coolly he assumes that there is some clearly defined distinction between individual differences and varieties. It is no wonder that a man who calls identical forms, when found in two countries, distinct species, cannot find variation in nature.[22]

Whereas Agassiz had denied any permanent effects to the selection of individual differences out of a belief in the fixity of species, the next speaker, Parsons, did the same, but from a belief in speciation through saltative changes in the specific character.

Darwin assumes, and reasons exclusively on the assumption, that the successive changes by which these great results have been brought about have always been minute and slow, and have only become sufficient to reach their consummation, by an indefinite accumulation of effects, through the indefinite periods of time which geology affords them.[23]

In denying such a possibility Parsons offered, as an alternative, speciation by embryonic saltation which, in turn, had as its cause "some influence of variation acting upon the ovum" so that from some group of animals, like wolves, foxes, hyenas, or jackals "a brood will come forth puppies and grow up like dogs and produce dogs."[24] As we have seen, Darwin answered Parsons, employing the argument against monstrosities.

It was Professor Bowen, the last speaker in the anti-Darwinian group, who summed up most succinctly by noting that:

Variations, if slight, are seldom transmitted by inheritance, and so cannot act by accumulation, and cannot therefore effect permanency of type.[25]

It is not difficult to see how the attacks of Agassiz, Parsons, and Bowen could have been discounted by Darwin. In the first place they were put forward by men who were anxious to demonstrate either the general immutability of species or else speciation by saltation. In the second place, their criticisms of selection revolved chiefly around the belief that only the noncontinuous variations were inheritable. Darwin, of course, denied all three alternatives.

The one American whose opinion Darwin valued most highly was Asa Gray, who, at this meeting, was the lone spokesman defending the *Origin*.[26] Yet even Gray could not see how selection could operate on individual differences. His vast, firsthand knowledge of botany had impressed upon him two apparent facts of nature: that individual variations remained slight changes in the individual and were therefore rarely transmitted, and also that, where there were some which were heritable, there still existed some formidable specific barriers preventing their cumulative selection, of which inter-specific sterility was only one manifestation. Said Gray summing up in the same journal:

> These [Darwin's individual] variations are supposed to be mere oscillations from a normal state, and in Nature to be limited if not transitory.[27]

Darwin wrote back:

> I declare that you know my book as well as I do myself; and bring to the question new lines of illustration and argument in a manner which excites my astonishment and almost my envy! Every single word seems weighed carefully, and tells like a 32 lb. shot.[28]

Though a gracious compliment, it was not really an acknowledgment that Darwin had been impressed enough to alter his stand regarding slight differences.

A similar forum on Darwinism took place in England the following June. It was at this Oxford meeting of the British Association for the Advancement of Science that Dr. (and Reverend) Samuel Wilberforce began his virulent attack of the theory of natural selection later extended into a thirty-page review of the *Origin* in the *Quarterly Review*. His concluding remarks give the core of his argument:

> We have already shown that the variations of which we have proof under domestication, have never, under the longest and most continued system of selection we have known, laid the first foundation of a specific difference, but have always tended to relapse, and not to accumulated and fixed persistence.
>
> We come then to these conclusions. All the facts presented to us in the natural world tend to show that none of the variations produced in the fixed forms of animal life, when seen in its most plastic condition under domestication, give any promise of a true transmutation of species; first, from the difficulty of accumulating and fixing variations within the same species; secondly from the fact that these variations, though most serviceable for man, have no tendency to improve the individual beyond the standard of his own specific type, and so to afford matter, even if they were infinitely produced, for the supposed power of natural selection on which to work; whilst all variations from the mixture of species are barred by the inexorable law of hybrid sterility.[29]

The last commentary on the subject appearing in this summer of heated debate came to Darwin in October in the form of a reprint from William Henry Harvey, the Dublin professor of botany with whom he had had previous correspondence on the subject of monstrosities. Said Harvey:

> It strikes me that there is a fallacy at the very base of Mr. Darwin's argument; and that his whole superstructure rests on the *assumption* that Variability acts indefinitely and continuously, without check or hindrance.[30]

In his copy, Darwin noted: "Good to admit that continued

variation is an assumption" and when, a few weeks later, he started the third edition of the *Origin*, he added:

> That varieties more or less different from the parent stock occasionally arise, few will deny; but that the process of variation should be thus indefinitely prolonged is an assumption, the truth of which must be judged of by how far the hypothesis accords with and explains the general phenomena of nature.
>
> On the other hand, the ordinary belief that the amount of possible variation is a strictly limited quantity is likewise a simple assumption.[31]

While Gray, like Agassiz and the rest, had based his criticism mainly on the transient nature of individual differences, both Wilberforce and Harvey stressed rather the limits they felt existed to the selection of such differences. It was to their remarks that Darwin directed his attention when looking back over his earlier editions. The fact that he made but one allusion to the subject in the new edition indicates, first, his general unwillingness to change* and, second, his intention to wait until he had a chance to go into the matter more thoroughly in his work on *Variation*. For it was this on which he had been engaged when he started the third edition.

Yet Darwin was not so much unwilling to change on general principles as he was convinced, through having entertained many alternative possibilities years before, that the process as he had outlined it (in the first *Origin*) was still a perfectly effective means. It was his critics, he felt, that had been unable to see clearly the manner in which natural selectivity operated.

Darwin's view of organic nature, looking from the remotest

* On the grounds that his reviewers did not clearly apprehend the process as he saw it.

period of biological times to the present, was of a finely graded series of forms, each diverging slightly from the one previous, into the distinct ecological channels presently inhabited by those forms we now distinguish as "species." In each case, new forms arose from existing ones through a series of slightly graded differences. From within present species, said Darwin, one could see how species had arisen in the past. He said, in fact: "I believe a well-marked variety may be justly called an incipient species."[32] If one inspected the supposed differences demarcating the subspecific forms, said Darwin, one saw that "these differences blend into each other in an insensible series."[33] Thus the many taxonomically distinguishable types, such as species, subspecies, varieties, etc., were actually considered part of a finely graded series. Taxonomic labels were, in fact, superimposed over such groups within this natural series as could be seen to possess common sets of characters. In this view, the only "groups" which had any existence as real, discrete, recognizable forms were those which could consistently reproduce the same sets of characters. Thus, with Darwin, intermediary subspecific forms were those which could be as real and distinct as those higher groups recognized by taxonomists. In fact, in Darwin's view, two allied taxonomic species were no more than such self-reproducing forms as those extinct intermediary forms which had linked them. Conversely, each in the series of intermediary forms could be looked upon as a form as distinct as any taxonomic "species."*

Hence I look at individual differences, though of small interest to the systematists, as of high importance for us, as being the first step towards such slight varieties as are barely thought worth recording in the works on natural history. And I look at varieties which are in any degree more distinct and permanent, as steps leading to more strongly marked

---

* Distinct as discrete, not in terms of the divergence implied between two distinct species.

and more permanent varieties; and at these latter, as leading to sub-species, and then to species.[34]

Darwin had also been very careful to distinguish between the causes of variation on the one hand, and the cause of speciation on the other. Individual differences common to all forms in every generation were one form of divergence. And they had recognized environmental causes. But the differences resulting from their cumulative selection, over long periods of time, appeared a quite different form of divergence. These were changes in type that had been affected through natural selection. While these latter changes originated from, and were indeed dependent on, the selection of the former, the two had separate and distinct causes.

By thus recognizing two distinct sorts of change, Darwin was led to look upon the question of diversity under two separate categories: the sufficiency of individual diversity; and the extent of the diversity (or divergence) effected by the selective accumulation of such individual variation. If individual variability were limitless, there was no reason, said Darwin, to suppose any limit to the possible diversity achievable through selection (beyond, of course, that which was imposed by the conditions of life, or certain physiological laws).

For Darwin, the divergence of a species "$\emptyset$" from species "O" represented the selective accumulation of individual differences as they had appeared, from time to time, in each of several distinct, succeeding forms. Divergence was *not* the sum of the individual variations as they appeared within any single form. That is, the variations $O_a - O_z$ were not seen as individual differences arising in the original specific form "O," but as each an individual variation occurring within a distinct intermediary form. Thus, $O_a - O_z$ each appeared as an individual variation within a particular form, entirely independent of any other, though appearing together on the same genetic chain which connects the new species "$\emptyset$" with the original "O."

While it remains true even in this view that the variations on the chain, all the way up to and including O_z, must all appear as individual differences, they are not supposed to have appeared as such in the same form. This was possible on Darwin's assumption that each new intermediate form became a fixed, subspecific group. At some later date, he assumed, this recently fixed form would again present individual variations that could be selectively accumulated to produce the next new form required. But such a view was not to prove satisfactory to his critics. For them, these intermediate forms, whether temporarily fixed or not, were the cumulative effects of the selection of individual differences. Additionally, and because of their admittedly temporary nature, they were looked upon as differences appearing in the species "O." In their view, each of these differences amounted to a variation of as diverse a nature as the full extent of their departure from their specific type "O." Thus, in our example, twenty-six variations, each differing only slightly from its immediate parent form, are at the same time each increasingly divergent from its predecessors in terms of actual departure from the original type.

If, as was true with Darwin, each is seen in relation only to its parent form, then the question of sufficient diversity appears to be accounted for by the universality of individual differences. On the other hand, if looked at in relation to the original specific type, each one must be as individually divergent as the total divergence between the new form it represents and the original specific form from which it has departed.

Darwin felt that both views could be held at the same time, there being a question only of the vantage point from which one was compared with the other. His critics, on the other hand, saw that the two views must be consistent, that the variation (from within whatever form it arose) was still a variation from its own specific type. The essence of their disagreement with Darwin involved viewing the intermediate forms as distinct, semi-permanent biological entities. Since these forms were admittedly below the level of species (indeed, were included *within* the species), it was difficult for them to see how variations arising within such forms could be looked upon as anything other than variations of that specific type.

Darwin had stated that variations, having once arisen, were reproduced in the same manner as normal characters. Yet, in various scattered parts of the first *Origin,* one finds implied something more than the mere heritability of a new character.[35] At one point Darwin added that "its descendants would probably inherit a tendency to a similar slight deviation of structure,"[36] indicating that the character itself need not be passed on, for "the tendency to variability is in itself hereditary, consequently they [previous changes] will tend to vary and generally to vary in nearly the same manner as their parents varied."[37] While this held true when the offspring had been exposed to the same conditions as their parents, Darwin, speaking of "an innate tendency to further variability of all kinds"[38] implied that this would hold true generally. Again, in his summary, he remarked: ". . . we have evidence that variability, when it has once come into play does not wholly cease."[39] Darwin appeared to be implying some general principle of continued variation among those forms which had already varied. Indeed, when he spoke of the descendants of the newly modified forms he noted: "We might surely expect to find them still often continuing to vary in those parts of their structure which have varied within a moderately recent period."[40] Thus, a few paragraphs later, he put into somewhat axiomatic form his reference to "parts which have recently and largely varied being more likely still to go on varying than parts which have long been inherited and have not varied."[41] This possibility, only mentioned in passing in the *Origin,* he intended to make the subject of further investigations when he got into the study of variation and inheritance.

The attacks asserting a limit to variability, however, made this belief in the tendency to further variability on the part of already variant forms appear even more attractive as an asset to the process of natural selection.

It was in reviewing his work prior to replying to his critics that Darwin saw clearly for the first time that in the process of speciation as he outlined it, the newest variant form produced the next. That is, it was from within, say, form O_j that the individual variations O_k (the forerunners of the next form) arose. In this way he saw that, in the wider view of the process, it was the variant forms which, in their continued variation, produced all the requisite variations and then, after having been fixed as established forms at each stage, produced the intermediate forms all the way up to, and including, new species. It was, in short, a matter of the variants varying again and again. From this view, it would certainly have been helpful for the selective process if the variant forms could be shown to have such a tendency toward continued variation (greater than the normal tendency to individual variation possessed by all organisms). It would eliminate considerable difficulty if Darwin could show some underlying basis for believing in a greater tendency toward continued variation. In the meantime, all he could add in the third *Origin* was the statement "that the process of variation should thus be indefinitely prolonged is an assumption, the truth of which must be judged of by how far the hypothesis accords with and explains the general phenomena of nature."[42] It must wait for his future researches to uncover such an underlying cause.

THE *Variation*

The researches that went into the making of the *Variation* (1861–1866) appeared to confirm Darwin's views on variability. Devoting whole chapters to the subject, he set forth in a kind of axiomatic form the many basic principles which bore on the problem. The first of such "rules" was

that all characters of all kinds, whether new or old tend to be inherited, and that those which have already withstood all counteracting influences and been truly transmitted, will, as a general rule, continue to withstand them and consequently be faithfully inherited.[43]

The implication in the first *Origin* that some predisposition to further variation could be passed on was proposed here in greater detail and in a tone of greater confidence.

The tendency to mere general variability or plasticity of organisation can certainly be inherited, even from one parent.[44]

In the following quotations Darwin seemed to feel that the underlying reason for this phenomenon had something to do with a general plasticity accompanying variation:

We must believe structures, which have already varied, would be more liable to go on varying, rather than structures which during an immense lapse of time have remained unaltered.[45]

That the same parts do continue varying in the same manner we must admit, for, if it were not so, there could be no improvement beyond an early stage of excellence, and we know that such improvement is not only possible, but is of general occurrence.[46]

But Darwin could find no underlying genetic cause to explain this empirical phenomenon and he offered no such explanation through his theory of pangenesis.

In October 1862, Darwin read Hugh Falconer's manuscript on fossil elephants which was, in part, a criticism of his theory. Two matters which seemed to trouble Falconer were, first, the lack of variation in certain specific types; and, second, the way in which variability could coexist with persistence of type.[47]

These remarks came just at the time Darwin was working on this subject. He had seen that the tendency to continued variability was a definite asset to the selective process. Yet it appeared that this phenomenon, which assured the continued variation within the already improved forms, would prevent that equally important goal of persistency of type. In recognition of Falconer's remarks, Darwin added in the fourth *Origin* (prepared March–May 1866) the idea "that the periods during which species have been undergoing modification, though very long as measured by years, have probably been short in comparison with the periods during which these same species remained without undergoing any change."[48] In other words, while individual variability might itself continue, actual modification of the species took place only at widely spaced intervals. During these intervals, variations which had arisen previously became assimilated into the population, increased in numbers, and fixed into a new form.

> It is generally believed, though on this head we have little or no evidence, that new characters become fixed; and after having long remained fixed it seems possible that under new conditions they might again be rendered variable.[49]

In the *Variation,* Darwin described two phenomena which do not appear to be mutually consistent: that new characters tend to be as consistently and faithfully inherited as the old; and that recently varied structures tend to continue varying. Darwin felt, however, that he had reconciled them in two ways: first, in pointing out that by continued variation he meant the tendency to vary again *after once having become fixed* and having remained so for a considerable time; second, in pointing out that by further variability he meant *general* variability, *individual differences,* and not necessarily a change in the form of the species (the result of selection). In this manner, Darwin accounted for the coexistence of variability and persistence of type that had troubled Falconer and a number of others.

Having thus confirmed his earlier assumptions regarding the continuing tendency to further variability among recently varied intermediate forms, Darwin stood his ground on the subject, entering no further changes in the fourth *Origin*. To his critics, however, these axiomatic statements on the causes of variability seemed completely *ad hoc*. They appeared to describe what must have happened in order that the process of natural selection could effectively create new species from old by way of individual differences. Darwin's phrases "we must believe," "it is necessary to believe," "we must admit, for if it were not so, there could be no improvement" indicated to them a rather prejudiced, one-sided attitude of saving his theory of natural selection no matter what unfounded, unproved assumption had to be postulated. But it was not so much his blatantly *ad hoc* postulations that riled his critics as their belief that such assumptions were just not valid.

It was the appearance of the fourth *Origin,* unchanged in its stand on the subject, that served as the object of Fleeming Jenkin's review in the *North British Review* the following spring. The delay between the publication of the *Origin* and the appearance of the review was a sign of the pains taken by its author to gather all his critical evidence.

JENKIN'S REVIEW

Jenkin's rather long paper was, without doubt, the best critical review of the Darwinian theory that had appeared up to that time. The penetrating insight and extensive knowledge of Darwin's works shown by this Scots engineer-mathematician produced a formidable denouncement of the basic assumptions on which an effective theory of natural selection depended.

Only the first ten pages of Jenkin's forty-page review tackled the problem of variability. Jenkin never wavered from a strictly logical dissection of the bases of Darwin's mechanism.

Darwin's theory requires that there shall be no limit to the possible difference between descendants and their progenitors, or at least, that if there be limits, they shall be at so great a distance as to comprehend the utmost differences beween any known forms of life. . . . But if man's selection cannot double, treble, quadruple, centuple any special divergence from a parent stock, why should we imagine that natural selection should have that power? The rate of variation in a given direction is not constant, is not erratic; it is a constantly diminishing rate, tending therefore to a limit.[50]

Jenkin went on to illustrate the grounds for a belief in such a limit by employing a model which in its implications anticipated great knowledge of genetics (particularly the work of Francis Galton, William Johannsen, and William Bateson):

A given animal or plant appears to be contained as it were, within a sphere of variation; one individual lies near one portion of the surface, another individual, of the same species, near another part of the surface; the average animal at the centre.[51]

Jenkin felt that the existence of a definite perimeter-barrier in his model had been established, first on the grounds of increasing reversion as the limit approached (to final cessation), and second, on the basis of existence of inter-specific sterility as the demarcation of such a boundary.

However slow the rate of variation might be, even though it were only one part in a thousand per twenty or two thousand generations, yet if it were constant or erratic we might believe that, in untold time, it would lead to untold distance; but if in every case we find that deviation from an average individual can be rapidly effected at first, and that the rate of deviation steadily diminishes till it reaches an almost imperceptible amount, then we are entitled to assume a limit to the possible deviation.[52]

Darwin's conception of this process contained two points on which he placed special emphasis. His view was that after an initial change—that is, during the great lapse of time before another beneficial variation of the exact nature required would appear—the new form multiplied (within the old), at first gradually consolidating itself within the parent form, then supplanting it. The first point of his concept was that there were long intervals of time occurring between the stages of change during which each form became fixed; and, second, he thought that each further variation in the process was seen, not as a variation of the original form, but as a difference occurring within each new, fixed intermediate form. Jenkin, however, was quick to reply,

> But not only do we require for Darwin's theory that time shall first permanently fix the variety near the outside of the assumed sphere of variation, we require that it shall give the power of varying beyond that sphere. . . . Experiments conducted during the longest time at our disposal show no probability of surpassing the limits of the sphere of variation, and why should we concede that a simple extension of time will reverse the rule?[53]

It can be seen that, viewed separately, the individual aspects of Jenkin's criticism were not original with him, but are nearly identical to those of Agassiz, Gray, Wilberforce, and Harvey. It was Jenkin's gathering of all relevant points into a single review, forcefully illustrated by his particular model of variability (seen as a sphere encompassing definite specific limits), which proved him a more effective critic.

Thus, for Jenkin the outer surface of his sphere-model was the all-important limit. For within its confines, Jenkin was willing to go a long way with Darwin:

> We freely admit, that if an accumulation of slight improvements be possible, natural selection might improve hares as hares, and weasels as weasels, that is to say, it might produce animals having every useful faculty and every useful organ of their ancestors developed to a higher degree . . . but . . . the origin of species requires not the gradual improvement

of animals retaining the same habits and structure, but such modifications of those habits and structure, as will actually lead to the appearance of new organs.[54]

Almost as if the two were in direct conversation, Darwin marginally interrupted Jenkin right after he had said: "If an accumulation of slight improvements be possible" with "That is all that is wanted." Said Darwin to the remainder of his commentary: "No." But, Jenkin continued:

> We will go even further: if, owing to a change of circumstances some organ becomes pre-eminently useful, natural selection will undoubtedly produce a gradual improvement in that organ, precisely as man's selection can improve a special organ. . . . Thus it must apparently be conceded that natural selection is a true cause or agency whereby in some cases variations of special organs may be perpetuated and accumulated, but the importance of this admission is much limited by a consideration of the cases to which it applies. . . . Such a process of improvement as is described could certainly never give organs of sight, smell or hearing to organisms which had never possessed them. It could not add a few legs to a hare, or produce a *new* organ, or even cultivate any rudimentary organ which was not immediately useful to an enormous majority of hares. . . . Admitting, therefore, that natural selection may improve organs already useful to great numbers of a species, does not imply an admission that it can create or develop new organs, and so originate species.[55]

As if this were not effective enough, Jenkin continued for yet thirty more pages, detailing still other facts of nature which would prevent speciation in Darwinian terms. His acutely logical attack made him the most dogged and unrelenting critic Darwin had yet met. For example, it was possible, even after Jenkin's critical remarks, that speciation could still be brought about by calling upon some form of saltation as a way of "jumping" the species barrier. But Jenkin anticipated this possibility too; in the seven pages that followed, he brought the implications of blending to bear against just such a view. Little wonder Darwin exclaimed: "Fleeming Jenkin has given me much trouble, but has been of more real use to me than any other essay or review."[56]

Despite Darwin's comment, Jenkin's value as a critic was rather limited. It is true, as mentioned in the previous chapter, that Jenkin's employment of the swamping argument against saltations resulted in Darwin's final rejection of saltative changes, but Darwin remained convinced that there was another way to pass the species barrier. The fixation of a form near this border, followed by further variation at some later date, was thought sufficient to pass beyond it. After all, Jenkin had admitted that permanent change could be accumulated up to that point. Who was to say that, after some considerable time, the necessary variation would not appear? It was on the basis of this belief, inserted into the fifth edition, that Darwin managed to save his theory of natural selection:

> Some authors have maintained that the amount of variation in our domestic productions is soon reached, and can never afterwards be exceeded. It would be somewhat rash to assert that the limit has been attained in any one case; for almost all our animals and plants have been greatly improved in many ways within a recent period; and this implies variation. It would be equally rash to assert that characters now increased to their utmost limit, could not, after remaining fixed for many centuries, again vary under new conditions of life.[57]

Backing up this simple assertion was Darwin's former principle that variant forms were capable of passing on a tendency to further variability. In this addition, however, there appear some very subtle, but highly significant changes.

It should not, however, be overlooked that *certain varia-*

tions, which no one would rank as mere individual differences, frequently recur owing to a similar organisation being similarly acted on,—of which fact numerous instances could be given with our domestic productions. In such cases, if a varying individual did not actually transmit to its offspring its newly-acquired character, it would undoubtedly transmit, as long as the existing conditions remained the same, *a still stronger tendency* to vary *in the same manner.*[58]

While this passage was intended primarily as a reply to the swamping effect of blending, it is for the most part merely a reiteration of previous comments. What are worth noting are the four italicized additions: large-scale variations, frequency of appearance, passing on of a still stronger tendency to vary, and an identity of manner. The implication of such changes is impressive in view of Darwin's previous stand. Darwin had commented earlier on the tendency to continue variability; but never mentioned that it would be "still stronger . . . in the same manner." For some reason this may have been due to the fact that this tendency was the result of its progenitor having "variations which no one would rank as mere individual differences." From whatever cause, it was definitely stated that they "frequently recur." All this was certainly brought about by Jenkin's criticism of the blending theory and Darwin's consequent realization of possible weakness in his stand on variability.

When, after much delay, the *Variation* finally appeared in January 1868, it did little to allay the suspicions of many critics that Darwin would be unable to demonstrate the effectiveness of selection in creating permanent species or varieties. In fact, it confirmed them.

Not merely has man never originated a species, he has never permanently varied a species—not having been able to produce varieties even, but only breeds—and having, whilst producing them, found that species are without variableness or the shadow of turning. The immutability of species is maintained by two unconquerable laws—the ultimate sterility of breeds, and their reversion to type when let alone.[59]

It was becoming painfully obvious that Darwin was either mistaken in his belief that the process of natural selection could effectively work upon individual differences or that his exposition failed to make clear the process as he envisioned it. Certainly the continued criticism eliminated the possibility that here was just a handful of imperceptive critics haggling over trivialities.

Of the criticisms in the year 1868, the one that most echoed Jenkin's perspicacity was that of August Weismann. Upon his return from another convalescence at the beginning of October, Darwin found the manuscript of Weismann's pamphlet *A Justification of the Darwinian Theory* awaiting him. In this paper, Weismann's ideas closely paralleled those of Jenkin, with the main exception that it was the former who correctly saw individual differences as the effects of conditions (from embryonic life to maturity) acting upon the inheritable specific characters.

The whole argument of Weismann's paper was that there was a definite and decisive limit to what could be effected through the selection of superficial differences. He pointed out[60] that the physical and physiological constitution of the organism was fixed in its development [*Entwicklungsrichtung*] and, though it had a wide margin of possible superficial variation in all directions, it was nonetheless limited. These were chemical and physiological limits which were impossible to pass. Within these limits, said Weismann, are what we call individual differences; but to go beyond these, passing into the form of a new species, is impossible. He gave the example that one cannot make a dog from the individual differences presented among cats.

Again like Jenkin, Weismann agreed that natural selectivity could operate within a limited sphere. But the fact that further accumulation beyond a certain point could not be effected indicated to him that the process of natural selection is really only a form of limited change—an adjunct—to whatever real process effects speciation. Recognizing individual differences as merely superficial modifications, Weismann pointed out the necessity for some true form of variation—a change in the very foundation of the individual's (and the species') make-up—in its prototype.[*]

Weismann's paper, Darwin remarked marginally, "is justly directed against what I have vaguely said of indefinite variability. In all cases, the variability, within a large circuit is definite and thus certainly overrides the power of selection." In his letter of reply he stated: "It must, I think, be admitted that the variations of most species have in the lapse of ages been extremely diversified, for I do not see how it can otherwise be explained that so many forms have acquired analogous structures for the same general object, independent of descent."[61]

Such was the state of things when the fifth *Origin* appeared in the summer of 1869. After reading his copy, Hooker forwarded to Darwin the information that the botanist William Hallett had been unable, in a series of experiments involving wheat, to gain much continued improvement along certain selected lines beyond what appeared to be a certain discernible limit. Yet Darwin could not be daunted by experiments which permitted so little time for their results. He replied to Hooker:

> I am not at all surprised that Hallett has found some varieties of wheat could not be improved in certain desirable qualities as quickly as at first. All experience shows this with animals; but it would, I think, be rash to assume, judging from actual experience, that a little more improvement could not be got in the course of a century, and theoretically very improbable that after a few thousands [of years'] rest there would not be a start in the same line of variation.[62]

Darwin had not moved very much from his original view on variability. In his conception of things, the limit was far enough removed to allow of sufficient material for species-formation. As

[*] Weismann's distinction between the somatoplasm and the germ plasm was not made until 1883.

long as forms continued to produce enough individual differences of a beneficial nature, selection could and would operate to modify species. This belief was firmly rooted in the two basic assumptions which he continued to hold: (1) that individual differences were inheritable; and (2) that their fixation was equivalent to the production of a distinctly new, heritable intermediary form which could, upon further variation at some later date, produce yet newer forms capable of passing any supposed barriers.

From all this, one point remains clear: Darwin had apparently not been impressed by one of Jenkin's most cogent remarks: since time alone could not account for the fixation of a variety at the species boundary, how could one suppose that the mere passage of time would give to the form the power of varying further to pass such a barrier?*

Even Francis Galton, his cousin, had been led to criticize Darwin regarding the limits of variation. Galton, though favorably enough impressed with the idea of pangenesis to incorporate it into his work *Hereditary Genius* (1869),[63] nevertheless felt obliged to point out what he saw as a singular weakness in Darwin's view. Like Jenkin, Galton had (at least in theory) anticipated Johannsen's later experimental proofs of the limit to the selection of strictly somatic variation. His belief that a definite limit to the selective extenuation of such variations did exist led Galton to think about saltation. It was in this work of 1869 that he likened the stable nature of the specific characters to a heavy, rough stone lying on the ground. Its position could be altered slightly—yielding to a push, as it were—but it would tend generally to fall back to its original position. The occasion of a saltation was, he felt, as if one suddenly and with great pressure succeeded in pushing the stone so that it came to rest on a new face. It was

* Though not true of all of his contemporaries, in all fairness to Darwin it must be said that the existing state of genetic knowledge would have led most people to suspend judgment on this subject.

a point which he made more strongly and in greater detail in his work *Natural Inheritance* (1889), but which had been repeated in several papers throughout the 1870s.[64] Whether or not the criticisms of either Galton or Jenkin caused any fundamental change in Darwin's thought (and this can safely be doubted), they nevertheless contained within them the kernels of several lines of criticism that were to confront Darwin again in but a short time.* In fact, they marked the beginning of a period which saw ceaseless and unrelenting criticisms of Darwin's theory, which criticisms ultimately precipitated Darwin's total withdrawal from the scene of the debates on the theory of evolution.

* Jenkin mentioned, in passing, the failure of the theory of natural selection to account for totally new features; incipient (useless) stages of new structures; rudimentary organs. (See chapter 5, pp. 121 *et seq.*)

7. The Role of Isolation

Darwin's contribution to the subject is particularly difficult to evaluate since he was more plagued with doubts on this than on almost any other evolutionary question.

—Ernst Mayr, "Isolation as an Evolutionary Factor" *in* Proceedings of the American Philosophical Society

*I*n determining the extent and importance of isolation in Darwin's theory, it will be necessary to consider isolation in the fullest and broadest meaning of the term. This includes more than Darwin himself understood by the term; for there is a great deal more isolation (as viewed in its component elements of separation and confinement) in Darwin's writings than he expressly recognized. His conclusion that isolation is *not* a necessary condition for speciation was a result of shortsightedness. It was also to prove a source of some difficulty after 1859 because this relegation of isolation to a secondary position—as merely a "favourable circumstance" for evolution—led critics to believe that he counted upon no isolating mechanisms whatever as playing any necessary role in speciation.

There are three types of evolutionary isolation which, at their extremes, appear to blend into one another. In the broadest and largest sense, there is geographical or spatial isolation; in the narrowest and most intricate sense, there is physiological or functional isolation. Between the two there is that combination of both physical and organic characteristics which results in ecological isolation.

Geographical isolation is exemplified by cases involving separation by such topographical barriers as oceans, mountains, rivers, and deserts. Physiological or functional isolation is based largely on such sexual incapacities as inviability of gametes or inability to copulate. Ecological isolation results when either the life habits or habitats of two forms do not overlap although the organisms themselves are nonetheless spatially contiguous (sympatric).

While Darwin demonstrated much perspicacity in the matter of ecological and physiological separation, he nevertheless restricted his application of the term "isolation" to those situations involving the geographical or spatial separation of organisms.* What's more, Darwin further restricted use of the term to the spatial separation of rather small organic segments from the general population.† It was this restricted view of isolation that led Darwin to overlook his own description of nature divided into numerous organic enclaves as a prime example of isolation.

In order to take the full measure of the role of isolation in Darwin's theory, it will be necessary to start at the very foundations of his mechanism of evolution.

---

* Darwin's own early training and work in geology, together with the great influence of Lyell's work, no doubt went a long way toward predisposing him to see isolation more in physical than in functional terms. In those sections of the *Principles of Geology* (vol. 2, chaps. 5-10) which Lyell devoted to the habitats and distribution of species, the more subtle ecological and physiological aspects of isolation were not mentioned.

† When one speaks of isolation one tends to think in terms of, first, "that which is isolated" and, second, "that from which the isolated portion has been separated." Darwin thought of isolation in this way. However, this distinction is not entirely accurate. While it is common practice to refer to the smaller of the two entities involved as the isolated element, it is actually the case that both elements are mutually isolated, one from the other. In fact, the magnitude of either portion is not a condition of isolation; both may be large, or they may even be equal in size.

THE CONDITIONS FOR EVOLUTION

The first element of isolation is that of the containment implied in Darwin's use of certain terms to denote the locale in which the first stages of the evolutionary process began. He saw the process of natural selection as operating on certain forms within particular locations. In fact, the various topographical features of a continent seemed automatically to encompass such natural subdivisions as would *contain* endemic fauna and flora. It was these geographical subdivisions which Darwin referred to as "regions" or "areas." In such instances, however, the isolation implied is only that of a rather broad containment; it would not be necessary to think of such areas as isolated in any but the broadest sense. Yet, on the very premise that local forms are contained (citing the dependency of organism on habitat as well as purely physical confinement), Darwin went on to describe what necessarily follows in the process of evolution.

Balance of Nature: In the implicit assumption that all organisms inhabit (however broadly) confined regions, Darwin described the highly complex "balance of nature" that exists in each. This local balance results from a struggle for existence under relatively static conditions.[1]

The result of the conflict between the ever-present tendency toward reproductive overproduction on the one hand and the several agents of natural destruction on the other is a competitive struggle for existence among all organisms for the limited number of places in the local polity of nature. Darwin believed that within each of the world's innumerable geographical areas, a form of equilibrium would soon be reached. This he considered a dynamic balance: the establishment of a vital and complex network of interrelationships among the endemic species, and between them and their regional environment. In Darwin's words, "the intimate and complex manner in which the inhabitants of each country are bound together" follows from the fact that "all the inhabitants of each country are struggling together with nicely-balanced forces."[2] Each species stands in a definite relationship to every other species, and is, in this sense, "contained" within its natural habitat.

> A corollary of the highest importance may be deduced from the foregoing remarks, namely, that the structure of every organic being, is related, in the most essential yet often hidden manner, to that of all the other organic beings with which it comes into competition for food or residence, or from which it has to escape or on which it preys.[3]

The Concept of "Place": Bound up with the element of containment implied in such terms as "habitat," "area," and "region" is the notion of "place." "Place" is a rather vague term but one which Darwin frequently used. He gave it no express definition, leaving only the implication that it represents the totality of those conditions of life necessary to sustain the existence of one organism within the economy of a given area. "Place" was intended to be to the individual organism what "habitat" was to the species. In this sense, unlike the other terms mentioned above, it was (together with "habitat") not meant to designate a particular locale or region. It was, in fact, a totally non-specific term, the greatest part of whose intended meaning arose out of the equally vague notion of "balance of nature." A balance or equilibrium having been struck among the several species of a region, each organism has, as a result, its own "place" within this complex. Furthermore, within any region, the relative constancy of physical and organic conditions prescribes a finite number of such places for each species.

Since every species tends (through its natural tendency to overreproduce) to expand to the full limits allowable within the nature of the surrounding conditions of life, all possible places within a region will be occupied by a member of one species or another. Thus, as Darwin said, the tendency of each area is to "always be fully stocked with inhabitants."[4]

Several types of isolation-as-containment can be noted in the *Origin.* First (as implied in Darwin's use of the terms "area" and "region"), there is that of purely physical containment—by topographical barriers of one kind or another—which amounts to the confinement or "localization" of species. Second, there is that of the functional or ecological attachment of a species to its habitat so that it is confined to a particular region through its vital requirements. For the individual organism this condition is implied by the concept "place." Third (and Darwin's most subtle ecological contribution), there is that implied in the complex network of inter-specific relationships and dependencies that further serves to contain all the endemic forms within the common region.

The Importance of "Place": Since the Darwinian process began with the notion of individual variation, the concept of individual place is of key importance to his theory. The struggle for a place in the local economy of nature is the sole reason for the struggle for existence, and the place itself is the sole objective of that struggle. One of the most fundamental axioms set down by Darwin was that the process of natural selection "depends on there being places in the polity of nature which can be better occupied by some of the inhabitants of the country undergoing modification of some kind."[5]

One might have thought that, in a nature so abundantly occupied, some agent would be necessary to remove old forms and create room for new. However, Darwin expressly stated that selection did not depend on the existence of unoccupied places in the natural economy, only that there must be places that could be *better occupied* by some new form.* Thus there need not necessarily be such agents of destruction or removal. This is not to say that Darwin ignored the possibility that there were such agents; he actually listed several. He merely took special care to distinguish those conditions which, taken together, were them-

---

* Darwin often lapsed on this point and in many places seems to imply that such agents are sometimes necessary. See *Origin*. IX:75.13e and the marginal comment in Moritz Wagner's reprint (DRC Q 258): "Species do not change unless new places for them."

selves *sufficient* for speciation: all others were relegated to subsidiary positions as "circumstances favourable to natural selection."

THE BEGINNINGS OF THE EVOLUTIONARY PROCESS

The Struggle for Existence: The motive force of the process of evolution is the competitive struggle for existence. Darwin interpreted this as arising from the phenomena of overreproduction, natural destruction, and containment. During those periods of time when the physical and organic conditions were relatively static, this struggle became adaptively resolved into a form of dynamic, inter-specific equilibrium. Such would be the situation without the introduction of adaptive novelty in the form of individual variation, or without change in some physical aspect of the environment.

The Struggle for Existence as the Result of Upsetting the Balance of Nature: From Darwin's picture of the local balance of nature as the adaptive result of the opposition of two natural forces (overpopulation and destruction), one can see that whatever agents may act to disrupt this equilibrium will, by so doing, redirect the original forces involved and thereby precipitate the struggle for existence once again. The balance, once tipped in favor of one form over others, will be restored only by further changes in the organic conditions. This procedure is best described in Darwin's own words:

> As all the inhabitants of each country are struggling together with nicely balanced forces, extremely slight modifications in the structure or habits of one inhabitant would often give it an advantage over others; and still further modifications of the same kind would often still further increase the advantage.[6]

From this, he continued, there invariably follows an increase in numbers among these competitively successful forms. And following from this:

> We may conclude, from what we have seen of the intimate

and complex manner in which the individuals of each country are bound together, that any change in the numerical proportions of some of the inhabitants, would most seriously affect many of the others.[7]

Exactly how seriously in some cases, Darwin stated a few paragraphs below:

If some of these many species become modified and improved, others will have to be improved in a corresponding degree or they will be exterminated.[8]

The relationship between the notion of natural containment and the ensuing struggle for existence now becomes clear. Each natural subdivision, region, or area, being isolated from all others, is a unit in the process of evolution, containing within it a balanced network of specific interrelationships. Any disturbance involving any of the endemic elements will act to upset the balance of the whole. As they were initiators of the struggle for existence, the several factors cited by Darwin as disturbing this equilibrium are of great importance to an understanding of his theory.

Factors Upsetting the Balance of Nature; Change in Physical Conditions (see Figure 7.1): Every species is surrounded by organic as well as by purely physical elements. Darwin considered changes in the physical conditions, independent of any change in the local organic network, as of no importance to the process of evolution, because the struggle for existence results from some change in the organic situation, either intrinsic or externally caused. However, since the organic elements are intimately bound up with the physical environment, almost any change in that environment would effect some change among the resident species. The effect on the population in these cases is purely extrinsic, involving either the destruction of local forms, the influx of forms from outside the region, or the emigration of local forms.

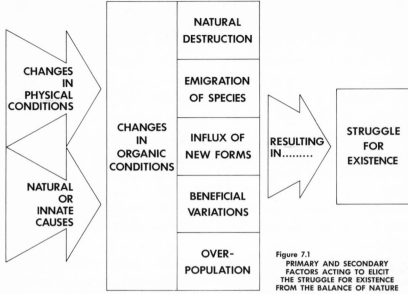

Figure 7.1
PRIMARY AND SECONDARY
FACTORS ACTING TO ELICIT
THE STRUGGLE FOR EXISTENCE
FROM THE BALANCE OF NATURE

1. THE DESTRUCTION OF FORMS. Like any disturbance in an intricate system, change in conditions almost always has a deleterious effect, and, said Darwin: ". . . no one will dispute that the physical conditions of each country, as well as the number and kind of its inhabitants, are liable to change."[9] In citing an example involving horses, he noted: ". . . if the conditions had gone on, however slowly, becoming less and less favourable, we assuredly should not have perceived the fact, yet the fossil horse would certainly have become rarer and rarer, and finally extinct."[10]

2. THE FAVORING OF FORMS. The obverse of the theory of natural destruction is that of nature's favoring of certain forms. The constitution of one form may be better suited than that of an allied form to cope with changed conditions. Because of the inter-dependencies that exist among endemic species, Darwin saw that if "enemies or competitors be in the least degree favoured by any slight change of climate, they will increase in numbers, and, as each area is already fully stocked with inhabitants, the other species will decrease."[11] The universality of individual differences, some of which will no doubt prove adaptively bene-

ficial under the change of conditions, assures that such new (variant) forms will also be favored by the environmental change.[12]

3. THE EMIGRATION OF FORMS. Of particular relevance to the discussion of isolation is the indirect influence of physical change on the organic populations—principally with regard to organic migration. Although it is dealt with in greater detail in a later section, Darwin's recognition of this phenomenon is worth noting in this context. First, in discussing the new, beneficially varying forms that arise from time to time within an area, Darwin saw that under a change in conditions (affecting the physical barriers) ". . . new forms would certainly immigrate and this also would seriously disturb the relations of some of the former inhabitants."[13]

4. THE IMMIGRATION OF FORMS. The obverse of this was the immigration of better adapted forms from outside that followed "after any physical change, such as of climate, etc."[14]

Generally speaking, Darwin saw changes of conditions slowly reshaping the local topography—by redefining areas and shifting barriers—thereby altering the areas of confinement.

Changes in the Organic Conditions: While the organic conditions surrounding any local form could be affected by most physical changes in the environment, Darwin stressed the fact that such purely physical changes are by no means necessary to initiate organic changes. "The most important of all causes of organic change is one which is almost independent of altered and perhaps suddenly altered physical conditions, namely, the mutual relation of organism to organism—the improvement of one being entailing the improvement or the extermination of others."[15] He saw the existence of such intrinsic factors as the natural tendency to spontaneous individual variation as singularly sufficient to precipitate a local imbalance. "The slightest difference of structure or constitution may well turn the nicely-balanced scale in the struggle for life."[16]

Throughout this section of his work Darwin stipulated that

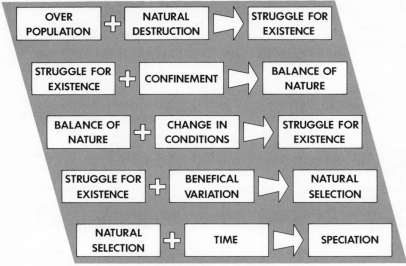

Figure 7.2
THE CONDITIONS FOR SPECIATION

a change in physical conditions was not a *necessary* condition of bringing about the struggle for existence. His earlier statement, ". . . changes in the conditions of life, by specially acting on the reproductive system, causes or increases variability,"[17] was, in this chapter, prefaced with the qualification "Not that, as I believe, any change of conditions is necessary to induce variability."[18] (See Figure 7.2.)

THE ROLE OF ISOLATION

As stated in chapter 5, Darwin had been aware of the difficulties attached to blending inheritance ever since his early *Transmutation Notebooks* of 1838 and 1839. The prevention of free crossing among breeds, so essential in the domestic state, led him, by analogy, to see the necessity of natural isolation. Describing how, among domesticated animals and plants, "the offspring are picked out & not allowed to cross," Darwin was led to ask:

—Has nature any process analogous[?]—if so she can produce great ends—But how[?]—even if placed on Isld. if &c, &c . . .[19]

Again, writing of the breeder in the *Sketch of 1842* Darwin noted:

> He knows only way to make a distinct breed is to select and separate. . . . He would endeavour therefore to get his cows on islands and then commence his work of selection. According to this analogy, change of external conditions, and isolation either by chance landing of a form on an island, or subsidence dividing a continent, or great chain of mountains, and the number of individuals not being numerous will best favour variation and selection.[20]

Two years later, in the *Essay of 1844,* in a special section devoted to considering "circumstances most favourable for selection" Darwin noted one in particular:

> Isolation as perfect as possible of such selected varieties; that is, the preventing their crossing with other forms; this latter condition applies to all terrestrial animals, to most if not all plants and perhaps even to most (or all) aquatic organisms. It will be convenient here to show the advantage of isolation in the formation of a new breed by comparing the progress of two persons (to neither of whom let time be of any consequence) endeavouring to select and form some peculiar new breed.[21]

By the time Darwin reached the similarly titled section in the considerably expanded *Origin,* his views had changed somewhat. Darwin began by pointing out not one but four ways in which the process of natural selection would be favored by isolation.

First of all, the swamping effect of blending would be considerably mitigated if pocket populations containing the variants could somehow become separated from the general population. With far fewer numbers of unmodified organisms to breed with, the variant form not only could establish itself nearly undiluted in nature, but it could do so in a reasonably short space of time.

Second, since the physical and climatic conditions of a small

area are both uniform and stable, their direct influence "will tend
to modify all the individuals of a varying species throughout the
area in the same manner in relation to the same condition."[22]

Third, isolation aids "in checking the immigration of better
adapted organisms, after any physical change, such as of climate
or elevation of the land, etc.; and thus new places in the natural
economy are left open for the old inhabitants to struggle for."[23]

Fourth, by checking immigration and consequently competition, isolation allows the new variety to establish itself, until
the whole population, despite some blending, becomes similarly
modified.

In spite of these apparent advantages, Darwin rejected the
necessity of isolation in small pocket populations to ensure speciation. "Although I do not doubt that isolation is of considerable
importance in the production of new species, on the whole I am
inclined to believe that largeness of area is of more importance."[24]
Now, in the section of the *Origin* in which Darwin dealt with this
matter,[25] he listed also the advantages of variety formation within
large areas, at the same time implying the several disadvantages
of isolation.

First, because of the larger number of individuals in each
species, there would be a greater chance for the appearance of
the requisite variations.

Second, the more complex conditions of life (due to the
larger numbers of species) would produce a more sensitive balance of nature and a more violent struggle for existence.

Third, largeness of area would afford greater opportunity for
new forms, successful within their own habitats, to spread into
new areas within the same region.

Fourth, there would be more places in the polity of nature
within large areas.

SPECIATION WITHOUT ISOLATION

Unconscious Selection: In concluding that it was within sizeable areas containing a large number of endemic forms that new

forms became established, Darwin had still to face the problem
of blending. Having thus specifically chosen speciation within
large areas as the alternative to isolation, there remained for
Darwin the task of demonstrating how new forms could maintain
their integrity in the presence of the far larger unmodified population. As noted in chapter 5, Darwin had long been aware of
the swamping tendency inherent in blending inheritance. The
Origin differed from his earlier writings in the attempt to demonstrate possible ways in which speciation could be effected without
isolation.

The chapter on the process of natural selection began with a
comparison of natural selection to man's "methodical and unconscious means of selection." Methodical selection, as Darwin had
described it in his first chapter, involved both the destruction of
inferior forms and the complete separation of the superior forms.
Unconscious selection involved neither. In this latter process,
merely by neglecting the inferior individuals while breeding only
the superior, man could ultimately effect a slow but permanent
change of form.

> But when many men, without intending to alter the breed,
> have a nearly common standard of perfection, and all try to
> get and breed from the best animals, much improvement and
> modification surely but slowly follows from this unconscious
> process of selection, notwithstanding a large amount of cross-
> ing with inferior animals. Thus it will be in nature. . . .[26]

Blending inheritance lay at the basis of unconscious selection.
While the inferior forms, whose selective neglect meant death
by slow extinction, were not actively destroyed, neither were the
superior forms in any way separated from the main population.
Instead, the superior variants mixed their qualities with the general population and therefore blended them. Despite this blending, at each generation there followed, through the continued
appearance and reappearance of the variation,* the increased

* See chapter 6, pp. 146 *et seq.*

modification of the whole population. It was blending that en-
sured the equal and widespread distribution of the advantageous
quality throughout the whole population.

> I believe that during the slow process of modification, the
> individuals of the species will have been kept nearly uniform
> by intercrossing; so that many individuals will have gone on
> simultaneously changing, and the whole amount of modifica-
> tion will not have been due, at each stage, to descent from a
> single parent.[27]

Yet Darwin did not appear to be fully convinced that the only
way to circumvent swamping was to incorporate blending into
the process of modification:

> For I can bring a considerable catalogue of facts, showing that
> within the same area, varieties of the same animal can long
> remain distinct, from haunting different stations, from breed-
> ing at slightly different seasons, or from varieties of the same
> kind preferring to pair together.[28]

It was the method within the process of evolution of bringing
about this endemic *apartheid* that Darwin had to demonstrate.
And it was at this point that Darwin exhibited considerable
ecological insight in intimating that the occupation of new
places by new forms might prove a source of isolation from
the parental forms. In the same chapter he described:

> . . . varying descendants seizing on places at present occupied
> by other animals; some of them, for instance, being enabled
> to feed on new kinds of prey, either dead or alive; some in-
> habiting new stations, climbing trees, frequenting water, and
> some perhaps becoming less carnivorous.[29]

Beyond this implication of isolation as inherent in the pre-
adaptive nature of certain variations, Darwin ventured no further. From 1859 to 1867 he let matters hang, neither rejecting nor

fully accepting either unconscious selection or ecological separation. In May 1863, while writing part of the *Variation*,
Darwin pointed out:

> On the principle which makes it necessary for man, whilst
> he is selecting and improving his domestic varieties, to keep
> them separate, it would clearly be advantageous to varieties
> in a state of nature, that is to incipient species, if they could
> be kept from blending, either through sexual aversion, or by
> becoming mutually sterile.[30]

This indicated that blending modification was still to be avoided
if possible.

In preparing the fourth *Origin* in the spring of 1866, Darwin
repeated these sentiments: "It would be clearly advantageous
to two varieties or incipient species, if they could be kept from
blending."[31]

It was Fleeming Jenkin who, through his great stress on the
inevitability of swamping, committed Darwin more fully to the
use of unconscious selection. Yet, why was it that Darwin, from
this point forward, ceased to mention ecological differentiation as
a case of isolation and to employ it as such against the blending
of new forms? There is little doubt that, after Jenkin appeared,
wielding the swamping effect like a bludgeon against emergent
forms, positive selection became considerably more difficult to
demonstrate. A possible explanation is that Darwin's preoccupa-
tion with, and consequent emphasis on, geographical or spatial
isolation led him to believe that purely ecological barriers were
not sufficient to ensure against the sexual intercourse of two
forms. Yet his references to breeding seasons and preferential
matings definitely amounted to separation in this respect. However, Darwin's continued stress on the gradual and continual
assimilation of variation through blending selection indicates
his reluctance to employ any other explanation. Even in 1868,
when the latter explanation was vigorously attacked and shown

to be insufficient, Darwin's refusal to fall back on ecological isolation gives the impression that, for whatever reason, he did not see in it a suitable form of insulation against inter-crossing.

THE PROBLEMS OF SPECIATION WITHOUT ISOLATION

This repeated emphasis by Darwin that selection could operate perfectly efficiently without any isolation brought to the fore a further problem. So long as there was no form of isolation between the new forms and their parent-species, their confinement to the same area meant a continuous series of successive forms, each new emergent one gradually supplanting its parent. The selection of changes occurring within the population of a single species, to the point that the entire population has so diverged from its original type as to rank as a new specific form, is, however, only one type of evolutionary speciation. This historical metamorphosis of one species into another may be termed *orthoselective speciation*.[32] But it in no way accounts for either the multiplication of species (from a single ancestral species) or for their subsequent distribution. Without such multiple speciation there would have to have been as many ancestral as contemporary species and the true "origin of species" would remain unexplained.

Whether the new form supplanted the old, cohabited with it, or completely separated from it, depended *not* specifically on the operation of natural selection, but *on the conditions* under which selection operated. The divergence of two or more new specific forms from a common ancestor and their distribution, while in a sense secondary to an explanation of the creation of new species from old, were nevertheless phenomena which any theory of evolution *must* explain. Since it was also a fundamental principle of Darwin's theory that "all the species of the same genus, or even higher group, must have descended from common parents,"[33] the facts of organic distribution forced on Darwin the conclusion that the new species "must in the course of successive generations have passed from some one part to the others."[34] Again we see

Darwin employing isolation as an explanation, this time as in-
ferred in the phenomenon of migration.

MIGRATION

One can readily see a connection between the multiplication
and distribution of species: both depend, to varying degrees, on
the separation of variant from parent forms. True, distribution
can be accounted for by the separation of *identical* forms (two
portions of the same population) and their subsequent modification (if the two forms presently differ) in their new location. In
either case, however, there must be some form of separation, if
not through some external, then through some internal agent, or
a combination of both. His view of isolation as merely a fortuitous
occurrence led Darwin to look to some internal agency. This he
found in the tendency for successful forms to migrate.

> Widely-ranging species, abounding in individuals, which have
> already triumphed over many competitors in their own wide-
> ly-extended homes will have the best chance of seizing on
> new places, when they spread into new countries.[35]

It would seem as if Darwin were here denying his earlier
descriptions of containment—even if only to the extent that it was
merely the already successful, heavily (or over-) populated forms
that had the power to transcend natural barriers. But in the
earlier part of the same chapter, he saw such migrations occurring solely in "the case of a country undergoing some physical
change."[36] Only then, "if the country were open on its borders,"[37]
would the new forms emigrate. This is why, when giving fuller
consideration to the problem in chapter 10, he said:

> We know not at all precisely what are all the conditions most
> favourable for the multiplication of new and dominant species
> . . . the power of spreading into new territories . . . would be
> highly favourable. A certain amount of isolation, recurring
> at long intervals of time, would probably be also favourable.[38]

Thus it here became a condition—at least as far as multiplication and distribution of species was concerned: "The migration of the more dominant forms of life from one region into another having been effected with more or less ease, at periods more or less remote."[39] It is in this chapter that Darwin amalgamated his views concerning the site of speciation, isolation, and subsequent migration.

> The existence of the same species at distant and isolated points of the earth's surface, can in many instances be explained on the view of each species having migrated from a single birthplace; . . . Hence, it seems to me, as it has to many other naturalists, that the view of each species having been produced in one area alone, and having subsequently migrated from that area as far as its power of migration and subsistence under past and present conditions permitted, is the most probable.
>
> Undoubtedly many cases occur, in which we cannot explain how the same species could have passed from one point to another. But the geographical and climatal changes, which have certainly occurred within recent geological times, must have interrupted and rendered discontinuous the formerly continuous range of many species.[40]

Thus Darwin had to call upon periodic isolation not only to explain multiplication and distribution, but also as a protective factor to contain the members of the incipient species until the new form became established in terms of changing the entire resident population. As Darwin pointed out in this same chapter: ". . . the great majority of species have been produced on one side [of a barrier] alone, and have not been able to migrate to the other side."[41]

Though he disclaimed any necessity for isolation in the evolutionary process, isolation as a natural containment factor of organisms appeared as an essential element throughout Darwin's theory. It played a fundamental role in at least three situations described by him.

The first of these was the fact of the geological, ecological and functional containment of organisms within certain regions. This, together with overreproduction, was the basic condition for the struggle for existence.

Second, upon the appearance of a new form, a period of isolation allowed the multiplication and establishment of such variants (through blending selection) until they formed an entire resident population—after which time they could, if conditions permitted, migrate elsewhere. In this respect, isolation also eliminated excess competition, the influx of new forms, and generally created a favorable atmosphere for the process of natural selection.

Third, the separation of new from parental forms was necessary to ensure the independent modification of each into several new specific forms. This isolation was geographical (through the creation and destruction of barriers), ecological (variation as functional differentiation), and physiological (preferential matings, different breeding seasons). Yet, save for the cases of purely physical containment, Darwin called upon none of these instances of isolation in the process of natural selection.

AFTER 1859

Fleeming Jenkin (1867): As suggested in chapter 5, Jenkin's arguments served to confirm Darwin's original conviction that selection did not depend on the appearance of any single, strongly marked variation. It was, in fact, the cumulative selection of numerous individual differences and their assimilation through the entire population by means of a heritage of blending that brought about the significant evolutionary changes in Darwin's process. "I saw the great importance of individual differences, and this led me fully to discuss the results of unconscious selection."[42] This cumulative selection, the natural analogue of the unconscious selection of domestication, necessitated confinement to one area during the process. And so, Darwin noted in his reply to Jenkin: ". . . it should be borne in mind that most animals and plants keep to their proper homes and do not needlessly wander about" so that "similarly modified individuals would exist in a small body together . . . being firstly local . . . afterwards . . . as a newly-formed variety it would slowly spread from a central spot, competing with and conquering the unchanged individuals."[43] This required not only isolation, but the continual addition of more of the same type of variation at nearly every generation. It was Jenkin's commentary that extracted for the first time from Darwin an admission that it was necessary to think in terms of "the preservation during many generations of *a large number of [variant] individuals* and the destruction of a still larger number [of normal forms]."[44]

It also became necessary, at this time, for Darwin to repeat his earlier remarks on the tendency for variations to reappear in subsequent generations.[45] Now that he was fully committed to modification-with-blending, it was necessary that he go back over earlier statements and adduce all the supporting factors for his new view of selection.*

Moritz Wagner (1868): In Germany, the naturalist Moritz Wagner had been greatly impressed by the blending arguments against Darwin's theory. To him there seemed no solution to the swamping tendency short of complete isolation. Since, without some form of spatial isolation, mere variation occurring in a population would be genetically absorbed and obliterated through crossing at the first generation, the first condition for permanent variation from original type *had to be* isolation. Wagner had thought about the problem as early as 1851,[46] and by 1868 he had become convinced that isolation was the all-important condition for speciation. On March 7 of that year he delivered a paper putting forward that opinion and criticizing Darwin for his failure to emphasize the importance of isolation.[47]

---

*See chapter 9 for an assessment of the effects of Jenkin's review and the criticisms of others on Darwin's theory.

Wagner started by citing the fundamental differences between Darwin's theory of separation and his own. He referred to
the Darwinian theory of natural selection as the "theory of transmutation"; to his own he referred as the "theory of separation."
In making this distinction he had, in fact, put his finger on Darwin's greatest weakness regarding isolation. Darwin's singular
emphasis had been that of demonstrating how any single new
specific form could have emerged from a previous form. Any
species, a population of which was confined to a certain locale,
while, at the same time, undergoing modifications in a particular
direction from within, could be transformed into a new specific
form.* But Wagner saw this as, at best, merely the modification
of an existing species. But even this process was subject, from its
inception, to what appeared to Wagner insurmountable obstacles.
If the new variant forms lay in or close to the station of its parents,
said Wagner:

> a constant variety or new species cannot be produced, be-
> cause the free crossing of a new variety with the old unaltered
> stock will always cause it to revert to the original type; in
> other words, will destroy the new form. Free crossing, as the
> artificial selection of animals and plants incontestably teaches,
> not only renders the formation of new races impossible, but
> invariably destroys newly formed individual varieties; it is
> moreover, the principal cause that individual variability does
> not, after several generations, effect a lasting change. The
> unlimited sexual intercourse of all individuals of a species
> must always result in uniformity.[48]†

---

* Both Darwin and Wagner left their readers to believe that if a new form,
differing from its parent in only a single character, established itself and eventually
transformed the existing population (through time) in its entirety to its own
form, it would be considered a completely *new* species.

† These arguments were the same as those put forward by Lyell in the first
five (1830–34) editions of the *Principles of Geology* (see above, pp. 129–130).
Yet both Darwin and Wagner owed a great debt to Lyell's treatment of isolation
and migration in that same work. Darwin, however, was later able to bring Lyell
around to a conditional acceptance of his theory, and subsequent editions of the
Principles were revised.

Thus, for Wagner, speciation *in situ* was out, if not on the ground that it failed to account for either the multiplication or the distribution of new species, then on the ground that it was practically impossible for the variant form to establish itself as a new form within the parent population.

Wagner's alternative—his "separation theory"—was based on what he called "the law of the migration of organisms." For any number of reasons—some of which Darwin himself had put forward—organisms tend to migrate. This is due either to intrinsic factors—the drive to seek new sources of food, instinct, or accidental wandering—or to such external pressures as a change in conditions, the struggle for existence, or some natural trauma. In any case, a small segment of the general population which has migrated finds itself cut off, isolated from the parental stock. Wagner further noted that the migratory relocation of a population automatically entails a change in its conditions of existence:

> The migration to a new district where the species appear for the first time, must always involve a certain amount of change in the conditions of life, especially in the quantity and quality of the food. Darwin, in his latest work on the variation of animals and plants in a state of domestication, rightly attaches the greatest importance to the influence of food. . . . Under these altered conditions of life—on which the climate has but slight direct influence—the quality of individual variability inherent in every organism and without which natural selection is not conceivable, must be greatly enhanced.[49]

Thus Wagner's equation emerges: migration + isolation + variation = speciation. Though his emphasis was, like that of Darwin when he employed it, strictly on geographical or spatial isolation, his examples would have applied equally to any form of isolation. It should also be noted that Wagner was not so much denying the operation of natural selection[50] as he was transposing it, with that of isolation, to a secondary role. He viewed isolation as the prior, primary condition in the process of speciation.

The migration of organisms and their colonization, according to my conviction, are necessary conditions of Natural Selection. The former confirm the latter, set aside the most important objections which have been raised to the theory, and render the whole natural process of the formation of species much clearer than was previously the case.

The law of migration of organisms and natural selection are closely connected. The geographical distribution of forms could not be explained without Darwin's theory. On the other hand, selection without the migration of organisms, and without long isolation of single individuals from the station of their species could not be called into action. Both phenomena are in close correlation.[51]

DARWIN'S REPLY TO WAGNER
Darwin wrote back to Wagner that same month:

You well show, in a manner which never occurred to me, that it [isolation] removes many difficulties and objections. But I must still believe that in many large areas all the individuals of the same species have been slowly modified, in the same manner, for instance, as the English race-horse has been improved, that is by the continued selection of the fleetest individuals without any separation.[52]

Yet, in underlining Darwin's inability to explain the multiplication and diversification of species if confined within the same area without isolation, Wagner managed to elicit one admission from Darwin:

But I admit that by this process two or more new species could hardly be found within the same limited area; some degree of separation, if not indispensable, would be highly advantageous; and here your facts and views will be of great value.[53]

At the same time Darwin wrote his impressions of Wagner's paper in a letter to August Weismann:

> I thought M. Wagner's first pamphlet very good and interesting but I think he overrates the necessity for emigration and isolation. I doubt whether he has reflected on what must occur when his forms colonise a new country, unless they vary during the very first generation. . . .* Nor does he attach, I think, sufficient weight to the cases of what I have called unconscious selection by man; in these cases races are modified by the preservation of the best and the destruction of the worst, without any isolation.[54]

In turn, Darwin, in his reading of Wagner, had seen the latter's main omission—and a very important one it was. In his concentration on the *conditions* for speciation, Wagner completely overlooked the nature of the *process* itself—the evolution of adaptation. In terms of explanatory difficulties, Darwin's theory shone most brightly in its capacity of throwing light on the origins of the manifold complexities of natural adaption—a subject which Wagner's separation theory failed even to mention and, from its context, did not appear remotely capable of explaining. This was why, in his later paper of 1875, which went not a step further than that of 1868, Darwin scrawled across the front "Most Wretched Rubbish," and alongside the appropriate paragraph: "There does not appear the least explanation how e.g. a woodpecker could be formed in an isolated region."[55]

In his preparation of the fifth edition of the *Origin*,[56] Darwin had to consider the points raised by Jenkin as well as those by Wagner. After Darwin had committed himself to the concept of production of new and permanent species without the necessity of isolation, his reading of Jenkin resulted in his complete commitment to speciation through a type of blending selection. The result in the fifth edition was that, while paying some tribute to Wagner's championing of the role of isolation ("Moritz Wagner

---

* Darwin certainly saw the necessity of the pre-adaptability of variation.

. . . has shown that the service rendered by isolation is probably greater even than I have supposed"),[57] he nevertheless felt compelled to add that he could "by no means agree with this naturalist, that migration and isolation are necessary for the formation of new species." Then followed Darwin's earlier arguments.

On the matter of isolation, things stood more or less in abeyance until 1875, when Wagner once again published on the subject.[58] This second paper differed very little from the previous one. Once again Wagner leveled the same criticism at Darwin: his theory described only "the gradual morphological metamorphosis of the *whole* existing species in the same region."[59] Were this the case, he said, there would have to have been "numerous middle forms and connecting links," adding acidly, "the rarity or complete lack of these more delicate transition forms contradicts such a process of formation. Also the compensating effect of free crossing most certainly disproves the theory of selection."[60]

In his letter of reply to Wagner, Darwin reaffirmed his belief "that all the individuals of a species can be slowly modified within the same district, in nearly the same manner as man effects by what I have called the process of unconscious selection."[61] And once again, he was forced to admit Wagner's point on multiple divergence: "I do not believe that one species will give birth to two or more species as long as they are mingled together within the same district." But perhaps recalling his own words on ecological isolation, he added: "Nevertheless I cannot doubt that many new species have been simultaneously developed within the same large continental area." Whether he thought the agent was the ecological differentiation implied in pre-adaptive variation, he never said; but he did see the need for isolation in multiple speciation:

> There are two different classes of cases, as it appears to me, viz. those in which a species becomes slowly modified in the same country (of which I cannot doubt there are innumerable instances) and those cases in which a species splits in two or

three or more new species, and in the latter case, I should think nearly perfect separation would greatly aid in their "specification," to coin a new word.[62]

It does, at first, seem strange that the Darwin of the Galapagos Archipelago should feel so strongly about demonstrating speciation by natural selection, specifically *excluding* isolation as a vital condition. In fact, the difficulties which stemmed from this determination may make it appear that Darwin had forgotten the very context in which he had first glimpsed the selective means to evolution. In not accepting isolation as a necessary condition, Darwin took a middle ground between ecological separation and blending selection as alternative means to achieve speciation, but without citing either. Jenkin's criticism of 1867 must have convinced him that blending was better incorporated within his theoretical process than—as Jenkin had so forcefully put it—as "an insurmountable obstacle to the formation of new varieties." Yet, to such later critics as Wagner, Darwin's reliance on modification with blending seemed only to underline the need for some form of isolation.

We have pointed out the many genuine instances of isolation which formed part of the foundation of Darwin's evolutionary process without his conscious recognition of them. Nor was this Darwin's only oversight. In the earlier editions of the *Origin* (the four editions before that of 1868), Darwin dealt only summarily with the multiplication and distribution of species. He had been content to devote the major theoretical part of his work to a demonstration of the conditions and the process by which one species could become sufficiently modified to rank as a new specific form.

In employing against Darwin both the swamping argument and the explanatory failures of the theory regarding multiple divergences, distribution, and transitional forms, Wagner hit upon the theory's greatest weaknesses.* Only the isolation implied in his own "separation-migration" theory, Wagner felt, could account for these most important phenomena. Darwin, however, rightly expressed astonishment at Wagner's intimations that he had neglected isolation. He had, he felt, shown that it was not a *condition* for speciation, while at the same time it would provide an extremely useful situation not only for speciation, but (as he later recognized) for divergence and distribution as well.

To conclude, Darwin's position concerning the importance of isolation changed little from 1859 on. Although he rejected isolation completely as a necessary condition for the basic (ortho-selective) form of speciation that formed the core of his work, nevertheless he used the concept throughout without recognizing it for what it was. Darwin led us to believe that the multiple divergence and distribution of species can be accounted for by means of the fortuitous instances of natural geographical and spatial isolation that occur from time to time.

* Except for explaining transitional forms, it is in fact true that isolation in some form is necessary for the origin and distribution of new species.

8. Darwin and Wallace

*Although I maintain, and even enforce, my differences
from some of Darwin's views, my whole work tends
forcibly to illustrate the overwhelming importance of
Natural Selection over all other agencies in the
production of new species. I thus take up Darwin's
earlier position, from which he somewhat receded in the
later editions of his works, on account of criticisms and
objections which I have endeavoured to show are
unsound. Even in rejecting that phase of sexual
selection depending on female choice, I insist
on the greater efficacy of natural selection.
This is pre-eminently the Darwinian doctrine, and
I therefore claim for my book the position of being
the advocate of pure Darwinism.*

—A. R. Wallace, Preface to Darwinism (1889)

Wallace stayed on in Asia for four years after the publication
of his joint paper with Darwin, returning to England in the
spring of 1862. As he later declared in his autobiography, his
absence from England caused him to be unaware of the magnitude
of the controversy over evolution. On his return, Wallace settled
in London and began to work on his huge zoological collections.
Though he was quite self-conscious about his new position in the
scientific world, he was nevertheless sorely disappointed about
the lack of recognition given his earlier (1855) paper on evolu-

tion.[1] He did not mingle much with his scientific contemporaries, but worked steadily on his collections and papers. He continued his correspondence with Darwin but the two men met only on those rare occasions when Darwin ventured up to London for a meeting. Their relationship was limited to a rather sporadic correspondence during this period. Both naturalists were working at this time on organic variability: Darwin on domestic variations in preparing his work on that subject, Wallace on those of his Asian specimens. It would not be long before the two were brought headlong together once again by a common idea.

SEXUAL SELECTION (1864–1870)

Darwin's Conception: The idea of sexual selection occurred to Darwin almost through a process of elimination. Endeavoring, as always, to work from the facts to his hypotheses, Darwin looked upon the entirety of organic nature as a vast collection of factual data, each part of which he hoped to explain by means of the principle of natural selection. But, very early on, he had come to see phenomena which could not be explained on the basis of a natural selection. This led him to mention various "minor" causes of modification. He attributed each of these several phenomena to such factors as the direct effects of conditions, of habit, of use and disuse, of correlation, and of mere spontaneous variability, until he came to those often complex secondary sexual characters of beauty and ornamentation. These he felt necessary to ascribe to the process of sexual selection.* Yet, as already indicated, Darwin devoted little space in the first three editions of the *Origin* to sources of change other than that of natural selection.

While the original idea of sexual selection was referred to in his *Notebooks* before 1842, Darwin went little further than to

---

* In the introductory passages on sexual selection in the *Descent* (II:246 *et seq.*), Darwin demonstrated this process of elimination whereby he accounted for several phenomena unexplainable by selection alone, leaving those which seemed explicable only through sexual selection.

give a brief illustration of it until 1867. Until he began work on the subject of man, in fact, he did not become fully aware of the range of application of sexual selection and what he came to feel was its necessary place in evolution. Though it was this work on man that caused Darwin to extend his view of sexual selection, probably the greatest stimulus along these lines was the publication, during the 1864–67 period, of a number of papers by Wallace on the subject of organic coloration. Unfortunately, the long delayed and still incomplete *Variation* made it impossible to embark on any more side issues at the time. Finally, early in 1867, free at last of the *Variation*, he turned to the problem of man's origin. Then it was that the important and essential differences between man and other organisms, many of which seemed inexplicable on the basis of natural selection alone, suggested some auxiliary process at work. This he saw almost at the outset of his investigations. "As far as we are enabled to judge, not one of the external differences between the races of man are of any direct or special service to him."[2]

"Sexual selection," stated Darwin, "depends on the advantage which certain individuals have over other individuals of the same sex and species, in exclusive relation to reproduction."[3] Because the individual organism (of the opposite sex to the one being selected), rather than elements of the environment, constituted the source of the selective standard, Darwin saw that a distinctly different form of selection was involved. Since the features selected were exclusively related to sex and reproduction, he gave this the name "sexual selection."

Darwin began his case with observations of animal behavior. He described how females often showed preference for males of a particular coloring, of special singing ability, or for those who performed certain courtship rituals. Males sought the same characteristics in females, with the addition of an enticing odor. One distinctive feature of males was that they also battled other males for the possession of the females—they possessed structures of offense and defense. In short, whereas the process of natural selection was the basis for survival of the species, sexual selection was the basis for the goal of fertilization and reproduction of the individual.*

Once again, in bringing to bear supporting evidence, Darwin employed analogy to the role of man in a domestic situation:

> If man can in a short time give elegant carriage and beauty to his bantams, according to his standard of beauty, I can see no good reason to doubt that female birds, by selecting, during thousands of generations, the most melodious or beautiful males, according to their standard of beauty, might produce a marked effect.[4]

Wallace's Influence: The publication of Lyell's *Antiquity of Man* in 1863 acted as a stimulus to both Wallace and Darwin. Lyell's work, alternating as it did between geology and theology without any commitment concerning Darwin's theory of man's origin, only underlined the need for a clear and definite statement on the evolution of man. At this time, however, Darwin was still thoroughly occupied with, and committed to, his *Variation*. Once again it was to be Wallace who first tackled the problem in print.

At the beginning of 1864, Lyell, preparing his presidential address on "Man" for the British Association for the Advancement of Science, wrote to Wallace asking his opinion on the subject of man's origin. Stimulated by this query, Wallace decided to put down his ideas in the form of a paper which he sent to the *Anthropological Review*. "Human Races and Natural Selection" appeared in the May issue. It was a fact-filled essay whose main thesis was that man's body could be explained only by the theory of natural selection up to the time he became a social animal, but that man's peculiar attributes of mind and soul could be explained only on grounds of intervention of the deity. On May 10 Wallace sent Darwin a copy of this paper and asked for his criticisms.

---

* In the fourth and later editions of the *Origin*, this method of selection included plants as well.

There was little in it to indicate that Wallace was himself occupied with the problem of explaining the acquisition of secondary sexual characters. Since he confined himself to speculations on man's origin without reference to any process necessary to account for the facts other than that of natural selection, there was no basis for any trepidation by Darwin on this account. Yet Darwin must have been somewhat disconcerted by Wallace's independent endeavor in a realm whose exploration by anyone save himself he had not anticipated. The magnanimity of Wallace's repeated references to natural selection as "Darwin's theory" could do little to assuage the feeling of being once again somehow anticipated. The limited scope of Wallace's paper, however, and Darwin's growing awareness of the importance of sexual selection in the human species, seemed to allow a more generous attitude toward his younger colleague. In his return letter, Darwin indicated his awareness of having supplanted Wallace in the public mind as the author of the theory of selection, and in a gesture of personal restitution, Darwin made an offer of assistance: "I have collected a few notes on man, but I do not suppose that I shall ever use them. Do you intend to follow out your views, and if so, would you like at some future time to have my few references and notes? I am sure I hardly know whether they are of any value, and they are at present in a state of chaos."[5] It seemed, however, a typically polite offer anticipating an equally gracious refusal. Wallace was himself anxious to press on regarding the seemingly inexplicable acquisition of sexual characteristics. At the same time, there was his large work on his Asian travels still unfinished. Thus, on the grounds of his "present work" Wallace declined the offer, and, save for the odd personal letter, their correspondence dwindled for the next few years.

During these intervening years Wallace had papers published on the variability of Malayan fauna. Those on pigeons and butterflies written in 1865 showed his increasing interest in sexual characters and the question of their origin. It was also becoming more obvious that he was thinking along causal lines different from that of sexual selection. In his butterfly paper of January 1866,[6] Wallace first demonstrated selection on the basis of protective resemblance. He described the evolution of mimicry in certain species by the selection of those variations representing an increasing resemblance to certain inanimate aspects of the environment. He saw that the more the species acquired mimetic camouflage, the less an object of predation it would be, surviving over less well-endowed forms and thereby subject to the process of natural selection. He went further, trying to explain differences in coloration according to sex: a problem that had long been troubling Darwin and which he (Darwin) felt could best be explained by sexual selection. "The reason why the females are more subject to this kind of modification than the males is, probably, that their slower flight when laden with eggs, and their exposure to attack while in the act of depositing their eggs upon leaves, render it especially advantageous for them to have some additional protection."[7]

Having begun on man early in 1867, Darwin reopened correspondence on evolution with Wallace with a query on sexual characters. He had now come to believe that sexual selection was "the main agent in forming the races of man" and as such, it was taking up increasingly more of his time. When it came to studies of color and other sexual characters, Wallace was obviously *the* man to consult for information. (No doubt he was also anxious to ascertain the extent of Wallace's own researches into the subject.) Darwin's request was for examples illustrating the action of sexual selection. Recalling Wallace's own views on selection-for-protection, he added: "I am fearfully puzzled how far to extend your protective views with respect to the females in various classes. The more I work the more important sexual selection apparently comes out."[8] Darwin wanted to know how caterpillars came so often to be brightly colored. Since Wallace had postulated that coloring in certain species amounted to a mimicry for protection (when the colors resembled the surroundings), how could he account for such obvious cases that would seem to have quite the opposite effect? Wallace saw the answer instantly, however. Certain insects are inedible or unpalatable or, in some other way, prove undesirable as a food source for certain predators. By making themselves conspicuous through bright and outstanding coloration, they warn away or discourage predators and so survive unmolested. Wallace was quite satisfied with his reply since he now felt that two distinct classes of phenomena were both explained on the basis of selection-for-protection. Furthermore, this explanation, in both cases, bypassed explanation on the basis of sexual selection. This latter mechanism, rooted as it was in the element of choice on the part of organisms themselves, seemed to Wallace a dubious way of effecting evolutionary change.

Wallace had been busily at work gathering his thoughts on mimicry for a paper which he hoped to submit shortly. As he continued in his preparation, he became more firmly convinced of his central theme, writing to Darwin:

> I have lately hit upon a generalisation connected with sexual characters which pleases me very much and I make no doubt will interest you. I have become more than ever convinced of the powerful effect of *"protective resemblances"* in determining and regulating the development of colour. [Examples follow.] I think this proves that the primary action of sexual selection is to produce colour pretty equally in *both sexes,* but that it is checked in the females by the immense importance of *protection* and the danger of conspicuous colouring.[9]

Again Darwin saw Wallace entering a realm of discussion which he had hoped to develop himself and once more he stepped forward to establish a form of priority. "I have been greatly interested by your letter, but your view is not new to me. If you will look at p. 240 of the fourth edition of the *Origin* you will find it briefly given . . . a more general statement is given at p. 101 or at p. 89 of the first edition, for I have long entertained this view, though I have never had the space to develop it."[10] He went on:

"I have collected all my old notes, and partly written my discussion, and it would be flat work for me to give the leading idea as exclusively from you. But, as I am sure from your greater knowledge of Ornithology and Entomology that you will write a much better discussion than I could, your paper will be of great use to me. Nevertheless I must discuss the subject fully in my Essay on Man." Darwin went to great lengths to remind Wallace of his prior thoughts on the subject: "When we met at the Zoological Society, and I asked you about the sexual differences in kingfishers, I had this subject in view; as I had when I suggested to Bates the difficulty about gaudy caterpillars." What is more, Darwin persisted in attributing the origin of unusual coloration to sexual selection. "The conclusion to which I have been leaning is that in some of these abnormal cases the colour happened to vary in the female alone, and was transmitted to females alone, and that her variations have been selected through the admiration of the male." In concluding, he added: "It is curious how we hit on the same ideas."

As one historical commentator has put it: "Wallace still anticipated ideas in the most embarrassing manner."[11] Darwin's letter, with all its recollections of printed references, personal comments, etc. amounted to quite a plea. This time, however, things were different. Darwin was now a man of world renown, one who had been at work on the subject for nearly thirty years: he certainly could not have relished the idea of being anticipated again. His statement about intending to publish, his remark about gathering his "old notes," and his comment that it would be "flat work" if he must cite the leading idea as coming exclusively from Wallace, all indicate that it would have been flat work indeed. Though there is no comparison in merit between the theories of natural selection and sexual selection, Darwin nevertheless saw the work of nearly twenty years in the balance. His reaction was decidedly less generous than that of 1858. But, while it may not have been the same Darwin writing, it was the same Wallace. He replied by sending all his notes to Darwin; there was no preliminary of a polite offer, but an immediate acquiescence through direct action. "I was afraid you had rather misunderstood my letter on first reading; for I assure you I never for a moment imagined that any of the more obvious facts connected with sexual selection could have been new to you."[12] Again he chose to defer to his senior. "I had thought of a short paper on 'The Connection between the Colours of Female Birds and their Mode of Nidification'—but had rather leave it for you to treat as part of the really *great* subject of Sexual Selection—which combined with *protective resemblances* will I think when thoroughly worked out explain the whole colouring of the animal kingdom."

Wallace's unabashed deference had its effect on Darwin. He felt quite embarrassed at having been too transparent in his feelings—it seemed like 1858 all over again.

> The offer of your valuable notes is most generous, but it would vex me to take so much from you, as it is certain that you could work up the subject very much better than I could. Therefore I earnestly, and without any reservation, hope that you will proceed with your paper, so that I return your notes. You seem already to have investigated the subject. I confess on receiving your note that I felt rather flat at my recent work being almost thrown away, but I did not intend to show this feeling.[13]

Darwin continued, discounting his own efforts on the subject and lauding the younger Wallace's abilities: "I am surprised at my own stupidity, but I have long recognised how much clearer and deeper your insight into matters is than mine," and concluded: "Forgive me, if you can, for a touch of illiberality about your paper." Darwin had been recognizably oversensitive in the matter.

Wallace's studies of mimicry and bright coloring under the theme of selection-for-protection had little or no direct bearing on sexual selection. In fact, Wallace was steadfastly avoiding such an explanation. What the two men had in common was that they sought to explain the same class of phenomena. Darwin's implication that there might be some question of priority at stake was an error in judgment, the realization of which caused him no little embarrassment. Their mutual correspondence ceased for some months while both men set to work at writing up their respective views. Shortly afterward (in July 1867), Wallace's paper on mimicry and protection appeared and was followed in October by his review of Jenkin's paper and the Duke of Argyll's book, both of which attacked the theory of natural selection.[14]

Wallace had never felt comfortable over Darwin's notions of sexual selection, his chief reason being that the whole process was based on the agency of (male or female) choice or individual preference. This dependency on the exercise of animal will in the form of choice disturbed Wallace. In his own later compendium on the subject—published, one should note, *after* Darwin's death— he remarked that Darwin "has extended the principle into a totally different field of action, which has none of that character of constancy and of inevitable result that attaches to natural selection."[15] While this was the underlying cause of Wallace's dissatisfaction, he was also impressed by what he felt were large numbers of explanatory inadequacies in the new theory.

Wallace saw the principle of sexual selection as operating in two distinct ways: first, in the combat in nature between males for the possession of females, and, second, in the element of choice exercised over musical or ornamental features. He declared:

> The first is an observed *fact,* the second is an *inference* from the observed facts. The first kind of sexual selection I hold as strongly and as thoroughly as Darwin himself; the latter I at first accepted, following Darwin's conclusions from what appeared to be strong evidence explicable in no other way; but I soon came to doubt the possibility of such an explanation, at first from considering the fact that in butterflies sexual differences are as strongly marked as in birds, and it was to me impossible to accept female choice in their case, while, as the whole question of colour came to be better

understood, I saw equally valid reasons for its total rejection even in birds and mammals.[16]

Wallace's disinclination to accept the theory of sexual selection became complete disavowal as a result of his work on mimicry and coloration for protection. When he came to realize that the principle of natural selection would operate equally well to attain qualities of self-protection, and that most, if not all, secondary sexual characters could be thus explained, he saw no necessity whatever for calling upon such a process as sexual selection. The principle of natural selection, as originally postulated by both Darwin and himself, seemed perfectly adequate. Thus the combination of three factors put Wallace in the curious position of espousing the cause of natural selection against Darwin's sexual selection: first, its dependency on the exercise of choice; second, its explanatory inadequacies; and, third, the fact that the same phenomena could be explained on the basis of natural selection for protection. Throughout most of Darwin's lifetime, Wallace remained extremely tactful in expressing his opinions, so that Darwin became only gradually aware of his rather strong views on the subject. In October 1867, commenting on Wallace's review, Darwin remarked: "By the way, I cannot but think that you push protection too far in some cases."[17] Wallace's endeavor to subsume sexual selection completely appeared to Darwin a gradual encroachment of Wallace's explanatory mechanism upon his own. Because Darwin had come to attribute to sexual selection not only man's external characters but an ever-increasing amount of zoological and botanical phenomena, he found himself ever more strenuously defending his new theory, with the result that the two men drifted apart in their ideologies concerning evolution.

The Variation (*1868*): The greatest part of their correspondence in 1868 was given over to discussions of the natural selection of sterility. The correspondence on sexual selection resumed with Wallace on March 19, 1868. On February 4, Darwin mentioned in passing that he had "begun on Man and Sexual Selection," to which Wallace later replied:

> I am glad you have got good materials on Sexual Selection. It is no doubt a difficult subject. One difficulty to me is, that I do not see how the constant *minute* variations, which are sufficient for N. S. to work with, could be *sexually* selected. We seem to require a series of bold and abrupt variations. How can we imagine that an inch in the tail of the peacock, or ¼-inch in that of the Bird of Paradise, would be noticed and preferred by the female?[18]

Darwin answered by referring to "an over-all sense of appreciation of features," adding that the naturalist Jenner Weir gave good evidence that even details are noticed.[19]

April of 1868 saw the publication of a short paper by Wallace on birds' nests, in which he repeated his views on the acquisition of coloring for protection. He felt his hypothesis further proved by the general rule that both sexes are conspicuously colored when the nest is concealed, but that the sitting bird is of dull or obscure color when the nest is exposed to view. In a letter praising this paper, Darwin remarked that Wallace did "not lay much stress on new characters spontaneously appearing in one sex (generally the male), and being transmitted exclusively, or more commonly only in excess to that sex. I, on the other hand, formerly paid far too little attention to protection. I had only a glimpse of the truth; but even now I do not go quite as far as you." Darwin put a question to Wallace: "When female butterflies are more brilliant than their males you believe that they have in most cases, or in all cases, been rendered brilliant so as to mimic some other species, and thus escape danger. But can you account for the males not having been rendered equally brilliant and equally protected?"[20] Darwin offered his own explanation of transmission of characters being often limited to only one sex and sat back to await Wallace's reply. He did in fact succeed in extracting an admission from him:

I fully admit *all* sexual differences of colour cannot be explained in this way. There seems to be some production of greater vividness and condensation of colour, in the male, independent of protection.

I think all the evidence goes to show that though special variations of colour may sometimes be transmitted to one sex only, yet no *great accumulation* of such variation can occur in one sex only, unless it is injurious to the other sex and therefore weeded out by Natural Selection.[21]

Wallace could see no justification for calling upon such a rule of inheritance. Such limitation concerning sex indicated to him that possession by members of one sex only meant that possession by the opposite sex must have constituted some danger at some time in their history and thus have been eliminated by the process of natural selection. Darwin, however, maintained his position, adding: "We shall never convince each other." He did however complain of one inconsistency in Wallace: "I do not think you lay nearly enough stress in your articles on what you admit in your letters: viz., 'there seems to be some production of vividness . . . of colour in the male independent of protection.' This I am making a chief point; and have come to your conclusion so far that I believe that intense colouring in the female is often checked by being dangerous. I am not shaken about the female protected butterflies. I will grant (only for argument) that the life of the male is of very little value,—I will grant that the males do not vary, yet why has not the protective beauty of the female been transferred by inheritance to the male?"[22]

Wallace replied by, in effect, turning the tables on Darwin:

I hardly see your difficulty or your objection to the case of the female protected butterflies. You argued before (and have proved) that "characters appearing in one sex are sometimes transmitted to that sex exclusively." The case of these female protected butterflies (by mimicry) are so few that we may

well suppose the proper variations to have occurred sufficiently in that sex only. But there is also the important *fact* to
be considered, that in most (perhaps all) these cases the female has different habits and the *same variation* would *not* be
useful to the male because he *does not frequent the stations*
where the *mimicked species abound.* He also has the strength
of flight which does not accord with the slow weak flight of the
Heliconidia which that of the female does. In cases where the
difference of *habit and action* does not exist, both sexes are
equally protected as in the leaf butterfly which is protected in
repose.

My theory of colour in nature is somewhat as follows:

(1)   Colour is ever varying and is generally transmitted to
both sexes.
(2)   It protects, by simple concealment
by mimicry
by making conspicuous.
(3)   It is also useful sexually, to the female by attracting
the male and vice versa.
(4)   It is therefore selected and accumulated.
(5)   Owing to the special structures, functions and habits
of the female sex, this often requires more protection
than the male and is also more important in the
preservation of the offspring. Protection by colour is
therefore often acquired by this *sex alone.*
(6)   This occurs by subduing or checking the colour as
acquired by the male or by the accumulation of entirely distinct colours or markings.

I really do not think we shall ultimately differ much on this
point. . . .[23]

Darwin did not relent on the position of sexual selection: "I
am glad to say that I agree almost entirely with your summary
except that I should put sexual selection as an equal or perhaps

as even a more important agent in giving colour than Natural Selection for protection."[24] He had noticed Wallace's increasing estrangement from sexual selection: "What I rather object to in your articles is that I do not think anyone would infer from them that you place sexual selection even as high as No. 4 in your summary. It was very natural that you should give only a line to sexual selection in the summary to the *Westminster Review,* but the result at first to my mind was that you attributed hardly anything to its power."

Their correspondence was interrupted by Darwin's ill health, lasting this time for nine weeks. At the end of that period Darwin wrote to Wallace that he was coming to differ more and more from him, to the point that he could support his hypothesis hardly at all. Wallace replied: "I am certainly surprised that you should find so much evidence against protection having checked the acquiring of bright colours in females."[25] Their correspondence on sexual selection dropped until the publication of the *Descent,* of which more than half was devoted to its exposition.

The Descent of Man *(1871):* Wallace spent over two weeks poring over his copy, giving a temporary verdict on January 27:

> On the subject of "sexual selection" and "protection" you do not yet convince me that I am wrong; but I expect your heaviest artillery will be brought up in your second volume . . . my view is, as I thought I had made it clear, that the female has (in most cases) been simply prevented from acquiring the gay tints of the male (even when there was a tendency for her to inherit it), because it was hurtful; and that, when protection is not needed, gay colours are so generally acquired by both sexes as to show that inheritance by both sexes of colour variations is the most usual, when not prevented from acting by Natural Selection. The colour itself may be acquired either by sexual selection or by other unknown causes.[26]

Whereas Wallace had tried earlier to substitute selection-for-protection for sexual selection; it was seen here as only a more basic, limiting factor to sexual selection. He was admitting that the actual acquisition of sexual coloration now was achieved through sexual selection. Yet, only six weeks later, Wallace was writing to Darwin: "You will not be surprised to find that you have not convinced me on the 'female protection' question, but you *will* be surprised to hear that I do not despair of convincing you."[27]

In the *Academy* of March 15 there appeared Wallace's review of the *Descent,* in which he gave several examples where female insects did not appear to exercise any choice of males. Remarked Darwin in reply: "I have been much impressed with what you urge against colour in the case of insects, having been acquired through sexual selection. I always saw that the evidence was very weak; but I still think, if it be admitted that the musical instruments of insects have been gained through sexual selection, that there is not the least improbability in colour having been thus gained. Your argument with respect to the denudation of mankind and also to insects, that taste on the part of one sex would have to remain nearly the same during many generations, in order that sexual selection should produce any effect I agree to."[28]

Wallace never succeeded in convincing Darwin any more than he had up to 1871 and the subject was rarely even discussed after that. Darwin's theory of sexual selection, it should be noted, is not very important by itself. Its importance in Darwin's thought on evolution lies in two facts. First, it was a sort of test case, being, after all, a process of modification other than that of natural selection, and one whose wide range of application was described by Darwin himself. While it appeared to Darwin to fill the important explanatory gaps left by the theory of natural selection, it would nevertheless appear to some critics as a well-documented admission that the process of natural selection was merely one of a large number of processes at work in nature—a view certainly not in keeping with Darwin's original thesis on natural selection. Second, and not unrelated, is the point that in sexual selection it was the organisms themselves that were the agents of selection—just as was the case in the inherited effects of habit, use, and disuse, in which Darwin also came increasingly to believe. As such, it was looked upon by many later critics as implying that the species (or form) was the agent of its own evolution—another problem that would plague Darwin in the years that followed.

PHYSIOLOGICAL ISOLATION AND STERILITY (1859–1868)

The story of Darwin and the problem of inter-specific sterility is somewhat similar to that of saltations and sexual selection. It is another case of one of Darwin's close friends urging him to recognize a phenomenon which would strongly support the theory of natural selection (and which Darwin himself had expressly rejected). In this case, it was how inter-specific sterility was gradually acquired. By demonstrating how sterility might have been gradually acquired through the process of natural selection, Wallace saw that Darwin would have achieved two important ends: first, he would have explained the important fact of such sterility —"the very physiological test of a species which is wanting for the complete proof of the *'origin of species.'* " Second, he would have found an additional isolating process to prevent the blending that was contingent upon free inter-crossing. The latter reason was as important as the former, because Darwin had come to consider isolation as a mere fortuitous circumstance aiding selection. Too many sister-species cohabited in the same locality, yet remained distinct. A more subtle, perhaps non-physical, isolation was needed—a role which Wallace saw the selective acquisition of sterility filling admirably.

The Origin (*1859*): Darwin began his chapter on hybridism with the statement: "The sterility of the hybrids could not possibly be of any advantage to them, and therefore could not have been acquired by the continued preservation of successive profitable degrees of sterility."[29] The origin of such sterility Darwin saw as "incidental on other acquired differences."[30] That is, sterility was acquired through correlation with other important structural and functional changes effected through selection. In other words, as the new form diverged from its parent species, so, as a consequence of the total differences arising, it became less fertile. Thus, Darwin saw the *fact* of sterility as emerging from the physiological discrepancies of "two different structures and constitutions having been blended into one."[31]

More important, considerations of inter-specific sterility led Darwin to remark on one significant feature. Whether or not the direct object of selection, sterility seemed to occur in nature to varying degrees:

> It is certain, on the one hand, that the sterility of various species when crossed is so different in degree and graduates away so insensibly, and on the other hand, that the fertility of pure species is so easily affected by various circumstances, that for all practical purposes it is most difficult to say where perfect fertility ends and sterility begins.[32]

The varying degrees of sterility found in many inter-specific crosses (hybrids), together with the "close general resemblance between hybrids and mongrels" led Darwin to conclude "that there is no fundamental distinction between species and varieties."[33]

Wallace's Influence and the Fourth Origin *(1866):* On January 22, 1866, Darwin had just finished reading Wallace's paper on the geographical distribution and variability of the Malayan Papilionidae.[34] He had been intrigued by Wallace's comments on the results of inter-crossing dimorphic forms. The crossing of what amounted to two distinct varieties of the same species, said Wallace, often exhibited dominance in the characters of one of the forms.

> I doubt whether your criterion of dimorphic forms not producing intermediate offspring will suffice, for I know of a good many varieties which must be so called that will not blend or intermix, but produce offspring quite like either parent.[35]

Wallace, long since aware of the potential advantages implied in the gradual selective acquisition of sterility, jumped at what he thought might be the key to such a possible explanation:

> If you "know varieties that will not blend or intermix, but produce offspring quite like either parent"—is not that the very physiological test of a species which is wanting for the *complete proof* of the "origin of species"?[36]

Wallace had apparently seen some connection between the causes underlying dominance and those effecting sterility. Unfortunately, there is no trace of any reply from Darwin.[37] Having made this query just at the time Darwin was revising his chapter on hybridism, Wallace must have reawakened Darwin's interest in the subject, for there followed a rather lengthy addition to the chapter, which began:

> At one time it appeared to me probable, as it has to others, that this sterility might have been acquired through natural selection. . . . For it would clearly be advantageous to two varieties or incipient species, if they could be kept from blending, but it could not have been of any direct advantage to an individual animal to breed poorly with another individual of a different variety.[38]

He went on in reference to plants. He noted the isolative value in the hermaphroditic conditions being self-sterile (that one form of pollen should be prepotent over others) adding "we do not know whether sterility is a consequence of prepotency."[39] He therefore concluded:

> . . . that with animals the sterility of crossed species has not been slowly augmented through natural selection; and as this sterility follows the same general laws in the vegetable as in the animal kingdom, it is improbable, though apparently possible, that crossed plants should have been rendered sterile by a different process from animals . . . and we are driven to our former proposition, that the sterility . . . is simply incidental

on unknown differences in the reproductive systems of the parent species.[40]

Nothing further was mentioned until early 1868 when the *Variation* appeared. Darwin's views remained unchanged: the selective acquisition of sterility, while a desirable process (particularly now with blending recognized as such an overwhelming force against individual variation), remained outside the realm of selection. Darwin felt that too much stress had been laid on sterility. Even among recognized species it was not, after all, a universal attribute. Besides, he had recognized other factors preventing the crossing of different forms, stating " . . . that some domestic races are led by different habits of life to keep to a certain extent separate, and that others prefer coupling with their own kind, in the same manner as species in a state of nature, though in a much less degree."[41]

Darwin's commitment to the very slight individual differences and his total rejection of strongly marked changes (those which might render their possessors sterile at the same time) made the sterility problem important. There was more need, though less opportunity, for sterility when the differences between parent and variant forms were only slight.

The criticisms of Jenkin, followed by Darwin's unchanged position in the *Variation,* led to Wallace's writing Darwin once again:

> I do not see your objection to sterility between allied species having been aided by Natural Selection. It appears to me that, given a differentiation of a species into two forms, each of which was adapted to a special sphere of existence, every slight degree of sterility would be a positive advantage, not to the individuals who were sterile, but to each form.[42]

Wallace proffered the example of a species producing two new forms, A and B—form A fertile with the parent form, form B rendered to some degree sterile. Wallace claimed that B had a much greater chance of supplanting the parent form, A a better chance of being absorbed by it.

One can see that the fundamental difference between Darwin and Wallace lay in the fact that the former based his utilitarian principle of selection on the basis of the individual organism, while the latter thought in terms of the species. Darwin believed that in nature it is only the individual which exists as a real entity. He could not see how the inability to breed properly, to breed in lesser numbers, or to yield abnormal offspring could be selected as advantageous to any organism. Thus the problem revolved around the separate viewpoints, Wallace basing his principle of utility on the form or species itself, Darwin on the individual.

On February 27, Darwin replied:

> I grant, indeed it is certain, that the degree of the sterility of the individuals of A and B will vary; but any such extra-sterile individuals of, we will say A, if they should hereafter breed with other individuals of A, will bequeath no advantage to their progeny, by which these families will tend to increase in number over other families of A, which are not more sterile when crossed with B.[43]

Darwin never failed to recognize that "Natural Selection" and the "Survival of the Fittest" meant the possession of some advantage that would bring about the increase in numbers of those possessing it. In other words, the advantage must be one which increases the animals' adaptation to, or utilization of, its environment. But Wallace was not to be daunted. By return mail on March 1, he sent Darwin a long letter painstakingly setting forth, in a series of nineteen propositions, "a demonstration on your own principles, that Natural Selection could produce sterility of hybrids."[44]

Wallace felt that the whole problem could be solved by demonstrating two main points: (1) to show that partial sterility is more useful or possesses a selective advantage over perfect fertility; and (2) to show that a perfect sterility has the same selective advantage over a partial sterility. By recognizing sterility as following upon other changes, Wallace saw it as an additional factor, a characteristic occurring in already established new forms. Thus, if emergent forms are also found to possess the *additional* characteristic of lessened fertility (or partial sterility), this would prove advantageous. Whatever hybrids were formed would be inferior (not having the full measure of the beneficial characters of the variant parent) and would die out. There would be no absorption of the new form by blending with the old. To this he added, in his tenth proposition: "Now let a fresh series of variations in the amount of sterility occur . . . exactly the same result must recur."[45] He went on to say:

> It seems probable that the variations in amount of sterility would to some extent concur with and perhaps depend upon the structural variations; so that just in proportion as the two forms diverged and became better adapted to the conditions of existence, their sterility would increase. If this were the case, then N. S. would act with double strength, and those varieties which were better adapted to survive both structurally and physiologically, would certainly do so.

Darwin tried to grapple with Wallace's argument, but, said he: "I have tried once or twice, and it has made my stomach feel as if it has been placed in a vice."[46] It was his son George who took over the refutation, with Darwin dispatching his response to Wallace. On March 24 Wallace replied, repeating in shorter form his previous line of argument. He pressed Darwin on the point that free crossing would render both improvement and selection impossible "so that the species is in danger of extinction."[47] At the end, Wallace could only ask of Darwin: "If Natural Selection can *not* do this, how do species ever arise except when a variety is isolated?" None of Wallace's urging, however, could persuade Darwin to change his views. "Let me first say that no man could have more earnestly wished for the success of Nat. Sel. in regard to sterility than I did; and when I considered a general statement (as in your last note) I always felt sure it could be worked out, but always failed in detail. The cause being, as I believe, that N. S. cannot effect what is not good for the individual, including in this term a social community."[48]

Wallace must have been disappointed at Darwin's failure to be moved by his arguments. To him, effective speciation required not some fortuitous instance of physical isolation (such as he had seen Darwin himself reject), but a form of intrinsic isolation such as that resulting through the selective acquisition of sterility. Wallace replied by return mail with his characteristic graciousness: "If you are not convinced, I little doubt but that I am wrong. . . . I will say no more, but leave the problem as insoluble, only fearing that it will become a formidable weapon in the hands of the enemies of Natural Selection."[49]

THE TWO EVOLUTIONISTS DRIFT APART (1871)

On July 9, 1871, Darwin sent Wallace a copy of the reply of Chauncey Wright, an American, to St. George Mivart defending the principle of natural selection. Darwin was considering the idea of having it published in England at his own expense, thereby rendering it the "official" rejoinder to Mivart. In asking Wallace's opinion, both as to the paper itself as well as to its promulgation in England, Darwin was probably hoping that Wallace would volunteer himself for the job of tackling Mivart in print. His reference to Wright's paper as "not very clearly written, and poor in parts from want of knowledge"[50] indicates a hope for something more satisfactory in the way of an "official" reply. Whether or not he recognized any such hint, Wallace responded with what he must have felt to be the only logical possibility:

> I am sure *your own answers* to Mivart's arguments will be so much more clear and to the point, that the other will be unnecessary.[51]

Wallace went on to compliment parts of the review but noted that "some of Mivart's strongest points—the eye and the ear for in-

stance, are unnoticed in the Review. You will, of course, reply to
these." The matter was dropped right back into Darwin's lap.
Yet Darwin remained as ill-disposed to taking on the job himself
as he had been before and, in a long letter back to Wallace, he
made this quite clear by frequent references to his "daily dis-
comforts, or rather miseries . . . bad attacks . . . wretched health,"
concluding:

> I feel very doubtful how far I shall succeed in answering
> Mivart, it is so difficult to answer objections to doubtful points,
> and make the discussion readable. . . . I wish I had your power
> of arguing clearly.[52]

He went on to mention the caustic review which had just
appeared in the *Quarterly* and which he believed was also by
Mivart. "This 'Quarterly Review' tempts me to republish Chauncey Wright, even if not read by anyone, just to show that someone
will say a word against Mivart."[53] A few days later, when Wallace
still had not replied, Darwin went ahead in securing the publication of Wright's paper. On July 18 he also began on the sixth and
final edition of the *Origin*, whose greatly increased size was to
include a special section devoted to Mivart's comments. This
final edition appeared on February 19, 1872, and shortly there-
after Wallace paid Darwin his usual compliments, though remarking that he was still not satisfied with some of his replies,
particularly that on the evolution of the eye. This was effectively
the end of their close and detailed correspondence concerning
evolution.

Reviewing the relationship between the years 1864 and 1871,
one gains the impression that Wallace, while starting with a sincere veneration of the master and his views, gradually came to
look upon Darwin's stand on natural selection as far weaker and
less inclusive than his own. Where Darwin had found it necessary
to call upon the principle of sexual selection to fill what he thought
a gap in explaining the process of natural selection, Wallace believed he could give explanations of the same phenomena fully

consistent with the principles of natural selection (on the basis of protection). When it came to the selective acquisition of sterility, Wallace again thought Darwin was somewhat timid in his views. In his own theory of evolution (as put forward in his own *Darwinism*) he showed how he thought the latter could be selectively acquired.* Finally, on the question of natural selection and the origins of man, Wallace never could share Darwin's views. Wallace's belief in the intervention of the deity in the case of man put him in the same camp as Mivart on the issue. Generally speaking, on all three subjects his attitude was one of gradually increasing estrangement from Darwin and his views. However, throughout Darwin's lifetime, Wallace never failed in the end to defer to him on most matters. Strangely enough, in spite of all the modifications in his evolutionary thought after 1859, Darwin never accepted a suggestion resulting in any significant change in his theory from his personal friends of the "inner circle" of Darwinians. Instead, he made his greatest revision under the influence of his severest critics (Agassiz, Pouchet, Jenkin, and Mivart).

Darwin looked upon Wallace as the secondary discoverer of the theory of natural selection—a kind of junior partner, as it were, in an exclusive firm of evolutionists of which Darwin was the senior executive—and, in general, as a sounding board for his ideas. Their relationship was not without its moments of strain, and their scientific exchange terminated in 1872, although, on a personal level, they exchanged Victorian cordiality to the end of Darwin's life. On his part, Wallace was always deferential to the master of evolutionary theory, yielding and magnanimous almost to an extreme. When it came to expressing his own (often widely divergent) views, he always acted with tact, reserve, and caution —amounting, in fact, to a hesitancy which delayed his own thesis on evolution until after Darwin's death. On Darwin's part, the relationship was one of apparent receptivity, mingled with an underlying possessiveness about matters concerning evolution. He

* Though modern evolutionists support Darwin's view on the subject.

was generally unyielding in his attitude, and occasionally embarrassingly illiberal, though always full of praise for the younger naturalist. During the periods of their closest correspondence, discussions concerned three subjects principally: sexual selection; sterility and natural selection; and the origins of the races of man. On none of these matters did the two men agree, nor were their differences ever resolved.

9. The Origins of Useless Characters

*I have sometimes felt much difficulty in understanding
the origin of simple parts, of which the importance
does not seem sufficient to cause the preservation
of successively varying individuals.*

—*Charles Darwin,* On the Origin of Species *(first edition)*

*D*arwinian "natural selection" worked on a strict standard
of adaptive utility. The acquisition-through-selection of
every character must therefore be explicable as the cumulative
result of individual differences. The utility of each difference
entailed some element of competitive advantage in the struggle
for existence of the organism possessing it. Further, many extant
features of no *present* advantage could be explained on the
grounds of their *previous* utility to the ancestors of the forms
presently possessing them.* It was on such grounds that Darwin
had successfully accounted for all the most important structural
characteristics of a species. Yet, after having explained these,
Darwin was aware of a number of morphological features which
could not be explained on the principle of utility, either past or
present. They were nearly all of a trivial or superficial nature, and,

* Their perpetuation being merely the result of simple inheritance, or in the
case of vestigial characters, of the inheritance of the effects of disuse.

in accounting for such minor exceptions, Darwin merely alluded to any of several possible causes. First, they may have arisen as the direct effects of environmental conditions and as such have been either transmitted through the general law of inheritance, or, if correlated with some structure of selective value, have been indirectly selected. Still others (particularly those of a secondary sexual nature) could be accounted for on the principle of sexual selection. Thus, at the time of the first *Origin,* Darwin was able to make this assumption:

> . . . every detail of structure in every living creature (making some little allowance for the direct action of physical conditions) may be viewed, either as having been of special use to some ancestral form, or as being now of special use to the descendants of this form—either direct, or indirectly through the complex laws of growth.[1]

At this time, however, Darwin could devote but little time and space to such considerations, for he was principally concerned with explaining the selective origins of more important specific characters.

THE EARLY CRITICISM

Bronn (1860): The first person to criticize Darwin's theory for its inability to account for useless characters was the German paleontologist H. G. Bronn, at the end of 1860.[2] Darwin replied by restating his earlier point that present lack of knowledge often made it impossible to ascertain the purpose or utility of many characters. Again he repeated his comments about ancestral utility, and the possibility of correlated selection. He also plainly confessed to general ignorance of the causes of many minor characters. Despite all this, he confidently concluded:

> I believe in the doctrine of descent with modification, notwithstanding that this or that particular change of structure cannot be accounted for, because this doctrine groups to-

gether and explains, as we shall see in the latter chapters, many general phenomena of nature.[3]

It would only be when added to, and accompanied by, numerous other "minor" criticisms,* that the issue of such characters would attain an exigency necessitating Darwin's more detailed attention.

Nägeli (1865): In 1865, the botanist Karl Nägeli published a paper[4] in which he revealed a number of difficulties in explaining certain morphological features in the plant kingdom.[5] Both the fact that such features did not appear explicable on the basis of utility, and the fact that such apparently useless and trivial features were nevertheless constant in numerous species seemed to pose difficulties for selection theory. Said Nägeli, in conclusion:

> It is therefore noteworthy that the useful adaptation which Darwin suggests for animals and which one can find in quantity for the plant world, are exclusively physiological in nature; that is, they always exhibit the formation and transformation of an organ to a particular function.
>
> A morphological modification, which could be explained through the principle of utility is not known to me in the plant world; and I do not see how this could result, for the general process of formation is so indifferent to physiological function.
>
> The theory of utility demands the acceptance of the fact, which Darwin also expressed, that indifferent characteristics are variable while on the other hand the useful are constant. The purely morphological characteristics of plants should therefore be variable.[6]

In his copy of the paper, Darwin penned in the margin next to the above paragraph: "When part becomes variable, these variations [if] not useful, [are] not made constant."

---

* For example, that the theory of natural selection was unable to account for the useless incipient stages of what would become eventually highly useful and rather complex organs.

In concluding his paper, Nägeli intimated that there was not only a general tendency toward variation on either side of the mean (for any single character in a species), but that there was an innate tendency to vary in a *forward* direction—toward a greater complexity, to higher forms—in a word, a "progression." And it was this tendency, whether aided by natural selection or not, that accounted for the existence and perpetuation of apparently useless, purely morphological characters.

Darwin could not agree with this seemingly logical deduction, from the manifold phenomena of natural variation and the existence of useless characters to the idea of an innate progressive tendency. In a subsequent letter to Nägeli, he brought up the subject:

> The remark which has struck me most, is that on the position of the leaves not having been acquired through natural selection, from not being of any special importance to the plant. Although I can offer no explanation of such fact, and only hope to see that they may be explained, yet I hardly see how they support the doctrine of some law of necessary development, for it is not clear to me that a plant, with its leaves placed at some particular angle, or with its ovules in some particular position, thus stands higher than another plant.[7]

The whole matter, however, was held in abeyance while Darwin finished the *Variation,* and it was not until after Christmas 1868, that, beginning the fifth edition of the *Origin,* he reviewed the developments and criticisms concerning his theory that had arisen since the last edition.

PREPARING THE FIFTH *Origin* (1868)

In December 1868, about to begin on the fifth edition, Darwin wrote to Hooker for advice on the problem of useless characters. Looking back over the *Origin* he had seen that a significant number of unexplained phenomena remained, even after taking into account the several other possible causes. Darwin particularly wanted to hear Hooker's views on the possible origins of the alternate and spiral arrangement of leaves and of especially constant cellular arrangements in tissues. In his reply, Hooker was able to point out a number of instances where apparently functionless features were shown to play a vital role in the life of the plant. His answer raised Darwin's hopes and no doubt stimulated him to embark on a rather detailed reply to Nägeli. Within two weeks, on January 13, 1869, Darwin forwarded thirteen manuscript pages of his response to Hooker. They were read immediately and within forty-eight hours Darwin in turn had his reply. Hooker felt that even such apparently constant botanical phenomena as leaf angles and cellular arrangements exhibited random, fluctuating variation. Furthermore, he said, all such phenomena, whether useful or not, would still be passed on to the offspring on the general principle of inheritance.

Darwin expressed his gratitude, remarking that he had previously tried to show how such characters could have been acquired through the process of natural selection:

> Now I am much inclined to believe, in accordance with the view given towards the close of my MS., that the near approach to uniformity in such structures depends on their not being of vital importance, and therefore not being acted on by N. S. If you have reflected on this point, what do you think of it?[8]

Hooker agreed with Darwin but noted that this meant that "classification and system is founded on the least useful modifications" and concluded that there was, however, "something uncomfortable in the idea that system is based on modifications the active exigency of which is no longer in play."[9] A few days later, still following the same line of thought, Hooker passed on one further comment:

> Just one last thought anent genetic characters of no value

to the plant: is not the fact, that characters of primary value in system are so often of no use, an argument in favour of your conclusion, that such characters as are of no use, if not in any way detrimental, are not necessarily eliminated but may be retained *ad infinitum?*

On the other hand, is it not an argument against the theory of characters acquired by the *individual* being hereditary—thus, if hereditary modifications that never come into play do not die out, is it likely that non-hereditary modifications brought into play by the *individual* (for its own special use) should be transmitted?[10]

There is no record of Darwin's response; his published reply in the *Origin* shows that he concurred with Hooker on the first point. It is perhaps unfortunate that Hooker's comment on the unlikelihood of the inheritance of an individually acquired character did not appear within the context of a more general argument against such inheritance, for not only did Darwin appear to ignore it, but the subject failed to come up again between the two.

It was during this time (probably in December 1868) that Darwin read August Weismann's *Justification of the Darwinian Theory*.[11] In this lengthy pamphlet, Weismann considered the origins and causes of natural variation. One of his conclusions had been that "individual differences arise from the influence of external conditions on the inheritable evolutionary material; they are not accidental, but depend on the conditions of existence, together with the nature of the individual."[12] That this bore upon the matter at hand is shown by Darwin's marginal comment:

I think this means that "morphological" characters are the result of what I call the definite action of conditions. I do not feel quite satisfied with this—free inter-crossing would perhaps keep the characters which are not used, free from fluctuation.[13]

Thus, both Weismann and Hooker contributed to Darwin's

only slightly altered view as expressed in the new edition: Hooker, by suggesting that inconsequential characters could, once having arisen, be perpetuated purely by way of general inheritance (rather than for their selective value); and Weismann, by serving to confirm the possibility that many apparently useless variations arise through the interaction of environment and individual constitution.

In the chapter titled "Difficulties on Theory," in which he replied to various criticisms, Darwin started his reply by citing Nägeli's case and examples therein, after which he presented his own:

> Professor Weismann, in discussing Nägeli's essay, accounts for such differences by the nature of the varying organism under the action of certain conditions; and this is the same with what I have called the direct and definite action of the conditions of life, causing all or nearly all the individuals of the same species to vary in the same manner . . . we must admit that the organisation of the individual is capable through its own laws of growth, under certain conditions, of undergoing *great modifications, independently of the gradual accumulation of slight inherited modifications;* various morphological differences probably come under this head, to which we shall recur; but many differences . . .[14]

And he went on to repeat his earlier view that many presently useless characters may have formerly been of service and that there are numerous other factors which could account for most differences of a non-useful nature:

> Thus I am inclined to believe, morphological differences, which we consider as important—such as the arrangement of the leaves, the divisions of the ovary, the positions of the ovules, etc.,—first appeared in many cases as fluctuating variations, which sooner or later became almost constant through the nature of the organism and of the surrounding conditions,

as well as through intercrossing; for as these morphological characters do not affect the welfare of the species, any slight deviations in them would not be acted on or accumulated through natural selection.[15]

THE DARWINIAN PROCESS UP TO JULY 1869

Finally prompted as the result of cumulative criticisms to reply to the problem of useless characters, Darwin responded in much the same way as he had done with the problems of blending and isolation: he shifted his emphasis away from the process of natural selection and on to secondary, subsidiary processes of change.

Showing, as he did, the most probable manner of their origination, *independent* of natural selection, Darwin revealed the extent to which he was forced to compromise his original view of natural selection as the *sine qua non* of evolutionary modification.

It is interesting to note Darwin's inclusion of blending as leading to the constancy of a particular character in a given species. In fact his attitude toward non-useful characters and the particular processes called upon in explaining their origins reflect his general view of the causes of evolutionary modification at this time. Blending was now an ally, incorporated into, and in fact becoming an integral part of, the process of change. His references to "great modifications" being brought about "independently of the gradual accumulation of slight inherited modifications," as well as the fact that "all or nearly all of the individuals of the same species vary in the same manner" under environmental conditions, reflect the consistency with which Darwin now emphasized previously secondary mechanisms of change.

The overall impression generated from the first *Origin* is that the process of natural selection is *the* cause of speciation. The fact remains, however, that Darwin had said at the very outset that "natural selection has been the main but not exclusive means of modification,"[16] as Darwin himself was compelled to point out to his critics in 1872. Yet this is not the impression one generally gets from reading the first edition. Since the hypothesis of natural selection was based on the selective accumulation of variations on the basis of *utility,* and since Darwin himself put it so firmly "every detail of structure in every living creature" either was or is "of special use," it hardly seems as if he was entertaining any other possibility at the time. Later critics were therefore somewhat justified in rebutting him on this ground—particularly as he had so expanded the powers and roles of these secondary causes of modification.

Much, if not the greatest part, of the misunderstandings on this subject arose out of Darwin's failure to distinguish between the causes effecting primary, individual variation and those resulting in speciation. By including the two under the same general head of "causes of modification," the more phenomena that could be attributed to primary variation, the fewer could be attributed to selection. And indeed this was the case, because Darwin failed to see even a functional distinction between the two. As a consequence, application of the principle of natural selection was not only becoming more and more limited (to cases of useful characters alone) but, more important, it was becoming more apparent to Darwin's contemporaries that the other causes of modification recognized by Darwin were capable of assuming roles in the process of evolutionary modification that had previously been left to natural selection. The significance of the sum total of the changes made by Darwin up to and including the fifth edition was that they weakened his theoretical superstructure, principally because of his acceptance of certain views whose implications removed much of the power of modification through the natural selection process.

The mounting pressures on the explanatory virtue of his theory led Darwin to reconsider certain factors previously considered as playing an extremely minor role in modification of the theory of evolution. He had hoped to show that natural selection as a process was the major force causing speciation. His conviction that he had been able, in the first *Origin,* to demonstrate the way in which the most important and fundamental features of species originated, led him to believe that, in time, nearly all such phenomena could be similarly explained. Yet mounting criticism in the years afterward made Darwin increasingly aware that this would not be the case. By the time he had completed the lengthy revisions that became, in August 1869, the fifth *Origin,* the full extent to which his selection theory had changed became generally apparent.

The second edition, with its scant corrections, is hardly more than a reprint of the first. The third and fourth editions are noteworthy mainly insofar as they are evidence of Darwin's intent to use successive editions as vehicles for revisions in his own views. They do, as we have already seen, include a number of significant replies (cf. Bronn, Pouchet), but there is no attempt at a general, full-scale revision of the foundations of the Darwin theory. And this was precisely the point that lay at the basis of all his post-1859 difficulties: while he had been repeatedly altering many of his theoretical premises, he never undertook to revise or rewrite his theory in its entirety—from start to finish. Since each slight change in some lower, basic principle would affect his theory as a whole, critics would be free to fire away at the mass of contradictions and incongruities contained in it until such time as the entire work was rendered internally consistent. The fact that the *Origin* increased in size with each new edition, and that in the fifth edition alone nearly half of all the sentences had been either altered or deleted, signifies the structural weakness that had afflicted the *Origin of Species.*[17]

Among this mass of changes, Darwin's most noteworthy alterations in basic premises are as follows:

1. because of his complete rejection of saltations, his recognition of only very slight individual differences as the basis for all modification;
2. his belief in the inheritability of a tendency to further variation—and its general continuation in the same direction;

3. because of (1) + (2), his belief that beneficial variations would occur in sufficient numbers to modify a small population in a few generations;

4. his denial of any necessary or significant role to isolation, while at the same time implicitly including elements of separation and confinement in rendering natural selection operative;

5. his growing belief that the direct effects of environmental conditions could modify all or nearly all the members of an endemic population;

6. the increasing amount of modification attributed to the inherited effects of habit, use, and disuse;

7. his belief that a population could be modified without any segregation of variant from normal forms by a process analogous to what he called "unconscious selection by man"—which depended, in fact, upon a gradual modification through blending (and in which there was no overt form of selection);

8. his failure to distinguish between the several causes of individual variation and the causes leading to speciation, a fact which led to implied diminution in the power and scope of natural selection consequent upon increased emphasis on other causes of variation.

In order to show how speciation could be brought about through the process of natural selection, it was essential for Darwin to treat in some detail the several conditions making its operation possible. In so doing, he was led to investigate several subsidiary phenomena such as the size of variations, the causes of variations, the limits of variation, the laws of genetic transmission, the role of isolation, and secondary sexual characters. It was not until the years following 1859, when treating these subjects in some detail, that Darwin began to modify his original views. Since these were not only related to each other but related to the theory as a whole, the changes in them necessarily involved concomitant implications for the theory. That Darwin was well aware of most of these is shown by the further changes he found it necessary to make to achieve some degree of consistency among them. In this way, as he came to understand the great effects of blending, so he went on to modify his earlier views to allow for (1) a greater number of variations; (2) the tendency to continued variation in the same direction; and (3) the containment necessary for his process of "unconscious selection." There were two main reasons why he did not see the implications of these changes on the selective process. First, he did not see these several processes (which he recognized as leading to non-selective modifications) as exclusive to the process of natural selection, but as supportive of and subsidiary to it. That is to say, the fact that there were other recognized causes at work in no way lessened the importance of natural selection as the major cause of speciation. And, in the second place, these subsidiary factors were looked upon as the very conditions that made natural selection capable of achieving speciation.

The publication of the fifth edition in July 1869 saw the *Origin* so expanded, revised, and modified throughout as to result in a theory overburdened with inconsistencies and ambiguities. Indeed it provided a ripe target for a discerning critical eye. And, in fact, the years following 1869 were to see the foundations of the theory of natural selection under a critical fire so intense and so well directed at the weakest points that Darwin himself came to believe his theory might not survive.

10. The Crucial Years: Controversy with Mivart

*A worse fault than obscurity, in view of the wide faith
accorded by the nineteenth century and ours to
scientific works, is Darwin's hedging and self-contradiction;
for it enabled any unscrupulous reader to choose
his text from the* Origin of Species *with almost the
same ease of accommodation as if he had chosen
from the Bible.*

—*Jacques Barzun,* Darwin, Marx, and Wagner

*N*one of the many modifications which Darwin had thus
far made in the *Origin* gave it the internal consistency it so
sorely needed. Rather than changes, he saw his replies to
criticisms as clarifications and expansions upon his original
views. Yet, in almost every case, his finding support for one
weakened argument had, in effect, entailed his removing part
of the support from another.

By confusing the causes of variation with the causes of
speciation; by totally rejecting saltative changes, thereby committing himself completely to individual differences; by committing himself to speciation without (apparent) isolation; by
tacitly and (often) credulously assuming the heritability of
certain forms of variation; in all, by a gradual and cumulative
series of changes without full awareness of their implications,

Darwin made the later *Origin* a mass of "doubts, shifts of opinion, confused words, hedging, self-contradictions, endless shufflings with words, indecisiveness, hesitancies, inconsistencies."[1] As the same writer put it: "His power of drawing out the implications of his theories was at no time very remarkable."[2]

CALENDAR OF PUBLICATIONS IN THE DARWIN–MIVART CONTROVERSY

1.	(Darwin)	*Variation under Domestication*	January 1868
2.	(Mivart)	"Review of 4th *Origin* and *Variation*," *The Month* (DRC #R145)	July-September 1869
3.	(Darwin)	Fifth *Origin*°	August 1869
4.	(Mivart)	*Genesis of Species* (Darwin Library)	January 1871
5.	(Darwin)	*Descent of Man*†	February 1871
6.	(Mivart)	"Review of *Descent of Man*," *Quarterly Review* (DRC #174)	July 1871
7.	(Wright)	*Review of Mivart and Darwin*, privately printed by Darwin (DRC #R204) from *North American Review*, July 1871	September 1871
8.	(Huxley)	"Review of Wallace, Mivart and Darwin," *Contemporary Review* (DRC #R182)	November 1871
9.	(Mivart)	"Reply to Huxley," *Contemporary Review* (DRC #R183)	January 1872
10.	(Darwin)	Sixth *Origin*‡	February 1872
11.	(Mivart)	"Specific Genesis," *North American Review*	April 1872
12.	(Darwin)	Second *Descent*	September 1874
13.	(Darwin)	Second *Variation*	1875
14.	(Mivart)	*Lessons from Nature*	1876
15.	(Mivart)	*The Cat*	1881

Several of these shortcomings had been pointed out to Darwin, during the years which followed the first *Origin*, by men of widely varying qualifications. But of all these, both

° Fifth edition prepared from December 26, 1868 to February 10, 1869.
† *Descent of Man* prepared from February 10, 1869 to January 17, 1871.
‡ Sixth edition prepared from June 18, 1871 to November 9, 1871.

scientists and non-scientists who undertook to criticize the theory, none proved so formidable in the content of his remarks or so powerful in their effect as St. George Mivart, the English anatomist and zoologist.[3]

As an avid student of Huxley, Mivart had counted himself among the earliest supporters of the theory of natural selection. His opinion of Darwin's theory became, however, one of increasing dissatisfaction, culminating in 1869 with the complete disavowal and intensely vituperative attitude that characterized his *Genesis of Species.*

Mivart's disaffection had its origins within his religious beliefs, but at precisely what point he made his final (and *scientific*) break, it is almost impossible to determine. It is also reasonably certain that it was *not* Mivart's anatomical and osteological researches that led him to break with Darwinism. In fact, the conclusions to which he had been led as a result of these researches accounted for his general belief in evolution and for the token amount of credence he did give to the process of natural selection. It was mainly an ideological estrangement which prompted him to look for the theory's explanatory inadequacies—because Mivart never once disputed the *facts.*

The roots of Mivart's misgivings can be traced back to early in 1863. Lyell in his *Antiquity of Man* and Huxley in his *Evidence as to Man's Place in Nature,* both published at that time, had been extremely guarded in their discussions of the possible means by which man had evolved. Where Lyell suspended judgment, Huxley's firm belief that man *had* evolved was apparent—and it was here that Mivart differed so greatly from the Darwinians. In the introduction to his *Genesis of Species,*[4] Mivart stated the basis for his growing disbelief, remarking that he "found each successive year that deeper consideration and more careful examination have more and more brought home . . . the inadequacy of Mr. Darwin's theory to account for the preservation and intensification of incipient, specific, and generic characters. That minute, fortuitous, and indefinite variations could have brought about such special forms and modifications as have been enumerated . . . seems to contradict not imagination, but reason."[5] During the years between 1859 and 1869, Mivart read with great interest and absorption most of the pro- and con-Darwin literature. With even greater interest he read each subsequent edition of the *Origin,* watching Darwin attempt to counter each criticism as it arose and making careful note of the many changes—deletions, additions, and revisions—that were taking place in it. It is evident, from his later remarks, that he never at any time felt that Darwin had been effective in his replies to the more important attacks directed at the foundations of his hypothesis.

In Mivart's eyes, the sum total of these criticisms by early 1869 seemed to underline the overwhelming basic weaknesses of the theory of evolution-by-selection. One can see, throughout the pages of the *Genesis,* Mivart's unfathomable capacity for recalling former criticisms, as well as his astute faculty for apprehending their detailed bearing on and overall implications for the core of Darwin's theory.

When, in July 1869, Darwin's fifth edition appeared, with all its important replies to such critics as Jenkin, Wagner, and Nägeli, Mivart could keep silent no longer. The tone of his review the following month[6] showed the full measure of his condemnation of the Darwin doctrine. The apparently inextricable explanatory difficulties faced by the thesis of natural selection were, he felt, the result of an initial weakness: the fundamental inability of the theory to explain all specific origins by means of the natural selection process. It was on the basis of the points made in this review that Mivart set to work on the *Genesis.*

THE *Genesis of Species* (1871)

Style and Tone: The *Genesis* (as Darwin was himself to confess) was a formidable piece of scientific criticism. Together with Mivart's own contributions, it amounted to a collection of the most trenchant criticisms that had ever been leveled against the Darwin theory. No doubt his previous legal training had enabled Mivart to assemble so effectively an array of commentary whose results were to prove devastating. For within this small volume the several hypotheses of the theory were subjected, one by one, to a penetrating logical analysis, with weaknesses underscored. Mivart was, without a doubt, a master at argumentation. His marshaling the most telling of past criticisms, his citing even the contrary opinions of the Darwinians, and—perhaps most effective of all—his quoting of Darwin against himself, seemed almost to offset the rather peremptory tone of the book. Yet most of its scientific objectivity was lost because of the fact that it was permeated by a highly colored personal prejudice against Darwin and the Darwinians. This bias was made abundantly clear at the outset—in the introduction—when, speaking of the theory's numerous supporters outside of the Darwinian inner circle, Mivart remarked:

> It was inevitable that a great crowd of half-educated men and shallow thinkers should accept with eagerness the theory of "Natural Selection . . ."[7]

and, directing himself to members of the inner circle of evolutionists, specifically Huxley:

> If the odium theologicum has inspired some of its opponents, it is undeniable that the odium anti-theologicum has possessed not a few of its supporters.[8]

But the real nature of his acute antagonism was reflected in his tactless use of words and phrases and in his frequent disparaging asides. The dubious compliment that the Darwinian theory, like so many other errors, did contain *some* truth, and his references to the feasibility of natural selection as being "absolutely incredible" or "equal to impossibility" must certainly have raised Darwinian hackles. But for all its animosity, per-

230. *Charles Darwin: The years of controversy*

sonal and professional, the *Genesis* remained the most complete and cogent criticism during Darwin's lifetime.

Outline of Mivart's Argument: Mivart began by making two fundamental admissions. First, he said he believed that evolution of organic forms did take place; that one species may develop from and out of another, and further, that the *body* of man had arisen from a lower species. Second, he felt that natural selection could and did operate in this process.

Mivart then stated his two main intentions. First, said he, he would demonstrate that the process of natural selection as *the* explanation of the origin of species was not adequate to the task assigned it. Second, he would show that in certain cases natural selection did not operate at all. He then outlined ten points on which natural selection could be seen to fail.

The Size of Variations: Mivart did not miss a single one of the arguments against speciation through slight modifications that had appeared since the first edition. The accumulation of these arguments made a formidable case. He set down the following as the chief of his ten points:

1. If truly very slight or infinitesimal,[9] these modifications would more often than not be effectively useless (perhaps, hinted Mivart, even detrimental).

2. Since these extremely slight modifications could yield but equally slight advantages, the benefits they would impart to the individuals possessing them would, in their minute disparity from their brother-forms, prove of relatively negligible value in the struggle for existence.

3. There appeared ample evidence that potentially useful saltations did occur, and with some frequency. Here Mivart cited the works of the teratologists and, like Huxley, he saw no reason why nature (in the course of the natural selection process) should not avail herself of these saltations. He tended to play down even this possibility in favor of the view that saltations could cover, in a single instance, the gap between a

new variety and the old form, which would involve no selection at all—or, at best, a series of such jumps.

4. The fossil gaps, even when the links were seemingly plentiful, still afforded no evidence for the slow and gradual change implied in the selection of slight differences.

5. Mere "individual" differences were generally uninheritable.

6. As was also felt by both Jenkin and Galton, there were apparent limits to the selection of individual variations. What seemed to be required was a distinct, discontinuous change (like rolling to a new facet of Galton's die).

7. Changes that did take place by slight variation were merely insignificant "alterations" in which the basic, specific form remained intact. Such variation occurred on and about the specific theme with the form remaining recognizably the same.

The Limits of Variation and Specific Stability: The arguments cited above led Mivart almost imperceptibly into the problem of specific stability. Though he believed in specific change through saltation, Mivart employed all the usual arguments favoring specific stability, directing them against individual differences. He referred again to Galton and Jenkin, using both Jenkin's simile of a sphere of variation and Galton's model of the stone. Probably most effective of all was his comment: "The proposition that species have, under ordinary circumstances, a definite limit to their variability, is largely supported by facts brought forward by the zealous industry of Mr. Darwin himself."[10] Darwin's citations in the *Variation* of the many instances of failure to extend the range of certain selected features were cast back at him. Further, Mivart not only cited reversion (and Darwin's remarks thereon) as evidence for such a barrier, but struck at Darwin with his own remarks (made against Wallace) regarding his inability to account for the origins of inter-specific sterility—which Mivart saw as yet more evidence supporting the notion of a barrier.

Other Arguments: To describe the rest of Mivart's arguments at any length would be merely to repeat a composite of twelve years' previous criticisms, all of which had already been urged against Darwin. It is sufficient that both the inability to account for the early, incipient stages of ultimately useful structures, and Darwin's partial rejection of (and therefore implied inability to explain) selection for the purpose of mimicry and protection were among them.

It can be safely said that the real strength of the *Genesis* lay in the fact that at the same time as it penetratingly exposed the several weaknesses of the *Origin,* it marshaled, on a point-for-point basis, the most applicable and trenchant criticisms made against them. The effect of Mivart's book was not achieved through a direct assault by original criticism, but by the attention it focused upon Darwin's own undermining of his theory from within. It was the able critical strength of Mivart that, in pointing out these failings and contrasting them with the lucid critical opinions of his contemporaries, produced such an effect on Darwin.

Mivart's Alternative Hypothesis: Mivart saw an internal progressive force as the main agent in evolution. This was an innate tendency toward "derivation" (as he called it), which operated regardless of changes in external conditions. According to Mivart, the motive force stimulating the process of evolution was, in effect, the directly intervening hand of God. His hypothesis was an adjunct of his Deism. God, for him, was the great watchmaker who, having created His masterpiece, wound it fully with the force of His almighty power and set it down to unwind according to His ordinances.

To many of Darwin's facts Mivart undertook to give his own interpretation. The tendency to variation itself, for example, was seen as a manifestation of an internal force—as part of the original Divine plan of creation. Equally, he felt the tendency for many organisms to vary in the same direction was evidence of the operation of such a force. Even the *continued* tendency toward variation in the same direction—also espoused by Darwin—lent itself to such an interpretation. The facts remained indisputably the same; it was simply that they were as amenable to explanation through some inherent force as they were to the opposing view of some external, selecting mechanism.[11]

The Effect of the Genesis: It should be remembered that both the revised fifth edition of the *Origin* and the *Descent of Man* had been written before Darwin saw the *Genesis*. It was to be the sixth *Origin* which would show the full effects of Mivart's anti-Darwinian writings.

THE *Descent of Man* (1871)

The *Descent* is undoubtedly Darwin at a disadvantage—Darwin at grips with an uncongenial animal in uncongenial environments, Darwin without the miracles of inspiration and discovery, in large part without even the exhaustive first-hand research and the tireless, sympathetically understanding observation which were among his most dependable gifts.[12]

The several important modifications in his theory made by Darwin from 1859 to 1869 were largely obscured in their significance by the fact that they remained incorporated within the original work. By persistently altering the basic structure of the first *Origin,* rather than writing up afresh his much-altered views, Darwin made it difficult to gauge the full extent of his changes and the implications they held for the theory as a whole. The changes which signaled a shift in emphasis toward processes of modification other than natural selection appeared alongside his original statements, implying the latter's apparent all-sufficiency. Because these statements were embedded in the earlier text which had by then come to include an even greater amount of additional material, their real significance for the theory could be seen only by such well-trained eyes as Mivart's.

Thus it was in the *Descent*, whose very subject matter made it a distinctly separate work, that Darwin's later views could be clearly seen. In this work Darwin had to apply all the factors mentioned in the *Origin* to one particular organic subject, man.

The most striking feature of the *Descent* was Darwin's outright admission

> that in the earlier editions of my *Origin of Species* I probably attributed too much to the action of natural selection or the survival of the fittest. I have altered the fifth edition of the *Origin* so as to confine my remarks to adaptive changes of structure. I had not formerly sufficiently considered the existence of many structures which appear to be, as far as we can judge, neither beneficial nor injurious; and this I believe to be one of the greatest oversights as yet detected in my work.[13]

We need have no doubt that the phrase "as yet detected" was looked upon as anything but a challenge to St. George Mivart, for he saw more at fault with the *Origin* than was ever to be admitted by Darwin in the *Descent*. His review of the latter in the *Quarterly Review* was the inevitable consequence.

Yet Darwin went even further, explaining how and why he had come to this conclusion:

> I was not able to annul the influence of my former belief, then widely prevalent, that each species had been purposely created, and this led to my tacitly assuming that every detail of structure, excepting rudiments, was of some special though unrecognised service. Any one with this assumption in his mind would naturally extend the action of natural selection, either during past or present times, too far.[14]

From here Darwin proceeded to discuss those characters whose origins and development it had been impossible for him to explain on the basis of selection, and for which he felt it necessary to emphasize the action of Lamarckian factors of modification.

What had struck him most forcefully in his work on the *Descent* was the fact that "man, as well as every other animal, presents structures which seem to our limited knowledge, not to be now of any service to him, nor to have been so formerly, either for the general conditions of life, or in the relations of one sex to the other. Such structures cannot be accounted for by any form of selection, or by the inherited effects of the use and disuse of parts."[15] Thus was Darwin led to look back to factors which had been until then merely sources of variation, not of genuine evolutionary change.

The Direct Effect of Conditions: Even at the time of writing the *Descent* Darwin had not been at all clear as to how much genuine change, if any, he should attribute to:

> the direct and definite action of changed conditions, as shown by all or nearly all the individuals of the same species varying in the same manner under the same circumstances.[16]

He mentioned having "failed to obtain clear evidence in favour of much change effected in this manner." Yet, after a maze of assessments pro and con, he concluded:

> It cannot be denied that changed conditions produce some, and occasionally a considerable effect, on organisms of all kinds; and it seems at first probable that if sufficient time were allowed this would be the invariable result.[17]

"Time" was here seen as an important factor, for

> if these causes, whatever they may be, were to act more uniformly and energetically during a lengthened period, the result would probably be not mere slight individual differences, but well-marked, constant modifications.[18]

Although with useful and/or adaptive characters such modifications would be both preserved and perpetuated through the process of natural selection (together with inheritance, of course), there was only one possible way for this to be brought about with non-useful characters—through the inherited effects of the direct action of conditions. In those cases where there might not be sufficient time for the extensive modification of a whole population (and nowhere does Darwin indicate any specific periods of time), there was always the blending of free crossing to insure the uniform distribution of such environmentally acquired change.

> Uniformity of character, would, however, naturally follow from the assumed uniformity of the exciting causes, and likewise from the free inter-crossing of many individuals. The same organism might acquire in this manner during successive periods successive modifications, and these would be transmitted in a nearly uniform state as long as the exciting causes remained the same and there was some free inter-crossing.[19]

One can see more clearly here that Darwin was tackling two problems at the same time. First, he was showing how a sufficiently large number of initial variations of the same kind could be produced in a relatively short time. For this, the direct effects of conditions worked admirably. But in the second place, he had also to show how reasonably well-developed non-useful characters could have been brought to their present state without some such accumulating power as natural selection. And here he saw that the continued or *sustained* action of conditions could both amplify and extend the very modifications which it had initiated. Additionally, there were the uniformly distributive effects of blending inheritance which could be counted upon as additional means of securing the modification of the whole population. The various factors seemed to fit in very neatly. What must have been equally or even more satisfying for Darwin was that each of these factors had been both recognized and documented by him as far back as the first edition of the *Origin*. What Darwin had obviously not seen— and what it had been Mivart's strength *to see*—was that while these factors worked admirably in accounting for the origins of useless and/or incipient structures, they could nevertheless be applied with equal facility to account for structures which Darwin saw as strictly the objects and results of natural selection. However, what is important to note here is that it was in the *Descent* that Darwin first and most clearly enunciated views that had lain among a confusion of others in the much-modified *Origin*.

Use and Disuse: Of the non-selective processes of change so strongly reemphasized by Darwin at this time, those which seem to have struck modern readers are the processes of habit, use, and disuse. Said Darwin:

> We may feel assured that the inherited effects of the long continued use or disuse of parts will have done much in the same direction with natural selection.[20]

His reading of B. A. Gould's statistical survey of American servicemen[21] led Darwin to believe that the shortness of the sailor's arms "is due apparently to their greater use. Whether the several foregoing modifications would become hereditary if the same habits of life were followed during many generations, is not known, but is probable."[22] Darwin went further in cases not so securely anchored to observable details:

> The inferiority of Europeans, in comparison with the savage, in eyesight and other senses, is no doubt the accumulated and transmitted effect of lessened use during many generations.[23]

There is little doubt that the Darwin of the 1830s would have recoiled at such an explanation in this case. Was not the fact of the savage's more acute senses a perfect example of the results of natural selection? Was this, therefore, just an over-sight on Darwin's part? To quote a recent writer in this respect:

> Having dispensed with natural selection when there was no evidence of utility, he [Darwin] soon came to dispense with it even where he might have made out a case for utility. More and more the Lamarckian principle of the inherited effects of use and disuse came to replace natural selection. . . . Where once he would have reinterpreted these findings to make them conform to natural selection—and they are amenable to such reinterpretation—he was now easily per-suaded of the simpler Lamarckian idea.[24]

Not only does this tell but half the story—it gives a mislead-ing impression of Darwin's later attitude toward natural selec-tion. As was pointed out in the first chapter, Darwin, while rejecting Lamarck's notion of a *sentiment intérieur,* neverthe-less accepted two widely held axioms which had also formed part of the Lamarckian mechanism: the inheritance of the direct effect of conditions, and the inherited effects of habit, use, and disuse. On one page alone in the first *Origin* he cited what he felt were instances of the latter three.[25] Thus he had consistently, even in his earliest writings, given an interpreta-tion based on the inheritance of acquired characters to certain classes of facts. What does seem strange in the examples one finds in the *Descent* is that it was here that Darwin began for the first time to assign such causes (the limits of which he had previously restricted to the production of mere variation alone) to cases of modification, where he had before applied the theory of natural selection exclusively. It can be reasonably believed that this was the result of a logical extrapolation of these processes into the domain of natural selection—and it illustrates clearly the fact that Darwin was yielding to critical pressure to recognize such causes, while he was at the same time unable to distinguish where one mechanism came into play and where another left off. Though Darwin generally gave precedence to selection, Mivart saw little reason why the other factors could not—by themselves—apply to all cases.

Darwin had looked to these other factors only in those instances where he could not see selection as a possible means. To the inherited effects of habit and use, he attributed the origins of the slight incipient stages of useful structures; to those of habit he ascribed the development of apparently routine, non-useful instincts; to those of disuse he charged the presence of vestigial structures.

In summing up Darwin's reemphasized employment of non-selective factors in the evolutionary process, we can say that Darwin nearly always had an important and pressing reason for adopting them. With the effects of conditions were involved the explanatory difficulties presented by useless and/or purely ornamental (non-sexual) structures. With the effects of habit, use, and disuse were concerned the problems attached to explaining the first stages of incipient structures, the presence of vestigial organs, and the phenomena of instinct. There is also some indication that he saw in the action of use a means of achieving, within a shorter period of time, the increased development of certain incipient structures to the point at which their utility would render them objects of selection. Swamping-through-blending inheritance had also led to a difficulty which could be circumvented by invoking non-selective factors. For, whatever conditions provoked new habits or further uses, they would act as a stimulus to not one, but a majority of the members of the population. Thus, not only would the swamping of the few variants be eliminated, but at the same time the modification would appear almost simultaneously throughout the population (and, like the direct action of conditions, within a reasonably short period of time). Thus, considerations of the problems presented by swamping and shorter time intervals also contributed to Darwin's reemphasis of such factors.

All these ideas lay within the pages of the *Origin,* but only in the *Descent* did they emerge full-blown with renewed emphasis and, more important, in a new area of application. Much of this change of emphasis can be attributed to the contrasting text, so lacking was the *Descent* in the verbal undergrowth which had come to characterize the later *Origin*.

THE EVOLUTIONARY MECHANISM OF 1871

As a source of comparison with that of 1859, it will be worthwhile to summarize the complete mechanism of evolution, in axiomatic form, as Darwin had come to view it by 1871.

1. The raw material for evolutionary change consists of individual organic variations.
2. In their production, two elements are involved:
   (a) the conditions of the environment;
   (b) the nature of the organism.
3. The majority of variations—those slight but inheritable "individual differences"—arise, seemingly spontaneously, as the indirect response to the stimulus of environmental conditions.
4. Some amount of variation arises as the direct effect of conditions. This can be seen to produce a greater amount of modification in the organic population because:
   (a) the exciting environmental cause persists for some period of time;
   (b) the entire population would be exposed at the same time to the same set of conditions.
5. Some amount of variation is achieved through the results of increased or lessened use of parts; some through the organisms following—due to various reasons—new habits of life.
6. Some amount of variation arises from the fact that the tendency to vary in the same direction as the (variant) parents is itself hereditary.
7. Some amount of variation arises through the blending of a variant with a normal organism—inheritance itself

tending toward the distribution (through blending) of any variation throughout the population.

8. Some amount of variation arises as the correlated effects of other (primary) variation:
   (a) through the principle of correlations, or
   (b) through the principle of compensation.

9. The following classes of variation will be subject to the process of natural selection, through which their advantageous nature will be preserved and accumulated:
   (a) those variations which are useful or advantageous in the competitive struggle for existence;
   (b) those variations which aid in the struggle for, the acquisition of, and copulation with, a member of the opposite sex;
   (c) those variations which are correlatively linked in growth or development with either (a) or (b).

10. Variations of no apparent utility will often be perpetuated through the general law of inheritance. A few (9c) will be indirectly selected.

Though paraphrasing Darwin, the above axioms reflect both the tone and the general precepts of his mechanism. From this, a number of interesting details can be more clearly seen. First, there is Darwin's distinct dichotomy between the *causes of variation* on the one hand, and the process of natural selection as THE *cause of evolutionary change* on the other. Second, there is Darwin's recognition of primary and secondary causes of variation* in the form of correlation and compensation, although at the same time, he failed to recognize the effects of habit and use as such. This arose from his inability to see that use and habit cannot *initiate* variation, but can only *augment* it. Following upon this was Darwin's failure to see that certain

---

* Never a very distinct set of categories for Darwin, having only been mentioned in the *Variation* (see chapter 4 above, pp. 86 *et seq.*) and not brought up subsequently.

causal processes leading to *variation* may also result in an actual *modification* in the form of the species, since such causes did not necessarily cease after initiating variation, but could, through their persistence,* achieve genuine, large-scale, adaptive modification, not only of the individual but (through the encompassing nature of the provoking conditions and the natural process of blending) of an entire population and thereby, of an entire species.

All these latter remarks suffice to underline a more fundamental error in Darwin's outlook on the species question: his view of the biological entities involved.

Darwin never clearly defined the important differences denoted by the terms "individual," "variety," and "species." He saw a new species arising through the gradual supremacy of a new, specially endowed variety, and the variety, in turn, by the successful diffusion of individual variation throughout an entire population. By thus looking upon the form of an individual member of a species as representing the form of the species, thereby making the whole process of specific change hinge upon an almost indistinguishable degree of difference, Darwin had laid for himself a conceptual foundation infused with difficulties. This was, in fact, together with his view of the influence of heredity, the basis for most of his future difficulties.[26]

Though the *Descent* had gone to press before the *Genesis* was published, it nevertheless shows sufficient internal evidence to support the belief that Mivart had been instrumental in effecting several changes and eliciting a number of admissions. The heavily critical and condemnatory *Month* articles of 1869 had produced some effect.

Upon his reading of the *Descent*, Mivart was struck by the extent to which Darwin appeared to be retracting some of his earlier assertions. He saw, however, that most of these modifications amounted to little in his overall attitude toward the role

---

* Or, in the case of habit or use, through the organism's own persistence.

of natural selection. Stimulated no doubt by the headway he had made despite Darwin's avowed persistence in his original view, Mivart pushed forward in his campaign to get Darwin's total recantation. His review of the *Descent* in the *Quarterly*[27] was the next step in his planned controversy.

THE *Quarterly Review* (1871)

Darwin's apparent treatment of man as a single, detailed case—a demonstration, in fact—of the evolution of a new form through natural selection led Mivart to feel that the whole weight and value of the *Origin* itself would stand or fall on the explanatory success of the *Descent*. In his review, Mivart no sooner passed over what he felt were the basic incapacities of natural selection in the case of man* than he got down to its relevance to Darwin's theory as a whole:

> We shall endeavour to show that Mr. Darwin's convictions have undergone grave modification and that the opinions adopted by him are quite distinct from, and even subversive of, the views he originally put forth. The assigning of the law of "natural selection" to a subordinate position is virtually an abandonment of the Darwinian theory; for the one distinct feature of that theory was the all-sufficiency of "natural selection."[28]

Starting from Darwin's earlier premise: "if it could be demonstrated that any complex organ existed, which could not possibly have been formed by numerous successive, slight modifications, my theory would absolutely break down,"[29] it was easy. Mivart had a joyous excursion extracting conflicting quotes from various parts and editions of the *Origin,* contrasting them with the *Descent*. In effect, Mivart employed Darwin's hedging admissions as levers with which to topple over the entire theory:

* Its inability to account for the origins of man's soul and mental powers.

We may well pause before we trust ourselves unreservedly to a guidance which thus again and again declares its own reiterated fallibility. Mr. Darwin's conclusions may be correct, but we feel we have now indeed a right to demand that they shall be proved before we assent to them; and that since what Mr. Darwin before declared *"must* be," he now not only admits to be unnecessary but untrue, we may justly regard with extreme distrust the numerous statements and calculations which, in the *Descent of Man,* are avowedly recommended by a mere *"may* be."[30]

THE ATTACK AGAINST MIVART

Chauncey Wright: The reviews of the *Descent* having been for the most part generous and, at worst, tolerant, Darwin, in the summer of 1871, was quite content with the state of things. Before the rather pointed *Quarterly* review, he had faced the *Genesis of Species* with considerable equanimity: "I have just read (but not with sufficient care) Mivart's book, and I feel *absolutely certain* that he meant to be fair."[31] By the beginning of July, however, he was remarking to Wallace: "Mivart's book is producing a great effect against Natural Selection, and more especially against me."[32] The impression one gets from Darwin's correspondence during the first half of the year is that he did not himself feel any considerable enmity toward Mivart for the *Genesis.* In fact, the manner in which Darwin treated his opinions in the special section of the sixth edition of the *Origin*[33] suggests that he began with a rather respectful regard for Mivart's comments.

It was the American amateur naturalist Chauncey Wright who pointed out to Darwin what he felt was Mivart's calumny in the matter. In a letter of June 21,[34] he sent Darwin the proofs of his paper which reviewed Mivart as a gross distorter of facts, and upheld the position of natural selection. Struck by Wright's charges against Mivart of deliberate misrepresentation, and no doubt equally influenced by the fact that no similar review had thus far appeared in England, Darwin immediately set about, at his own expense, securing its publication. The tone of Darwin's subsequent letter to Wallace[35] showed that he had not previously given much thought to Mivart's motivations or intent. Seeing, however, that support against Mivart (from whatever basis) was at hand, Darwin became quite enthusiastic. Said he, when Huxley outlined to him the nature of his forthcoming review: "It quite delights me that you are going, to some extent, to answer and attack Mivart."[36] Between Chauncey Wright's allegations and the tone of Mivart's *Quarterly* review, Darwin's somewhat detached view became transformed into a distinct feeling of gross mistreatment at the hands of a Catholic fanatic.

Because of his position as the English publisher of Wright's review, we can infer Darwin's assent to most of its assertions. Particularly noteworthy were two remarks made therein: first, its recognition of the *Genesis* as "the most effective general criticism of the Theory of Natural Selection which has yet appeared,"[37] and, second, its denunciation of Mivart's stressing of the *Descent* as a reflection of Darwin's retreat from the views expressed in the *Origin*: "It is not an important modification at all, and does not change in any essential particular, the theory as propounded in the first edition of the *Origin of Species*."[38] Published in September 1871, Wright's review was followed by Huxley's caustic harangue against Mivart that November.

Huxley against Mivart: Mivart was right in his derogation of Huxley as anti-theological. A glance at the latter's review[39] shows the great delight Huxley took in combating Mivart's theological orientation. While recognizing Mivart's "acknowledged scientific competence," Huxley's emotional, non-scientific counterarguments were not themselves models of scientific detachment. He concluded his review with an extremely eulogistic appraisal of the master, intended to underline by contrast Mivart's disparagement. Huxley felt that to view Darwin's candor and intellectual honesty as implying hesitance, hedging, and halfhearted committal in such a man was indeed a despicable act.

Mivart's Reply: Essentially repeating the views in his *Genesis* and review, Mivart concluded with a paragraph which deserves repetition here in its entirety:

> Professor Huxley blames the Quarterly Reviewer's treatment of Mr. Darwin as "unjust and unbecoming" because he endeavours to show how Mr. Darwin has changed his ground without (in spite of his generally scrupulous candour) disavowing "natural selection" as *the* origin of species. I confess that it seems to me that the reviewer was fully justified in so doing, for Mr. Darwin's reputation as a man of science stands so high, that it was plainly the reviewer's duty to endeavour to prevent the public attaching, in mere deference to Mr. Darwin's authority, a greater weight to his assertions than the evidence adduced warranted. The reviewer sought to do this by showing, by Mr. Darwin's own words, that he had been compelled to admit that "abrupt strongly marked changes" may occur "neither beneficial nor injurious" to the creatures possessing them, produced "by unknown agencies" lying deep in "the nature of the organism." In other words, that Mr. Darwin has in fact, though not in express words, abandoned his original theory of the "origin of species."[40]

THE SIXTH *Origin* (1872)

The significance of the sixth *Origin* lies in the fact that it involved no distinctly new changes in Darwin's thought. There were, however, noticeable differences in this edition, chief among them a subtle change in tone. By substituting for his previous rash of qualifying adjectives more definite modifiers, or in dropping them completely, Darwin transformed statements previously appearing as mere speculation into firm commitments of belief. Thus, much of the hesitancy and hedging which had characterized the previous edition was gone, replaced by a more resolved (though still often inconsistent) exposition of his mechanism of evolution. In this, Darwin's last stand against his critics, one senses his attitude of full commitment to his original hypothesis as mixed with a slight but definite aura of resignation. Containing as it did Darwin's final and maximal concessions, this edition was to mark the end of his public appearances on behalf of his theory.

The main changes appearing in the sixth edition can be divided into two categories: those dealing with the hereditary mechanism and the causes of variation, and those involving Darwin's attitude toward non-selective processes of modification.

Heredity and Variation: The greater part of Darwin's views on these subjects remained essentially unchanged, but of the assertions whose importance had been implied for the first time in the fifth edition, there were a number of noteworthy alterations.

Where Darwin had in the fifth edition referred to "certain variations, which no one would rank as mere individual differences" as "frequently" arising due to similar organisms being similarly acted upon, these became "certain rather strongly-marked variations."[41] Since we know that Darwin maintained his rejection of saltative and discontinuous variations to the end of his life, we can assume that these strongly marked variations were of that middle range of variation. Yet Darwin's earlier statements implying that the difference between offspring and parent was "strongly-marked" was his only criterion for distinguishing between what he called "continuous" and "discontinuous" variations. Thus the last *Origin* leaves the reader in some confusion as to the *nature* of such changes: their *significance* at this stage of his thought is obvious; their production was suggested as a means of overcoming the problems of swamping and decreased time intervals.

Non-selective Processes of Modification: Darwin remarked on his surprise that Mivart had passed over all the changes that he (Darwin) had attributed to increased use and disuse of parts. He reiterated the many cases wherein he had recognized the action of such causes without their apparently involving any form of selection, and he remarked:

> it is scarcely possible to decide how much allowance ought to be made for such causes of change, as the definite action of external conditions, so-called spontaneous variations, and the complex laws of growth.[42]

In concluding this chapter in which he had catalogued all the non-selective processes and the structures for which they accounted, Darwin added the following qualification:

> We should keep in mind, as I have before insisted, that the inherited effects of the increased use of parts, and perhaps of their disuse, will be strengthened by natural selection. For all spontaneous variations in the right direction will thus be preserved; as will those individuals which inherit in the highest degree the effects of the increased and beneficial use of any part. How much to attribute in each particular case to the effects of use, and how much to natural selection, it seems impossible to decide.[43]

Yet, with all this hesitation and indecisiveness, the sixth *Origin* stands out in the development of Darwin's thought because it contains his firm and final stand regarding the role of natural selection. For even with all these other sources of both primary *and* secondary modifications, Darwin stated: "Such structures have often, as we may feel assured, been subsequently taken advantage of, and still further modified, for the good of species under new conditions of life.[44]

Where Darwin had said in the first *Origin* that species had changed through natural selection (modifying this in the fifth to "chiefly through natural selection"), he had by the sixth edition added "aided in an important manner by . . . ," followed by a list of the several non-selective processes.[45] In his final

statement he substantially repeated much of what he had concluded in the *Descent* regarding his neglect of non-selective
factors and repeated once again his firm belief in natural selection as "the main but not the exclusive means of modification."

It is unfortunate that Darwin was not able to grasp the
overall significance of the totality of changes that constituted
the core of the sixth *Origin*. In a way, what had happened
was a textual revolution. Each change was rendered continuous and consistent with the preceding one. But the cumulative
result of a long and interrelated series of changes was *not* consistent with the original version. Darwin never recognized
those aspects of his work in which he had unwittingly sacri-
ficed a total internal consistency in an attempt to account for
each part. He had always focused on the whole—and it would
have been better had his critics also done so.

Darwin never succeeded in reestablishing either the necessity or the sufficiency of the thesis of natural selection. At the
same time, he never for a moment considered abandoning his
concept of it. For Darwin the exceptions (and he saw no major
ones) unfortunately proved the rule. But also unfortunately—
for Darwin—Mivart was equally determined in his convictions.

MIVART'S REVIEW OF THE SIXTH *Origin*

Beginning with the very first in 1869, each of Mivart's writings dealing with Darwinism was essentially the same. Whole
sections of later reviews were identical with those of previous
reviews, the exceptions being the remarks addressed against
Darwin's continued failure to see the full force of his own
shortcomings as Mivart had pointed them out. None of the
concessions made by Darwin seemed to him to hit at the heart
of the matter. . . .

Mr. Darwin himself seems to have come round substantially,
though unavowedly, to the same opinion [as Mivart], and

has, in his *Descent of Man* implicitly admitted, though he has not yet explicitly declared that Natural Selection is not the origin of species.[46]

He went on, as he had done many times before, describing the limited role of selection as he saw it:

> . . . by a process of cutting off and limiting [it] fixed the characters of the different organic species, thus becoming their origin. *The* origin, not, of course, of the slight variations, but of the fixing of these in definite lines and grooves. . . . The assignment of the law of Natural Selection to a *subordinate* place is manifestly an abandonment of the Darwinian theory as originally proposed; for how can that be said to be *the origin* of species which only co-operates, in an inferior and comparatively uninfluential manner, in determining that origin?[47]

It was Chauncey Wright again who, in the following number of the *North American Review,* took up the task of replying to Mivart.[48] From Darwin, however, there was to be no further comment.

DARWIN'S RETIREMENT

Darwin's retirement from public participation in matters strictly concerned with the principle of evolution began shortly after he dispatched his revised manuscript of the sixth *Origin* in January 1872. As always, he had been glad to rid himself of the *Origin** and, also as before, he had found himself another subject to absorb his time. This time it was the research which ultimately led to *The Expression of the Emotions in Man and Animals.* Begun in February 1872, it occupied nearly all his time for the better part of a year. When Mivart's review appeared that April, Darwin could see that he was in a hope-

---

* There was a corrected edition of the sixth *Origin* made (presumably) by Darwin in 1876 but the few textual novelties amount primarily to corrections and insignificant word substitutions.

lessly deadlocked argument with this most persistent of his critics. Unable himself to counter his remarks on non-useful, non-adaptive characters, and feeling somewhat frustrated at his own difficulties in following the rather tenuous strains of logic involved (which he attributed to his increasing age and ill-health), Darwin relinquished his position to younger contemporaries. "I have resolved to waste no more time in reading reviews of my works or on evolution,"[49] he said to Wright. "There are so many good men fully as capable, perhaps more capable, than myself of carrying on our work,"[50] he had said to Ernst Haeckel upon finishing the last *Origin*.

While Mivart may have precipitated Darwin's withdrawal from the main arena of debate about evolution, Darwin might have soon retired anyway. His revolutionary work had been, by that time, generally accepted, his poor health was aggravated by years of controversy, and there was the lure of new, uncontroversial fields to investigate. These were all no doubt contributing factors. The year 1872 had been a most propitious and convenient period during which he could withdraw from the argumentative position into which he had been led. Mivart had not quite achieved what had been his greatest desire: to expose Darwinian natural selection as the ineffective hypothesis he believed it to be. Yet he must have found some satisfaction in knowing that he had been the prime instrument in badgering the elderly Darwin into the state of frustrating confusion which marked him on the eve of his retirement.

11. The Final Years: Darwin's Retirement

With the exception of the Coral Reefs, I cannot remember
a single first-formed hypothesis which had not after a time
to be given up or greatly modified.

—Charles Darwin (1876), Autobiography

Darwin's failures of logic and crudities of imagination
emphasized the inherent faults of his theory; a finer, more
subtle mind would only have obscured or minimized them.
The theory itself was defective, and no amount of tampering
with it could have helped.

—Gertrude Himmelfarb, Darwin and
the Darwinian Revolution

The last decade of Darwin's life was, in a sense, an anticlimax.
Having withdrawn from the controversy when he was already on the periphery of the mainstream of thought on evolution, he would no longer find his views of concern to anyone
save himself.

He had failed to refute Mivart's objections; he had merely
circumvented them by calling upon other mechanisms, thereby
relegating them (so he thought) to an area out of the domain of
natural selection. When Mivart persisted with unabated vehem-
ence, Darwin did what he had always been so prone to do—he
retired to the less taxing work of his botanical studies, leaving the
task of defending his theory to others more energetic than he.

The following table shows that Darwin's botanical work took up the greatest part of his time during these ten years. Each of these separate works represented the continuation of research begun many years before, and one (*Earthworms*) went as far back as 1837. Not one of these works made any *direct* contributions to his theory. Even *indirectly*, as supporting evidence for the action of natural selection, Darwin omitted all but the rarest allusions to aspects of his theory. When the first of these, *Insectivorous Plants*,[1] appeared, Wallace wrote straightaway to Darwin, expressing both surprise and concern over the lack of evolutionary references in the work:

> You do not make any remarks on the origin of these extraordinary contrivances for capturing insects. Did you think they were too obvious? I daresay there is no difficulty, but I feel sure they will be seized on as inexplicable by Natural Selection, and your silence on the point will be held to show that you consider them so![2]

Again, less than two years later, Darwin's opus *The Different Forms of Flowers of Plants of the Same Species*[3] carried almost no speculation as to the *origins* of the polymorphic forms of *Primula*. This was probably due to "the great difficulty" which he found "in understanding how any cause whatever could lead to the simultaneous reduction and ultimate suppression of the male organs in half the individuals of a species, and of the female organs in the other half, whilst all were subjected to exactly the same conditions of life."[4] In addition to the relaxation they provided him in his last years, Darwin's botanical works were intended to be strictly separate, non-evolutionary works.

THE MECHANISM OF INHERITANCE

Of the old evolutionary speculations that Darwin did reconsider during this last decade, one was concerned with the mechanism of inheritance. Having been requested to do so by John Murray, Darwin began the revisions for the second edition of

CHRONOLOGICAL TABLE OF DARWIN'S WORKS 1872–1882

February 1, 1872	*Expression of the Emotions* begun
August 22, 1872	*Expression* completed
	Insectivorous Plants begun
October 10, 1872	*Cross- and Self-Fertilisation* begun
November 26, 1872	*Expression* published
May 15, 1872	*Insectivorous Plants* resumed
November 20, 1873	Second *Descent of Man* begun
April 1, 1874	Second *Descent* completed
	Insectivorous Plants resumed
September 13, 1874	Second *Descent* published
March 1875	*Insectivorous Plants* completed
	Climbing Plants begun
July 2, 1875	*Climbing Plants* completed
	Second *Variation* begun
	Insectivorous Plants published
September 1875	*Climbing Plants* published
	Second *Variation* published
October 3, 1875	*Cross- and Self-Fertilisation* resumed
May 5, 1876	*Cross- and Self-Fertilisation* completed
November 10, 1876	*Cross- and Self-Fertilisation* published
April 1, 1877	*Different Forms of Flowers* begun
June 25, 1877	*Different Forms of Flowers* completed
	Power of Movement in Plants begun
July 9, 1877	*Different Forms of Flowers* published
March 10, 1879	*Erasmus Darwin* begun
July 1879	*Erasmus Darwin* completed
November 1879	*Erasmus Darwin* published
May 26, 1880	*Power of Movement* completed
November 6, 1880	*Vegetable Mould and Earthworms* begun
	Power of Movement published
April 16, 1881	*Earthworms* completed
October 10, 1881	*Earthworms* published
April 19, 1882	Darwin died

the *Variation* on July 2, 1875. Of these, the most important were those alterations in Darwin's view of pangenesis.

Certainly the most able and prescient of Darwin's critics on the theory of pangenesis was his cousin, Francis Galton. While at first he accepted the hypothesis as originally set forth, it was not long before Galton came to see the staggering physiological implications of the Darwinian "pangenes" or "gemmules." If each tiny part of every organism produces gemmules throughout its and the individual's lifetime, a fantastic amount of these will have been produced and stored in the reproductive organs. This, for him, seemed too farfetched a hypothesis merely to account for the inheritance of acquired characters, a belief which he repudiated anyway. Throughout the year 1870-71, Galton carried on a series of experiments with rabbits aimed at testing the truth of pangenesis. Assuming that the gemmules were passed from body to reproductive organs through the blood, he transferred blood from members of breed A into those of breed B hoping to "mongrelise" the offspring later conceived by B. When he failed to do so, he read what he felt was his disproof before the Royal Society that March, in 1871.[5]

Darwin responded in a letter to *Nature* on April 27, aimed at undermining the basis of Galton's disproof:

> In the chapter on Pangenesis in my "Variation of Animals and Plants under Domestication," I have not said one word about the blood or about any fluid proper to any circulating system.[6]

How then, one might ask, did Darwin see the transmission of the gemmules? As far as this letter was concerned, he did not commit himself beyond the fact that the gemmules obviously could not be carried by the blood. He added that had Mr. Galton been able to show their presence in the blood first, then his conclusions might have had some validity. Darwin saved his theory by logically sidestepping his cousin's argument. Yet the attack by Galton may have, in itself, contributed to a lessening in importance attributed to his ideas by Darwin.

In words which closely paralleled those of Weismann in the same year, Galton concluded:

> From the well-known circumstances that an individual may

transmit to his descendant ancestral qualities that he does not himself possess, we are assured that they could not have been altogether destroyed in him, but must have maintained their existence in latent form.[7]. . . The span of the true hereditary link connects, as I have already insisted upon, not the parent with the offspring but the primary elements of the two.[8]

In May 1875 Darwin read the first section of Weismann's *Studies on the Theory of Descent,* in which Weismann said:

We know for certain that one of these [phenomena of heredity] consists in the fact that peculiarities of the father do not appear in the son, but in the grandson, or still further on, and that they may be thus transmitted in latent form.[9]

In his letter to Weismann, Darwin noted that this agreed

with what I concluded with respect to the remarkable effects of crossing two breeds: namely, that anything which disturbs the constitution leads to reversion, or as I put the case under my hypothesis of Pangenesis, gives a good chance of latent gemmules developing.[10]

The difficulty was that pangenesis, with its inclusion of *both* the inheritance of somatic and germinal characters, had been so *ad hoc* as to withstand any criticism which sought to point up any fact inconsistent with it.

By the following November (1875), Galton had gathered his thoughts together in a paper titled "A Theory of Heredity,"[11] which Darwin read with consuming interest.

About all that remained of Galton's former belief in pangenesis was his belief in the existence of "gemmules." It was "the sum total of the germs, gemmules, or whatever they may be called" which comprised what Galton called the "stirp." To this he added the following assertions: "each of the enormous number of quasi-independent units of which the body consists, has a separate origin, or germ . . . the stirp contains a host of germs, much greater in number and variety than the organic units of the bodily structure that is about to be derived from them . . . comparatively few individuals out of the host of germs, achieve development . . . undeveloped germs retain their vitality; . . . they propagate themselves while still in a latent state, and contribute to form the stirps of the offspring."[12]

Galton was amazingly astute in his conceptualizing, and the net impression is one of a striking resemblance to the modern view of the hereditary mechanism. In his belief that the constituent germs or gemmules for a single potential feature represent an aggregation of varying ancestral units for that same feature, Galton was correct in all but amount.*

Nowhere had Galton been more clear in his rejection of the inheritance of acquired characters than when he said:

> It is indeed hard to find evidence of the power of the personal structure to react upon the sexual elements that is not open to serious objection.[13]

Darwin wrote back:

> If this implies that many parts are not modified by use and disuse during the life of the individual, I differ widely from you, as every year I come to attribute more and more to such agency.[14]

This was, and always had been, the key to their disagreement. For Darwin, any theory of inheritance must allow of the inheritance of acquired characters. In concluding, he wrote:

> I have admitted in [the] new edition (before seeing your

---

* In Mendel, there were seen to be only two units for a common feature. Insofar as number is concerned, modern genetics has come somewhat closer to Galton, it being now believed that genes at several chromosomal loci go into the determination of a single feature. The basic conception of *gene* itself, however, has changed significantly enough to be presently unlike the "germ" or "gemmule" of Galton. However, Galton's "stirp" (because of its broader, non-empirical nature) remains nearly synonymous with "genotype." Even his "germ" remains a good synonym for the non-operational part of the connotation of present-day "gene."

essay) that perhaps the gemmules are largely multiplied in the reproductive organs; but this does not make me doubt that each unit of the whole system also sends forth its gemmules.[15]

He was equally convinced on the results of inheritance:

If two plants are crossed, it often or rather generally happens that every part . . . of the hybrid are [sic] intermediates in character; and this hybrid will produce by buds millions on millions of other buds all exactly reproducing the intermediate character. I cannot doubt that every unit of the hybrid is hybridised and sends forth hybridised gemmules.[16]

Galton's letter of reply is amazing in its parallelism with Mendel's conclusions, and is worth quoting in full:

The explanation of what you propose does not seem to me in any way different on my theory, to what it would be in any theory of organic units. It would be this:

Let us deal with a single quality, for clearness of explanation, and suppose that in some particular plant or animal and in some particular structure, the hybrid between white and black forms was exactly intermediate, viz: grey—thenceforward for ever. Then a bit of the tainted structure under the microscope would have a form which might be drawn as in a diagram, as follows:—

black

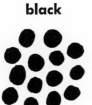

white

whereas in the hybrid it would be either that some cells were white and others black, and nearly the same proportion of each, as in (1) giving *on the whole* when less highly magnified a uniform grey tint,—or else as in (2) in which *each cell* had a uniform grey tint.

(1)   **(2)**

In (1) we see that each cell had been an organic unit (quoad colour). In other words, the structural unit is identical with the organic unit.

In (2) the structural unit would not be an organic unit but would be an organic *molecule*. It would have been due to the development, not of one gemmule but of a group of gemmules, in which the black and white species would, on statistical grounds, be equally numerous (as by the hypothesis, they were equipotent).

The larger the number of gemmules in each organic molecule, the more uniform will the tint of greyish be in the different units of the structure. It has been an old idea of mine, not yet discarded and not yet worked out, that the number of units in each molecule may admit of being discovered by noting the relative number of cases of each grade of deviation from the mean greyness. If there were 2 gemmules only, each of which might be either white or black, then in a large number of cases one-quarter would always be quite white, one-quarter quite black, and one half would be grey. If there were

3 molecules, we should have four grades of colour. This way of looking at the matter would perhaps show (a) whether the number in each given species of molecules was constant, and (b), if so, what those numbers were.[17]

While there is no trace of Darwin's reply, Galton's next letter shows Darwin's concern only with the implications of Galton's view on pangenesis. He was still preoccupied with mechanisms that would account for the inheritance of acquired characters—about Galton's general hypothesis he apparently said nothing. This was to be one of Darwin's very close brushes with a Mendelian approach to the subject.[18]

Though both Weismann and Galton had urged Darwin's attention to the importance of the actual inheritable part of the organic constitution, Darwin's long-held view which dichotomized the cause(s) of inheritance from the several causes of variation[19] led him to feel the latter subject more worthy of his attention at the time.

THE PROCESS OF SPECIATION

If nothing else, Mivart had shown the pitfalls that lay in proposing a general hypothesis and then accounting for exceptions as they arose by assigning an increasing number of supporting corollaries. Darwin's dedication to a method which emphasized "fact" as the starting point for all explanation had much to do with his future difficulties. In his endeavor to account for each new fact, Darwin had amassed a number of assumptions which no single theory could render consistent. Clearly, it was time to consider the whole question of speciation from a different point of view.

Thus, on those increasingly rare occasions between botanical researches when he inevitably returned to evolutionary speculations, Darwin did turn toward more general aspects of speciation. One of these was a detailed consideration of the process of change itself.

The process by which Darwin saw individual variation turned into the widespread, divergent change which denoted a "new species" had grown far more complex since 1859. By 1872 Darwin had come to recognize several causes producing variation. In all cases, however, the crossing of the variants with the normal forms would tend to soften their modifying effect on the population as a whole. Yet so effective were these several independent causes, and so often persistent the action of conditions, that a noticeable change in the population could be effected within a relatively short space of time. This had been Darwin's view of the process which he had called the analogue of "unconscious selection by man." That he still called it (and indeed felt it to be synonymous with) "natural selection" is a puzzle which can be explained only through his own peculiar outlook. For him, this *was* natural selection. It still acted to eliminate the unfit, it still set the selective criterion of adaptability, and through these, it still accounted for the accumulation and direction of the overall change.

In March 1872, August Weismann sent Darwin his pamphlet on the role of isolation in the formation of species.[20] Weismann had seen the value of the geographical isolation of a small segment from the main population of a species as one of the most important conditions for the formation of a geographical race of sub-species.[21] Unlike Moritz Wagner before him,[22] Weismann had seen the importance of variation both before and after isolation. Following his earlier rejection of the direct modifying effects of environmental conditons, he stated that the apparent uniformity among members of the same geographical race had *not* been due to the uniform action of the conditions to which they had been exposed. It was, he said, the result of the even distribution of variations through the blending effects of inter-crossing.

Darwin would have had good reason to assent to Weismann's view. For it had been the central part of *Wagner's* case for isolation (as the fundamental condition for speciation) that organisms migrate to a new region wherein they would then be modified by the new set of environmental conditions. In Weismann's assertion (a) that conditions induced change only *indirectly* and (b) that most uniform change was the result of blending, there was first-rate support for Darwin's having rejected isolation as a *necessary* condition in evolution. Yet, to go along with Weismann would have been to relinquish the idea of modification from the direct action of conditions, a source of widespread change which Darwin could not so easily give up in view of his latest theoretical position. As Weismann had indicated himself, the facts as they stood could be interpreted either as the effects of blending or of conditions. Perhaps both, thought Darwin. He uncommittedly wrote in the second edition of the *Variation:*

> Prof. Weismann has suggested that . . . in cases of this kind, it would falsely appear as if the conditions had induced certain definite modifications, whereas they had only excited indefinite variability.[23]

A few years later, Darwin outlined his view of the process of modification in a letter to the German zoologist Karl Semper:

> When a species first arrives on a small island, it will probably increase rapidly, and unless all the individuals change instantaneously (which is improbable in the highest degree), the slowly, more or less, modifying offspring must intercross one with another, and with their unmodified parents, and any offspring not as yet modified. The case will then be like that of domesticated animals which have slowly become modified, either by the action of the external conditions or by the process which I have called the unconscious selection by man—i.e., in contrast with methodical selection.[24]

Darwin had obviously chosen to accept both, as he had always done. The ambivalent nature of his position is shown elsewhere in the same letter:

> It is clear that the changed conditions of life have modified

the organisms in the different regions, so that they now form distinct races or even species. It is further clear that in isolated districts, however small, the inhabitants almost always get slightly modified, and how far this is due to the nature of the slightly different conditions to which they are exposed, and how far to mere interbreeding in the manner explained by Weismann, I can form no opinion.[25]

One thing, above all, remained clear. It was this gradual process of modification-through-blending, supplied through *several* causes of variation, that he now came to call "natural selection." This is further shown by Darwin's letter to W. R. Greg at the end of 1878, recapitulating the several considerations:

> With respect to new variations being obliterated by crossing, I have insisted on the improbability of such well-marked variations as that of the Ancon sheep being preserved under nature. I cannot doubt that the process of selection under nature is the same as that called by me "unconscious selection" when the *more or less* best fitted are preserved, or the *more or less* ill-fitted are destroyed. . . . By the way, he (Mivart) says I rest exclusively on natural selection; whereas no one else as far as I know has made so many observations on the effects of use and disuse. Nor do I deny the direct effect of external conditions, tho' I probably underrated their power in the earlier editions of the "Origin". . . .[26]

In October of the following year (1879) Semper sent Darwin a copy of the German edition of his *Natural Conditions of Existence*. In it, Semper's thesis was that the chief source of evolutionary change lay in the interaction between the environmental conditions and the organisms' innate capacity for transformation. The excitation provided by changing conditions acted as a stimulus or release for the realization of the organisms' own tendency toward progressive change. His view was decidedly Lamarckian, combining the notion of an innate tendency for progressive change with the inheritance of environmentally acquired characters.

> We perceive that most, perhaps all, of the characters now in a great measure hereditary, originated through modifications of those originally adaptive organs which bore within them the elements of continuous and extensive gradual transformation.[27]

Yet to this Semper added Darwinian natural selection:

> . . . no power which is able to act only as a selective and not as a transforming influence can ever be exclusively put forward as the proper efficient cause of any phenomenon. In all cases, including those of mimicry, the point finally must be to investigate the causes which may have availed to produce, by their direct action, any advantageous and protective change of colouring; it was not until the change had actually taken place that selection between the better or worse endowed individuals could lead to the further development of the advantageous character. *It is extremely difficult to decide,* in particular cases—in most indeed, it is impossible—*the precise point where one ceases and the other begins to act.*[28]

Semper's last sentence could easily have come from the last edition of the *Origin.* In his combining such elements, Semper had reached a theoretical position very much the same as Darwin's. His frequent citations of Lamarck, paralleled with those that he had taken from later editions of the *Origin* and the *Descent,* confirm this. Striking out the notion of an inner progressive force would make them nearly indistinguishable.

As late as the beginning of 1881, when the English edition of Semper had been published, Darwin wrote to him, agreeing

> . . . with what I gather to be your judgment, viz., that the direct action of the conditions of life on organisms, or the

cause of their variability, is the most important of all subjects for the future. . . . In far the greater number of points I quite follow you in your conclusions. . . .[29]

Only a few months after this letter had been written, there appeared a paper in which Hoffmann described his researches on the induction of botanical variations.[30] This was the work for which both Semper and Darwin had been waiting. If they expected any positive results, however, they were to be disappointed, for there were none. Hoffmann's work supplied nothing but negative results—not one uniformity between cause and effects. Hoffmann's painstaking work of twenty-five years was, however, a model of scientific method. If there had been any correlation between environmental conditions and variation—whether direct or indirect—he would certainly have detected them.* If one is searching for the point in the history of biology where the notion was finally overthrown that the direct action of conditions could produce definite, uniform variation, Hoffmann's paper provides that landmark. Said Darwin, half in consolation, to his fellow-believer, Semper:

It is really surprising how little effect he produced by cultivating certain plants under unnatural conditions, as the presences of salt, lime, zinc, &c., &c., during *several generations.* . . . No doubt I originally attributed too little weight to the direct action of conditions, but Hoffmann's paper has staggered me. Perhaps hundreds of generations of exposure are necessary. It is a most perplexing subject. I wish I was not so old and had more strength, for I see lines of research to follow. . . . I still *must* believe that changed conditions give the impulse to

* We know that there is no inheritable variation which arises as the direct and definite effect of conditions (in Darwin's senses of those words). That certain factors (chemical, X rays) can induce, indirectly and indefinitely, inheritable variations, is also known. One can say that, at least with the methods, materials, and subjects on which Hoffmann had been working, he would not have discovered the latter phenomena.

variability, but that they act *in most cases* in a very indirect manner.[31]

Darwin had lived to see another supporting assumption pulled out from under his general theory. By this time, he had weathered further attacks from Mivart and new assaults from Samuel Butler, who attacked both his originality and his theory's incapacity to explain the "real origin of species" (the origin of variations)— rather an unusual pair of points for a two-pronged attack.

By 1882, the science of evolution proper had almost gone out of vogue. Though both the layman and the scientist had become firm believers in the *idea* of evolution, and a host of old disciplines had been instilled with the vigor of a new *leitmotiv,* so important were the two missing links of knowledge of the mechanisms of inheritance and of the phenomenon of slight mutation that work on the actual process of evolution had slowed almost to a halt before a barrier of fundamental ignorance. While the principle of evolution was being documented by a host of scientists, nearly all the original Darwinians had left the field. Huxley, who had come nearer the truth than any, had let other scientific and educational activities carry him away. Wallace, the champion of pure Darwinism and the only original Darwinian to live to see Mendel rediscovered and the theory of natural selection attacked by the mutationists, had become so involved in totally non-scientific matters as to take the most divergent road of all.

Though he lived to see many of his beliefs undermined, and at the end was no longer able to demonstrate the supremacy of his theory of natural selection, Darwin died consistent in at least one thing—his faith in the theory that bears his name.

Epilogue

*F*ew histories are more difficult to write than that of an idea—
even of a single concept as formulated and developed in the
mind of one man. Such a concept as that of the mechanism of
evolution was as broad in its implications as the great system of
nature which it encompassed. It has also proved as complex in
its ramifications as any theory known to science.

The Newtonian world-machine may have been a vast and
intricate universal concept, but the laws which predicated its
operation had a basic logical and mathematical simplicity. Darwinian nature retained all the complexities of such a system in
addition to all those biological phenomena impervious to mathematical analysis. Time is also an element of great import, in the
Darwinian view, for it extends backward into a world of unseen
organisms moving in a dimly known environment. Clearly, the
scope of the Darwinian theory was (and is) too great for the
grasp of any one man. And this is precisely the point: Darwin's
unchallenged stature among the immortals of science rests upon
his introduction of the theory of the evolutionary mechanism and
upon the formidable and painstaking way he documented its action. Had Darwin died in 1859, his position in history would hardly be diminished. But just as this point underlines the magnitude

of his achievement in the *Origin*, it also carries implications for his work after 1859. As great as the *Descent of Man* has been judged, and as significant as his many botanical contributions are, it remains true that Darwin spent a great part of the last twenty-three years of his life trying unsuccessfully to establish the necessity and sufficiency of the process of natural selection as the sole mechanism of evolution.

What occurred between the *Origin* of 1859 and Darwin's retirement from the center of controversy swirling about the concept of evolution which followed the last edition of 1872 is itself an example of evolution.

The *Origin of Species* had, in the space of thirteen years, undergone a textual evolution. Variations, in the form of Darwin's changes, had appeared throughout the work in five successive editions. Despite the fact that each separate change was both a continuation of the general thesis, and consistent with it, it was nonetheless change. Consequently, just as in organic evolution, the cumulative result of a long, successive, and interrelated series of changes was a product no longer consistent with the original.

The fact that Darwin failed to see the inconsistencies which were mounting under his own reviser's hand was to bring him to a series of critical encounters from which he did not emerge with any feeling of self-satisfaction. The critical assaults of Agassiz, Pouchet, Jenkin, and Mivart which characterized the "critical years" were frustrating for Darwin.

The story that has been told here is paradoxical insofar as it documents a critical failure while at the same time illustrating a man's success. The genesis, exposition, and breadth of application of the theory of natural selection rank not only among the greatest of scientific achievements, but equally among the most profound concepts of man. Though Darwin failed to render his thesis internally consistent, and consequently was unable to demonstrate the necessity or sufficiency of natural selection as the causal agent of evolution, this is a failure which becomes less consequential when measured against Darwin's enduring achievement.

Whatever happened during Darwin's *personally* crucial years, a sufficient number of his scientific contemporaries became convinced of the efficacy of his theory of natural selection to ensure the revolution in biology that bears his name. Yet the story of Darwin's frustration over explanatory inadequacies remains important. This is not only because the time of crisis covered such a large portion of Darwin's life, but also because it reflects the thought of an era now past.

The last two decades of Darwin's life were testimony to the passing of the great period of the naturalist. Naturalists, it is true, have remained; but since the nineteenth century nearly all these men have been rigorously trained as scientists first. Round-the-world voyages exploring the far-flung corners of the earth have been replaced as apprenticeships by years of formalized university education. Darwin epitomized the nineteenth-century field naturalist and armchair theorizer. His brilliance as both is unquestioned. Though his naiveté in many instances was considerable, his assumptions often highly extrapolated from the evidence, his theory of pangenesis patently *ad hoc*, these are all minuscule weaknesses. A far greater weakness was his inability to disentangle the knotty confusions and inconsistencies he created in his theoretical framework. His genius was to construct, not to render consistent. Whether or not one relegates consistency to the limbo of the unimaginative, the construct of which Darwin was the author remains the achievement of the greatest of naturalists.

Perhaps this is one of the facets of a genius: an ability to weather all crises, those induced by criticism from outside, as well as those springing from an inner lack of consistency. Such a man never accepts defeat; he is therefore never defeated.

References

Note: Citations from Darwin's writings use roman numerals to indicate volume numbers and arabic numbers to indicate pages, separated by short dashes. Ex., LL–II–461 (Life and Letters of Charles Darwin, vol. 2, p. 461). References to The Descent of Man *and* The Variation of Plants and Animals under Domestication *also use this form. Ex.,* Descent. *I–248 (vol. 1, p. 248). However, as noted on p. ix, references to* The Origin of Species *use roman numerals to indicate chapters and arabic numbers to indicate sentences, divided by a colon, according to the Peckham edition of the* Origin. *Ex.,* Origin. *IV: 95–97 (chap. 4, sentences 95–97); references to the* Notebooks *use this same form, but to indicate* Notebook *number and page. Ex.,* Notebooks. *II:125 (second* Notebook, *p. 125).*

Chapter 1. The Darwinian Mechanism

1. *Darwin's notebooks on transmutation of species,* ed. Sir Gavin de Beer. *Bulletin of the British Museum* (Natural History), Historical Series, vol. 2, nos. 2, 3, 4, 5 (London, 1960). Hereafter cited as *Notebooks.*
2. Darwin's *Autobiography* as quoted in LL–1–83–84.
3. *Ibid.*
4. *Evolution by natural selection: Darwin and Wallace,* Foreword by Sir Gavin de Beer. Cambridge: University Press, 1958, pp. 41–58. Hereafter, the two separate papers by Darwin, as reprinted in this edition, will be cited as *Sketch of 1842* and *Essay of 1844.*
5. *Ibid.,* pp. 88–254.
6. *Geological observations on South America: being the third part of the voyage of the Beagle.* London: Smith Elder, 1846.

7. *Journal of researches into the natural history and geology of the countries visited during the voyage of HMS Beagle round the world.* London: Murray, 1845.
8. *A monograph of the sub-class Cirripedia . . the Lepadidae (T. the Balanidae . . the Verrucidae. . etc.).* London: The Ray Society, 1851 + 1854.
9. Darwin to Lyell. May 3, 1856. LL–II–67.
10. Darwin to W. D. Fox. October 3, 1856. LL–II–84.
11. *Notebooks.* Introduction, p. 40. De Beer here gives 1852 as the date which Darwin refers to in his autobiography as the time in which he solved the problem of divergence. His own testimony notwithstanding, it was a problem which Darwin was never fully to resolve. See chapter 7 for a more detailed discussion.
12. On the tendency of varieties to depart indefinitely from the original type. (Read July 1, 1858.) *Journal of the Linnean Society* (Zoology), 3rd ser. 58:45.
13. DPL, Boxes 8–15. Professor Robert Stauffer of the University of Wisconsin is currently preparing an edition of these eleven chapters.
14. *Origin.* IV:354.
15. *Origin.* I:4. "Darwin's thesis that species when domesticated start to vary is essentially or entirely wrong. Variation is not increased, but the changed environment allows the survival of many types of interest to man which in the wild state are removed by natural selection." See Arne Müntzing, *American Scientist* 47(1959): 314–319. Professor Ernst Mayr of Harvard, as well as a number of geneticists, disagrees with Professor Müntzing. The assumption of greater variability under domestication notwithstanding, the importance of the point lies in the fact that Darwin believed it was the conditions of the domestic state itself that produced this greater variation. As a point of information, those who aver greater variation in the domestic state are unanimous in their belief that this is *not* related to Darwin's "external" conditions, but to factors such as "gene pools," "genetic homeostasis," etc.
16. *Sketch of 1842*, p. 48.
17. *Essay of 1844*, p. 91. One of the earliest influences on Darwin on this point seems to have been that of Alexander Walker in whose book *Intermarriage* (London: John Churchill, 1838, p. 280–DL) Darwin noted this paragraph: "that, under certain circumstances, an offspring is produced with new properties, different from those of the progenitors; and that the most powerful of these causes is that artificial mode of life which we call the state of domestication."
18. *Essay of 1844,* p. 107.
19. *Ibid.*
20. *Origin.* V:305.
21. Darwin to Hooker. November 23, 1856. LL–II–87.
22. *Sketch of 1842,* p. 42.
23. *Essay of 1844,* p. 102.
24. *Origin.* I:322.

Chapter 2. The Study of Inheritance

1. T. A. Knight, An account of some experiments of the fecundation of vegetables. *Transactions of the Royal Horticultural Society* (London, 1799).

2. *Variation.* II–88.
3. *Ibid.* II–70.
4. *Ibid.* II–81.
5. *Loc. cit.*
6. *Ibid.* II–26.
7. *Ibid.* II–24, 25.
8. *Ibid.* II–1.
9. Some remarks on the supposed influence of pollen in cross-breeding. *Transactions of the Royal Horticultural Society* 5 (London, 1824).
10. On the variation in the colour of peas occasioned by cross-impregnation. *Transactions of the Royal Horticultural Society* 5 (London, 1824).
11. On the variation in the colour of peas from cross-impregnation. *Transactions of the Royal Horticultural Society* 5 (London, 1824).
12. *Annales des sciences naturelles* 10 (1826) and *Mémoires sur les Cucurbitaceae.* Paris: Huzard, 1826 (DL).
13. *History of the horse in all of its varieties and uses.* London, 1829 (DL).
14. *Intermarriage.* London: John Churchill, 1838 (DL).
15. *On the physiology of breeding* [pamphlet]. Sunderland: The Times Press, 1855 (DRC #144).
16. *Ibid.* p. 4. Only where specifically noted is reference made to a contemporary work *not* read by Darwin—this includes quotations (which, in such cases, had been marked by Darwin in his own copy).
17. *Philosophical and physiological treatise on heredity,* 2 vols. Paris: Huzard, 1847–50 (DL).
18. *Bastardzeugung im Pflanzenreich.* Stuttgart, 1849 (DL).
19. *Variation.* II–92.
20. *Ibid.* II–29 (paragraph heading).
21. *Ibid.* II–34 (paragraph heading).
22. *Ibid.* II–35.
23. *Ibid.* II–48.
24. *Ibid.* II–35.
25. *Ibid.* II–71.
26. *Ibid.*
27. *Ibid.*
28. *Ibid.* II–35.
29. *Ibid.* II–252.
30. Lucas, *Treatise on heredity,* p. 445 (DL).
31. *Histoire des anomalies.* Paris, 1832 (DL).
32. *Éléments de tératologie végétale.* Paris, 1841 (DL).
33. For an admirable study on this subject, see Conway Zirkle, The early history of the idea of the inheritance of acquired characters and of pangenesis, *Transactions of the American Philosophical Society* 35 (1946):91–151.
34. St. Hilaire, *Histoire des anomalies.*
35. *Histoire des progrès des sciences naturelles depuis 1789,* 1:310, as quoted in E. S. Russell, *Form and Function,* London: Murray, 1916, p. 73.
36. J. W. von Goethe, *Bildung und Umbildung organischer Naturen* 9 (1807): 466, as quoted in Russell, *Form and Function,* p. 37.

Chapter 3. The Nature of Variation

1. "The laws governing inheritance are quite unknown; no one can say why the same peculiarity is sometimes inherited and sometimes not so." *Origin.* I:57.
2. "Perhaps the correct way of viewing the whole subject, would be to look at the inheritance of every character whatever as the rule, and non-inheritance as the anomaly." *Origin.* I:56.
3. *Origin.* I:49.
4. Huxley to Darwin. November 24, 1859. LL–II–231.
5. T. H. Huxley, review of the *Origin. Westminster Review,* April 1860, p. 545 (DRC #R 3). In view of the fact that Huxley is referring to macroscopic anomalies, his position in the light of modern genetic knowledge is basically unsound. The saltative changes upon which selection does operate are primarily those arising from extremely slight gene mutations which, more often than not, are manifested (if at all) only by rather subtle visible alterations. Mutations of a larger order are generally deleterious and thus not utilized in the evolutionary process. These are usually the most obvious—seen on the empirical plane from which Huxley, Darwin, and their contemporaries viewed them.

   While this point might appear to have a great deal of bearing upon the saltation issue, from a historical point of view it is of only marginal significance.

   In the absence of such genetic knowledge, the arguments revolving around saltations and individual differences still retain a logical validity relevant to their context. Thus Darwin's position with regard to the employment of saltative or "discontinuous" variation must be weighted not against modern insights but against those contemporary with him.

   This applies equally to other issues debated at the time. When a nineteenth-century contemporary argued a point with Darwin in which that critic *did* possess a valid insight into modern scientific knowledge, then the historian would be justified in assessing Darwin's stand relative to presently accepted views. Unfortunately, this happened less often than many historians would lead us to believe. The remaining cases are judged by this author on the basis of considerations of their historical and scientific context. Where pertinent, however, aspects of presently accepted views are appended as footnotes.
6. For an interesting discussion of the merging of religious and scientific beliefs of the period which generated evolutionary ideas, see C. C. Gillispie, *Genesis and geology,* New York: Harper Torchbooks, 1959.
7. W. H. Harvey, A case of monstrous Begonia. *The Gardener's Chronicle,* February 18, 1860.
8. J. D. Hooker, A reply to Prof. Harvey. *The Gardener's Chronicle,* February 25, 1860 (not in DRC).
9. *Ibid.*
10. LL–II–272.
11. LL–II–275.
12. For the Gray-Darwin relationship, see A. Hunter Dupree, *Asa Gray,* Cambridge: Belknap Press, 1959. Gray's paper was not published. For details see Dupree, p. 285.

13. Asa Gray, review of *Origin. American Journal of Science and Arts,* March 1860, p. 155 (DRC #R 12).
14. Louis Agassiz (1807–73), Harvard Professor of Comparative Anatomy. The author is particularly indebted to Dr. Edward Lurie's *Louis Agassiz: a life in science,* Chicago: University of Chicago Press, 1960, and Prof. Dupree's *Asa Gray* for their discussions of this period of Darwinism in America.
15. *Proceedings of the American Academy of Arts and Sciences* 5 (1860):410 as cited in Dupree, *Asa Gray,* p. 461.
16. See C. C. Gillispie's *Genesis and geology,* pp. 165 *et seq.* for a precise description of Agassiz's geological views.
17. *American Journal of Science and Arts,* July 1860, pp. 150–151 (DRC #R 8).
18. As quoted in Dupree, *Asa Gray,* p. 273.
19. *North American Review,* April 1860, p. 500 (DRC #R 31).
20. On the origin of species. *American Journal of Science and Arts,* July 1860, p. 4 (DRC #R 9).
21. LL–II–274.
22. LL–II–275.
23. On the relation between the abnormal and normal formations in plants. *Minutes of the Weekly Meetings of the Royal Institution,* March 16, 1860 (DRC #216).
24. Masters to Darwin. Unpublished letter, in DRC #216.
25. ML–I–247.
26. A handwritten translation of a review of August 1860. See DRC #R 66, p. 31 (translation), p. 92 (review).
27. Unpublished letter, W. H. Harvey to Darwin, August 24, 1860. (DPL, Box 98.)
28. *Ibid.*
29. *Ibid.*
30. *Ibid.*
31. *Ibid.*
32. *Ibid.*
33. Unpublished letter, W. H. Harvey to Darwin. August 1860. (DPL, Box 98.)
34. Darwin to Harvey. August 1860. ML–I–160.
35. *An inquiry into the probable origin of the human animal on the principles of Mr. Darwin's theory* [privately printed]. Dublin, February 1860 (DRC #R 10).
36. Unpublished letter, W. H. Harvey to Darwin. October 8, 1860. See DPL, Box 98, p. 4.
37. *Ibid.*
38. *Ibid.* p. 8.
39. *Origin.* II:12.1.c.
40. *Ibid.* VI:173.
41. *Ibid.* IV:125.
42. *Ibid.* IV:173.a, c, and e.
43. *Ibid.* VI:178.
44. *Variation.* II–254.
45. *Ibid.*
46. *Plurality of the human race,* 2nd ed., London, 1864 (DL).
47. *Origin.* II:12.6.4.d.
48. *Ibid.* VI:173, XIV:10 + 116.

Chapter 4. The Causes of Variability

1. November 22, 1860. Murray was down to his last 350 copies of the second edition. However, sales had slowed down considerably since the January 1860 release. There would, of course, be further sales, and Murray was no doubt anticipating that a third edition, as opposed to a reprinting of the second, would promote renewed sales. LL–II–351.
2. The second edition, written less than two weeks after the appearance of the first, represented little in the way of a response to criticisms. As Peckham has noted on page 773 of his variorum edition of the *Origin,* the second edition contained but 7 per cent of the total changes of the five subsequent editions, and these were nearly all minor corrections.
3. The third edition contained 14 per cent of the total changes. Nearly half the corrections appeared in chapter 9 ("On the Imperfection of the Geological Record") and will not here concern us. The greatest part of the remaining changes appeared in chapter 4 ("Natural Selection"), where Darwin dealt with various objections, principally those of Bronn.
4. Of the adverse criticisms up to that time, Darwin was most favorably impressed with those of Bronn. This is borne out by the fact that replies to Bronn (in both chapters 4 and 9) constitute the bulk of third-edition changes. Only those points raised by Bronn involving the causes of variation will be discussed here. For Bronn's full commentary, see the German edition edited by him: *Über die Enstehung der Arten im Thier,* Stuttgart: Schweizerbart'sche Verlag, 1860 (DL and DRC #s 191, 292, and R 41).
5. Darwin to Lyell. October 8, 1860. LL–II–346.
6. *Origin.* IV:382.54.c.
7. "Probably the whole amount of difference has not been simultaneously effected; and the unknown laws of correlation will certainly account for, but not strictly explain, much simultaneous modification." *Origin.* IV:382.60.c.
8. *Ibid.* IV:382.54.c.
9. "I hope never again to make so many corrections, or rather additions, which I have made in hopes of making my many rather stupid reviewers at least understand what is meant." Darwin to Murray. December 1860. LL–II–356.
10. *Origin.* I:12.
11. *Ibid.* V:8.
12. *Ibid.* XIV:66.
13. *Variation.* II–270.
14. *Ibid.* II–267.
15. *Origin.* I:32.
16. *Ibid.* V:29.
17. *Variation.* II–285.
18. *Ibid.* II–290.
19. *Origin.* V:27.
20. *Ibid.* V:32.
21. *Ibid.* VI:190.
22. *Ibid.* I:29.
23. Darwin to Davidson. April 30, 1861. LL–II–368.
24. Hooker to Darwin. March 17, 1862. LLJDH–I–37.
25. Darwin to Hooker. March 18, 1862. ML–I–198.

26. Darwin to Hooker. March 26, 1862. ML–I–199.
27. Darwin to Hooker. November 24, 1862. ML–I–214. Darwin had been quite impressed with Mr. Thomas Meehan's paper, The uniformity of relative characters between allied species of European and American trees, *Proceedings of the Academy of Natural Sciences* (Philadelphia), January 28, 1862, calling it "a remarkable paper." His own copy (DRC #261) is heavily annotated. Meehan's observations on the differences between American and European members of the same species led Darwin to conclude that "these peculiarities cannot have been naturally selected. Hence we are led to infer that they have been definitely caused by the long-continued action of the different climate of the two continents on the trees." *Variation.* II–282.
28. *Variation.* II–250.
29. *Ibid.* II–290.
30. *Ibid.* II–292 (italics this author's).
31. "If we suppose any habitual action to become inherited—and I think it can be shown that this does sometimes happen—then the resemblance between what originally was a habit and an instinct becomes so close as not to be distinguished." *Origin.* VIII:20.
32. "If, on the other hand, it profited the young to follow habits of life in any degree different from those of their parent, *and consequently to be constructed in a slightly different manner . . . ." Origin.* XIII:304 (italics this author's).
33. *Origin.* V:96.
34. Called by him "correlation of growth" in the *Origin;* later called "correlated variability" in the *Variation;* finally called "correlated variation" in the fifth *Origin.*
35. *Origin.* V:98.
36. Cuvier, *Le règne animal,* 1817, 1:6.
37. *Origin.* V:111 (italics this author's).
38. *Ibid.* V:121–122.
39. Darwin's early view of correlation stemmed from his reading of Cuvier and I.G. St. Hilaire. Theirs, however, was mainly a rather static, descriptive outlook—though St. Hilaire's teratologic work (*Histoire des anomalies,* 1832, 3:392, *et seq.*) attempted a dynamic explanation of correlation through embryology.
40. Spencer's work was first released by his publisher in serialized form. Volume 1 was covered in six pamphlets, the first appearing in January 1863, the last in October 1864. The last issue, comprising volume 2, appeared in March 1867. Darwin started his chapter on the "Laws of Variation" in October 1864. The final ms. of the *Variation* did not get to Murray until February 1867.
41. *Principles of biology,* London, 1864, 1:289–292.
42. *Variation.* II–293.
43. *Ibid.* II–295.
44. E. S. Russell, *Form and Function.* London: Murray, 1916, p. 240.
45. *Variation.* II–535.
46. *Ibid.* II–353.
47. *Ibid.* II–302.
48. *Origin.* IV(VII):382.60.x.e.
49. *Ibid.*
50. *Ibid.* V:130.

51. *Annales du Muséum d'Histoire Naturelle* 10(1807):342 (anticipated by Goethe in 1795).
52. *Variation.* II–290.
53. *Ibid.* II–271.
54. *Ibid.* II–320.
55. *Ibid.* II–334–335.

Chapter 5. Blending Inheritance

1. Fleeming Jenkin, The origin of species. *North British Review* 46 (June 1867): 277–318 (DRC #R 89). Some of these authors are: Garrett Hardin, *Nature and man's fate,* New York: Rinehart, 1959, pp. 113–115; Loren Eiseley, *Darwin's century,* London: Gollancz, 1959, pp. 210–211; Sir Gavin de Beer, *Charles Darwin,* London: Nelson, 1963, p. 175; John Greene, *The death of Adam,* New York: New American Library, 1960, p. 291; W. P. Thompson (ed.), *Evolution: its science and doctrine,* Toronto: University of Toronto Press, 1960, p. 121; Phillip Fothergill, *Historical aspects of organic evolution,* London: Hollis & Carter, 1952, p. 132.
2. Sixty per cent of all Darwin's revisions in the *Origin* occurred in the last two editions, 29 per cent in the fifth alone. See App. I (p. 773) of Peckham's variorum text edition of the *Origin.*
3. ML–II–379 and LL–III–108.
4. Garrett Hardin, *Nature and man's fate.*
5. *Notebooks.* II:125.
6. *Ibid.* IV:118.
7. *Sketch of 1842,* p. 42.
8. *Ibid.* p. 44.
9. *Ibid.* p. 43. This means the inheritability of the effects of the environment on the individual.
10. *Ibid.*
11. *Essay of 1844,* p. 97.
12. *Ibid.* p. 102.
13. *Ibid.* p. 198.
14. *Ibid.* pp. 97, 122, 145.
15. *Ibid.* pp. 111–112.
16. *Ibid.* p. 196.
17. *Ibid.* pp. 228+247.
18. *Ibid.* p. 94.
19. To be published by Professor R. C. Stauffer of the University of Wisconsin, to whom this author is indebted for permission to see a great part of this work.
20. *Essay of 1844,* p. 111.
21. *Ibid.* pp. 85+93.
22. *Origin.* XIV:93.
23. *Ibid.* IV:196.
24. *Ibid.* IV:223, XIV:226, I:298.
25. *Ibid.* II:13.
26. *Essay of 1844,* p. 120.
27. Review, *American Journal of Science and Arts,* April 1860, p. 500 (DRC #R 31).
28. That Darwin did pass over much in Bowen's review can be seen in his reprint

281. *References*

copy. For a description of the Darwin-Agassiz relationship, see Edward Lurie, *Louis Agassiz: a life in science,* Chicago: University of Chicago Press, 1960.

29. See chapter 15 in A. Hunter Dupree, *Asa Gray,* Cambridge: Belknap Press, 1959.
30. Review of *Origin, American Journal of Science and Arts,* March 1860, p. 12 (DRC #12).
31. *Westminster Review,* March 1860; also see Huxley, *Darwiniana essays,* New York: D. Appleton, 1901, pp. 31 *et seq.*
32. *Westminster Review,* March 1860, pp. 546–547; *Darwiniana,* p. 21.
33. LL–II–231.
34. *Westminster Review,* March 1860, p. 548; *Darwiniana,* p. 38.
35. *Darwiniana,* p. 549.
36. W. C. Spooner, *On cross-breeding* [pamphlet], 1860 (DRC #208). This tract is not located in either the *Royal Society catalogue of scientific papers* or the *British Museum catalogue of printed books.*
37. Compare the quote from Bowen (above, pp. 111–112 at reference 27) with that of Darwin from 1842 (above, p. 102 at reference 7).
38. See above, p. 108.
39. Written February 1 to May 10, 1866.
40. *Origin.* IV:382.39.3.d.
41. Georges Pouchet, *Plurality of the human race,* 2nd ed., London, 1864 (DL). See above, p. 66.
42. *Ibid.* p. 142.
43. *Origin.* IV:382.39.6.c.
44. *Ibid.* IV:382.39.8.
45. *Ibid.* IV:382.39.7.
46. Darwin to Hooker. November 29, 1862. ML–II–212.
47. T. A. Knight, An account of some experiments of the fecundation of vegetables. *Transactions of the Royal Horticultural Society,* London, 1799, pp. 195–204.
48. Augustin Sageret, *Pomologie physiologique.* Paris: Huzard, 1830 (DL).
49. *Ibid.* p. 562 (not marked).
50. Charles Naudin, Observations concernant quelques plantes hybrides qui ont été cultivées au muséum. *Annales des sciences naturelles* 9, no. 5:1–24 (DRC # 161); Nouvelles recherches sur l'hybridité dans les végétaux. *Mémoires académie des sciences,* April 1862, pp. 180–204 (DRC #300).
51. *Ibid.* p. 181.
52. *Variation.* II–49.
53. Darwin to Hooker. September 13, 1864. ML–II–339.
54. *Variation.* II–50.
55. W. C. Spooner, *On cross-breeding in horses* [pamphlet], 1865 (DRC #363). Not listed in Royal Society or British Museum catalogue.
56. H. Madden and C. H. MacKnight, *On the true principles of breeding* [pamphlet], Melbourne, 1865. Not listed in either Royal Society or British Museum catalogue.
57. "When two species are crossed, one has sometimes a prepotent power in impressing its likeness on the hybrid offspring; and so I believe it to be with varieties of plants as it certainly is with varieties of animals—for a variety often has a prepotent power over another in impressing its likeness on their mongrel offspring" (from an unpublished letter of 1863 by Darwin—with no

indication of to whom addressed—in the collection of the New York City Public Library).

58. *Variation.* II–71. See above, pp. 35–36.
59. *Ibid.* II–35.
60. Garrett Hardin, *Nature and man's fate,* pp. 113–115; Loren Eiseley, *Darwin's century,* pp. 210–211.
61. Darwin to Carus. November 21, 1866. ML–I–272.
62. Darwin to Wallace. October 12, 1867. ML–I–283.
63. Jenkin, The origin of species, p. 282.
64. *Ibid.* p. 292.
65. *Ibid.* p. 288.
66. *Ibid.* p. 290.
67. ML–II–379 and LL–III–108.
68. *Ibid.*
69. Unpublished letter dated January 30, 1869. (DPL, Box 84.)
70. Darwin to Wallace. February 2, 1869. LL–III–108.
71. Jenkin, The origin of species, p. 291.
72. *Origin.* IV:95.4.e.
73. "The conditions might indeed act in so energetic and definite a manner as to lead to the same modification in all the individuals of the species without the aid of selection." *Origin.* IV:95.14.e. Compare this with his earlier remark in the *Variation* quoted above in chapter 4, p. 83 (reference 29).

Chapter 6. The Limits of Variation

1. *Origin.* IV:173.
2. *Essay of 1844,* pp. 111–112.
3. *Origin.* II:17.
4. *Ibid.* XIV:93.
5. *Ibid.* IV:84.
6. *Essay of 1844,* p. 106.
7. *Origin.* I:55.
8. Darwin left on the *Beagle* with the first volume of the first edition. He received vol. 2 of the first edition—which contains the relevant chapters on transmutation—at Monte Video on October 26, 1832. However, it was in the fifth edition of 1834 that Darwin made his copious marginal annotations. Thanks must be extended to Dr. Sydney Smith for providing this information, as well as for his transcriptions of Darwin's annotations.
9. *Principles of geology,* 1st ed. London: Murray, 1830–32, 2:26–28.
10. *Ibid.* p. 67.
11. *Ibid.*
12. *Essay of 1844,* p. 135.
13. *Ibid.*
14. *Origin.* XIV:185.
15. *Ibid.* II:67.
16. *Ibid.* IV:125.
17. *Ibid.* IV:252.
18. *Ibid.* IV:303.
19. *Ibid.* IV:259–261.

20. The comments of each appeared as papers in the July issue of the Academy's journal, *The American Journal of Science and Arts*. In Darwin's Reprint Collection they are DRC #'s R 8, -9, -10, and -31.
21. *American Journal of Science and Arts*, July 1860, pp. 150–151 (DRC #R 8).
22. Darwin to Gray. August 11, 1860. LL–II–333.
23. *American Journal of Science and Arts*, July 1860, p. 2 (DRC #R 9).
24. *Ibid.*
25. *American Journal of Science and Arts*, July 1860, p. 500 (DRC #R 31).
26. *American Journal of Science and Arts*, September 1860, p. 155 (DRC #R 12).
27. See above, p. 52 (reference 13).
28. Darwin to Gray. July 22, 1860. LL–II–326.
29. *Quarterly Review*, July 1860, pp. 237–247 (DRC #R 34).
30. See above, p. 63 (reference 35).
31. *Origin.* IV:42.2.c.
32. *Ibid.* II:69.
33. *Ibid.* II:65.
34. *Ibid.* II:66–67.
35. *Ibid.* XIV:70.
36. *Ibid.* IV:118.
37. *Ibid.* IV:309.
38. *Ibid.* V:174.
39. *Ibid.* XIV:70.
40. *Ibid.* V:199.
41. *Ibid.* V:212.
42. *Ibid.* IV:41.2.c.
43. *Variation.* II–64.
44. *Ibid.* II–241.
45. *Ibid.* II–64.
46. *Ibid.* II–23.
47. On the American fossil elephant. *Natural History Review*, January 1863 (not in DRC).
48. *Origin.* IX:159.1.d.
49. *Variation.* II–243.
50. On the origin of species. *North British Review*, July 1867, pp. 279–281 (DRC #R 89).
51. *Ibid.* p. 282.
52. *Ibid.*
53. *Ibid.* pp. 284–285.
54. *Ibid.* p. 288.
55. *Ibid.*
56. Darwin to Hooker. January 16, 1869. ML–II–379.
57. *Origin.* I:310.1–3.e.
58. *Origin.* IV:95.12.13.e (italics this author's).
59. On the variations under domestication. Anonymous review in the *Athenaeum*, February 15, 1868, p. 3 (not in DRC).
60. *Über die Berechtigung der Darwin'schen Theorie.* Leipzig, 1868, p. 27 (DL).
61. Darwin to Weismann. October 22, 1868. ML–I–311.
62. Darwin to Hooker. August 7, 1869. ML–I–314.
63. London: Trubner (DL). Read by Darwin sometime between December 1869

and January 1870. (See ML–II–41, which has, however, the wrong date attributed to it.)

64. In the *Journal of the Anthropological Institute* 1 (1875): Heredity in twins (DRC #1045) and (pp. 329–348) A theory of heredity (DRC #1046); also see Typical laws of heredity, *Proceedings of the Royal Institution,* 1877 (DRC #1246).

Chapter 7. The Role of Isolation

1. *Origin.* IX:159.1.d and XIV:23.
2. *Ibid.* IV:17+25.
3. *Ibid.* III:146.
4. *Ibid.* III:82.
5. *Ibid.* IV:221.
6. *Ibid.* IV:25.
7. *Ibid.* IV:17.
8. *Ibid.* IV:201.
9. *Ibid.* VII:382.39.2.d.
10. *Ibid.* X:63.
11. *Ibid.* III:82.
12. *Ibid.* VII:382.39.2.d.
13. *Ibid.* IV:18.
14. *Ibid.* IV:194. Similarities to sections on the same subject in the *Principles of Geology* show Darwin's indebtedness to Lyell.
15. *Ibid.* XIV:251.
16. *Ibid.* IV:37.
17. *Ibid.* IV:23.
18. *Ibid.* IV:22.
19. *Notebooks.* IV:118 (1839).
20. *Sketch of 1842,* p. 68.
21. *Essay of 1844,* p. 195.
22. *Origin.* IV:192.
23. *Ibid.* IV:194.
24. *Ibid.* IV:200.
25. *Ibid.* IV:201 *et seq.*
26. *Ibid.* IV:177.
27. *Ibid.* XI:78.
28. *Ibid.* IV:186.
29. *Ibid.* IV:266.
30. *Variation.* II–185.
31. *Origin.* VIII:159.2.d.
32. I am indebted to Professor Alfred E. Emerson for contributing this term in contradistinction to Professor G. G. Simpson's "orthogenetic speciation" (*The Meaning of Evolution,* New Haven: Yale University Press, 1949, pp. 30–51). The latter term is meant to apply to that form of speciation in which it is believed that the direction and final goal of a particular line of evolutionary development has been predetermined and directed at the outset in the primal genetic constitution. It may be worth adding the point, however, that Darwin's later allusions to a genetic tendency of the variant form "to vary again and in the same direction" (Simpson, p. 152) have serious orthogenetic connotations.

33. *Origin.* XIV:21.
34. *Ibid.*
35. *Ibid.* XI:38.
36. *Ibid.* IV:15.
37. *Ibid.* IV:16.
38. *Ibid.* X:111–112.
39. *Ibid.* XI:36.
40. *Ibid.* XI:63+69.
41. *Ibid.* XI:60.
42. *Ibid.*IV:95.3.e.
43. *Ibid.* IV:95.18.e.
44. *Ibid.* IV:95.11.e (italics this author's).
45. See above, pp. 143 and 171.
46. *Reisen in der Regentschaft Algier in den Jahren 1836, 37, und 38,* 3 vols. Leipzig: Leopold Voss, 1851 (not in DRC).
47. *Die Darwin'sche Theorie und das Migrationgesetz der Organismen.* Munich: Straub, 1868 (DRC #R 110).
48. *Ibid.* p. 29.
49. *Ibid.*
50. Wagner's second paper, in 1875, leaves the impression that he believed his own theory replaced that of Darwin in all but a few minor points. See below.
51. Wagner, *Die Darwin'sche Theorie,* p. 5.
52. Darwin to Wagner. 1868. LL–III–158. See *Origin* IV:177 for reference to unconscious selection of English racehorse.
53. Darwin to Wagner. 1868. LL–III–158.
54. Darwin to Weismann. October 22, 1868. ML–I–310.
55. Der Naturprozess der Artbildung. *Das Ausland,* May 1875, pp. 425–428 (DRC #Q 258). Darwin marginal annotation.
56. December 1868 to February 1869: appearing August 1869.
57. *Origin.* IV:193.1.e.
58. Wagner, Der Naturprozess.
59. *Ibid.* p. 426.
60. *Ibid.* p. 428.
61. Darwin to Wagner. October 13, 1876. LL–III–158.
62. Darwin to Semper. November 26, 1878. LL–III–160.

Chapter 8. Darwin and Wallace

1. On the law which has regulated the introduction of new species. *Annals and Magazine of Natural History* 7 (September 1855):184–196.
2. *Descent.* I–248.
3. *Ibid.* I–256.
4. *Origin.* IV:78.
5. Darwin to Wallace. May 28, 1864. LL–III–89 and ML–II–32.
6. On the phenomena of variation and geographical distribution, as illustrated by the Papilionidae of the Malayan Archipelago. *Transactions of the Linnean Society* [1865] 25:1 (published 1866) (not in DRC).
7. *Ibid.* p. 222.
8. Darwin to Wallace. February 22, 1867. LL–III–93.

9. Unpublished letter of A. R. Wallace to Darwin. April 26, 1867. (DPL, Box 83.)
10. Darwin to Wallace. April 29, 1867. ML–II–59.
11. William Irvine, *Apes, angels, and victorians.* New York: McGraw-Hill, 1955, p. 184. Irvine treats the Darwin-Wallace relationship of this period, but without benefit of the unpublished Wallace letters. It remains, however, a worthwhile study.
12. Unpublished letter of A. R. Wallace to Darwin. May 1, 1867. (DPL, Box 84.)
13. Darwin to Wallace. May 5, 1867. ML–II–61.
14. Mimicry and other protective resemblances among animals. *Westminster Review,* July 1867; Review of article in *Quarterly Review of Science,* October 1867, p. 472.
15. *Darwinism.* London: Macmillan, 1890, p. 283.
16. *Ibid.* p. 224.
17. Darwin to Wallace. October 12, 1867. ML–I–281.
18. Wallace to Darwin. March 19, 1868. ML–II–62.
19. Darwin to Wallace. March 19, 1868. ML–II–63.
20. Darwin to Wallace. April 15, 1868. ML–II–73.
21. Unpublished letter from Wallace to Darwin. April 28, 1868. (DPL, Box 83.)
22. Darwin to Wallace. April 30, 1868. ML–II–76.
23. Unpublished letter from Wallace to Darwin. May 1, 1868. (DPL, Box 83.)
24. Darwin to Wallace. August 19, 1868. ML–II–84.
25. Unpublished letter from Wallace to Darwin. August 30, 1868. (DPL, Box 83.)
26. Wallace to Darwin. January 27, 1871. LL–III–134.
27. Unpublished letter from Wallace to Darwin. July 12, 1871. (DPL, Box 83.)
28. Darwin to Wallace. March 16, 1871. LL–III–137.
29. *Origin.* VIII:7.
30. *Ibid.* VIII:8.
31. *Ibid.* VIII:184.
32. *Ibid.* VIII:26.
33. *Ibid.* VIII:285.
34. Wallace, On the phenomena of variation and . . . distribution.
35. Wallace to Darwin. July 2, 1866. ML–I–267.
36. Unpublished letter from Wallace to Darwin. February 11, 1866. (DPL, Box 83.)
37. There is, in fact, a gap in the extant Darwin-Wallace correspondence between this letter and that of July 2—when Wallace wrote to Darwin without any indication of any previous correspondence.
38. *Origin.* VIII:159.1.d.
39. *Ibid.* VIII:159.15.d.
40. *Ibid.* VIII:159.18–20.d.
41. *Variation.* II–104. LL–III–79.
42. Wallace to Darwin. February 1868. ML–I–288.
43. Darwin to Wallace. February 27, 1868. ML–I–289.
44. Wallace to Darwin. March 1, 1868. ML–I–289.
45. *Ibid.* p. 291.
46. Darwin to Wallace. March 17, 1868. ML–I–293.
47. Wallace to Darwin. March 24, 1868. ML–I–293.
48. Darwin to Wallace. April 6, 1868. ML–I–294.
49. Wallace to Darwin. April 8, 1868. ML–I–297.

50. Darwin to Wallace. July 9, 1871. LL–III–144.
51. Unpublished letter from Wallace to Darwin. July 12, 1871. (DPL, Box 83.)
52. Darwin to Wallace. July 12, 1871. LL–III–146.
53. *Ibid.*

Chapter 9. The Origins of Useless Characters

1. *Origin.* VI:220.
2. For a more detailed discussion of Bronn's objections, see above, pp. 73 *et seq.*
3. *Origin.* IV:382.63–65.c.
4. Enstehung und Begriff der Naturhistorischen Art. *Sits. Königl. Akad.,* Munich, March 1865 (DRC #393/671).
5. Number of leaf-axis revolutions, angle of leaves between revolutions, divisions of the ovarium, positions of the ovules.
6. Nägeli, Enstehung und Begriff, p. 27.
7. Darwin to Nägeli. June 12, 1866. LL–III–50.
8. Darwin to Hooker. January 16, 1869. ML–II–378.
9. Hooker to Darwin. January 18, 1869. LLJDH–II–122.
10. Hooker to Darwin. January, 1869. LLJDH–II–123.
11. *Über die Berechtigung der Darwin'schen Theorie* [pamphlet]. Leipzig, 1868 (DL). (The paper was read before the Academy of Sciences at Munich, July 8, 1868.)
12. *Ibid.* p. 27.
13. Darwin annotation in above copy.
14. *Origin.* IV:382.65.0.6–9.e (italics this author's).
15. *Ibid.* IV:382.65.0.48.e.
16. *Ibid.* p. 50 (Introduction).
17. The *Origin* had increased by more than 20 per cent in size by the fifth edition. Nearly 30 per cent of all changes were made in the fifth edition alone—60 per cent in the fifth and sixth editions together.

Chapter 10. The Crucial Years: Controversy with Mivart

1. Jacques Barzun, *Darwin, Marx, and Wagner.* New York: Doubleday Anchor Books, 1958, pp. 74–76.
2. *Ibid.* p. 84.
3. For details on the life and work of Mivart, see Jacob Gruber, *A conscience in conflict: the life of St. George Mivart,* New York: Columbia University Press, 1960. To this book the author is indebted for providing much background information on the Darwin-Mivart controversy.
4. St. George Mivart, *The genesis of species.* London: Macmillan, 1871. Hereafter referred to as *Genesis* (DL—nearly every second page has been annotated by Darwin).
5. *Ibid.* p. 61 (Introduction).
6. Anonymous review (by Mivart) in *The Month,* July-September 1869 (DRC #R 145—lightly annotated by Darwin).
7. *Genesis,* p. 11.
8. *Ibid.* p. 12.

9. Both Darwin and Wallace objected to Mivart's use of the word "infinitesimal" on the grounds that Darwin never employed the word describing variations, and Mivart subsequently apologized (see Gruber, *Conscience in conflict,* pp. 84–85); yet in the first two editions of the *Origin,* one can find the sentence: "Natural Selection can act only by the preservation and accumulation of infinitesimally small inherited modifications" (*Origin.* IV:125).
10. *Genesis,* p. 116.
11. *Ibid.* pp. 236 *et seq.*
12. William Irvine, *Apes, angels, and victorians.* New York: McGraw-Hill, 1955, p. 193.
13. *Descent.* I–153.
14. *Ibid.*
15. *Ibid.* II–388.
16. *Ibid.* I–113.
17. *Ibid.*
18. *Ibid.* I–153.
19. *Ibid.*
20. *Ibid.* II–387.
21. B. A. Gould, *Investigation in military and anthropological statistics.* Boston, 1869 (DL).
22. *Descent.* I–117.
23. *Ibid.* I–118.
24. Gertrude Himmelfarb, *Darwin and the Darwinian revolution.* New York: Doubleday, 1959, p. 346.
25. *Origin.* I:34–36.
26. This point is discussed by Professor Ernst Mayr in Isolation as an evolutionary factor, *Proceedings of the American Philosophical Society* 113 (1959): 221–230.
27. *Quarterly Review,* July 1871, pp. 41–53 (DRC #R 174).
28. *Ibid.* p. 47.
29. *Ibid.* and *Origin.* VI:208.
30. *Ibid.* p. 52.
31. Darwin to Wallace. January 30, 1871. LL–III–135.
32. Darwin to Wallace. July 9, 1871. LL–III–144.
33. The new chapter 7 which appeared in the sixth edition.
34. Darwin to Wallace. July 9, 1871. LL–III–143.
35. *Ibid.* p. 144.
36. Darwin to Huxley. September 21, 1871. LL–III–148.
37. Wright, review of Mivart and Darwin. *North American Review,* July 1871, p. 5 (DRC #R 204).
38. *Ibid.* p. 16.
39. Huxley, review of Wallace, Mivart, and Darwin. *Contemporary Review,* January 1872, p. 132 (DRC #R 182).
40. Anonymous reply to Prof. Huxley. *Contemporary Review,* January 1872, p. 172 (DRC #R 183).
41. *Origin.* IV:95.12.f.
42. *Ibid.* VI:220.f.
43. *Ibid.* IV:382.65.0.50.165–67.f.
44. *Ibid.* VI:257.f.

45. *Ibid.* XIV:183, 183.e, and 183.f.
46. Specific genesis. *North American Review,* April 1872, p. 452 (not in DRC).
47. *Ibid.* p. 453.
48. Reply to Prof. Mivart. *North American Review,* May 1872 (not in DRC).
49. Darwin to Wright. June 3, 1872. LL–III–164.
50. Darwin to Haeckel. December 23, 1871. ML–I–335.

Chapter 11. The Final Years: Darwin's Retirement

1. London: Murray, 1875.
2. *Alfred Russel Wallace: letters and reminiscences,* ed. J. Marchant. New York: Harper, 1916, p. 233.
3. London: Murray, 1877.
4. *The different forms of flowers of plants of the same species,* 3rd ed. London: Murray, 1892, p. 284.
5. On blood relationship. *Proceedings of the Royal Society* 20 (June 13, 1872): 394–402 (not in DRC).
6. *Nature,* April 27, 1871, p. 502.
7. On blood relationship, p. 394.
8. *Ibid.* p. 400.
9. *Studien zur Descendez-Theorie* [reprinting of 1872–74 papers]. Leipzig, 1875–76 (DL).
10. Darwin to Weismann. May 1, 1875. ML–I–356.
11. *Journal of the Anthropological Institute,* November 1875, pp. 329–348 (DRC #1046).
12. *Ibid.* p. 331.
13. *Ibid.* p. 345.
14. Darwin to Galton. November 7, 1875. ML–I–360.
15. Darwin to Galton. December 18, 1875. See Karl Pearson, *Life and letters of Francis Galton,* Cambridge: University Press, 1924, 2:157.
16. *Ibid.*
17. *Ibid.* p. 189.
18. Item number R 112 in Darwin's reprint collection is a 171-page pamphlet by the German botanist Heinrich Hoffmann entitled *Bestimmung des Werthes von Species and Varietät* (Giessen: Richter, 1869). It is a handlist giving synopses of botanical breeding experiments. The first item under Section 118 (p. 136) on the genus *Pisum* is an abstract of Mendel's 1865 paper. This was Mendel's classic paper. There is good internal evidence that Darwin read Hoffmann's pamphlet in its entirety. The presence of six citations of Darwin's work on the same genus (on the facing page) brought Mendel's citation right under Darwin's eyes. For further details, including photographs and translation, see Darwin and Mendel: a historical connection, by this author, in *Isis* 59:1 (Spring 1968), pp. 77–82.
19. See above, p. 90.
20. *Über den Einfluss der Isolierung auf die Artbildung.* Leipzig: Engelmann, 1872 (DL).
21. *Ibid.* p. 25.
22. See above, p. 178.
23. *Variation* (2nd ed.). II–262.

24. Darwin to Semper. November 30, 1878. LL–III–160.
25. *Ibid.*
26. Unpublished letter from Darwin to W. C. Greg. December 31, 1878. In the collection of the American Philosophical Society Library.
27. *The natural conditions of existence.* London: Kegan Paul, 1881, pp. 16-17.
28. *Ibid.* p. 404.
29. Darwin to Semper. February 6, 1881. ML–I–391.
30. Rückblick auf meine Variations-Versuche von 1855–80. *Botanische Zeitung,* 1881 (DRC #Q 319).
31. Darwin to Semper. July 19, 1881. LL–III–344–345.

Bibliography

I. Primary Sources

A. PAPERS AND LETTERS:

The Darwin collection of papers and letters in the University Library. Cambridge, England.

The Darwin letters in the collections of the library of the American Philosophical Society, the British Museum, and the New York Public Library.

B. LIBRARY:

Books from Darwin's library at the Downe House, Kent; at the University Library, Cambridge; and at the Botany School, Cambridge.

C. REPRINT COLLECTION:

Darwin's personal reprint collection, housed in the Anderson Room of the University Library, Cambridge.

D. WORKS:

1871 and (2nd ed.) 1874. *The descent of man.* London: Murray.

1868 and (2nd ed.) 1875. *The variation of animals and plants under domestication.* London: Murray.

1958. *Evolution by natural selection: Darwin and Wallace* [containing joint papers of 1858; Darwin's *Sketch of 1842*; and Darwin's *Essay of 1844*], Foreword by Sir Gavin de Beer. Cambridge: University Press.

1959. *The origin of species: a variorum text,* ed. Morse Peckham. Philadelphia: University of Pennsylvania Press.

1960. *Notebooks on transmutation of species,* ed. Sir Gavin de Beer. *Bulletin of the British Museum* (Natural History). Historical Series, vol. 2, nos. 2–5. London.

1961. *Notebooks on transmutation of species: addenda and corrigenda,* ed. Sir Gavin de Beer and M. J. Rowlands. *Bulletin of the British Museum* (Natural History). Historical Series, vol. 2, no. 6. London.

II. Biographical and Letter Sources

DARWIN, F., ed. 1897. *Life and letters of Charles Darwin.* 2 vols. New York: D. Appleton & Co.

DARWIN, F., and SEWARD, A. C., eds. 1903. *More letters of Charles Darwin.* 2 vols. New York: D. Appleton & Co.

HUXLEY, L. 1900. *Life and letters of Thomas Henry Huxley.* 2 vols. New York: D. Appleton & Co.

————. 1918. *Life and letters of Sir Joseph Dalton Hooker.* 2 vols. New York: D. Appleton & Co.

LITCHFIELD, H., ed. 1915. *Emma Darwin: a century of family letters.* 2 vols. New York: D. Appleton & Co.

LYELL, K. M. 1881. *Life and letters of Sir Charles Lyell.* 2 vols. London: Murray.

MARCHANT, J. 1916. *Alfred Russel Wallace: life and reminiscences.* New York: Harper.

WALLACE, A. R. 1905. *My life: a record of events and opinions.* 2 vols. New York: Dodd, Mead.

III. Secondary Sources

ALLEE, W. C., EMERSON, A. E., *et al.* 1949. *Principles of animal ecology.* Philadelphia: Saunders.

ANONYMOUS. 1902. *The primrose and Darwinism.* London: Richards.

ARGYLL, DUKE OF. 1867. *The reign of law.* London: Straham.

BAILEY, SIR E., 1963. *Charles Lyell.* London: Nelson.

BARLOW, LADY N., ed. 1958. *Autobiography of Charles Darwin.* London: Murray.

————. 1967. *Darwin and Henslow: the growth of an idea.* London: Murray.

BARNETT, S. A., ed. 1962. *A century of Darwin.* London: Mercury Books.

BARZUN, J. 1958. *Darwin, Marx, and Wagner.* New York: Doubleday.

BELL, P. R., ed. 1959. *Darwin's biological work.* Cambridge: University Press.

BIBBY, C. 1959. *Thomas Henry Huxley.* London: Watts.

————. 1959. Huxley and the reception of the *Origin. Victorian Studies* 3:1.

BREE, C. R. 1860. *Species not transmutable.* London. (DL)

BROCA, P. 1864. *Hybridity in the genus homo.* London. (DL)

BUTLER, SAMUEL. 1878. *Life and habit.* London: Trubner.

————. 1879. *Evolution: old and new.* London: Trubner.

CARTER, G. S. 1957. *100 years of evolution.* London: Sidgwick.

CLODD, EDWARD. 1897. *Pioneers of evolution.* New York.

COLEMAN, W. R. 1964. *Georges Cuvier, zoologist: a study in the history of evolution theory.* Cambridge: University Press.

DE BEER, SIR G. 1958. Further unpublished letters of Charles Darwin. *Annals of Science* 14:83–115.

————. 1958. The Darwin-Wallace centenary. *Endeavour* 17:65.

————. 1959. Some unpublished letters of Charles Darwin. *Notes and Records of the Royal Society* 14:83–115.

————. 1961. The origin of Darwin's ideas on evolution and natural selection. *Proceedings of the Royal Society* 115:321–338.

————. 1963. *Charles Darwin.* London: Nelson.

DIBNER, B. 1964. *Darwin of the Beagle.* New York: Blaisdell.

DOBBS, J. W. 1953. *The age of paradox 1841–51.* London: Gollancz.

DOWDESWELL, W. H. 1955. *The mechanism of evolution.* London: Heinemann.

DUPREE, A. H. 1959. *Asa Gray.* Cambridge, Mass.: Belknap Press.

EISELEY, L. 1959. *Darwin's century.* London: Gollancz.

————. 1959. Charles Darwin, Edward Blyth, and the theory of natural selection. *Proceedings of the American Philosophical Society* 103:108.

ELLEGÅRD, A. 1957. The Darwinian theory and nineteenth century philosophies of science. *Journal of the History of Ideas* 18:362–393.

————. 1958. *Darwin and the general reader.* Göteborg: Elanders.

FISHER, SIR R. A. 1929. *The genetical theory of natural selection.* Edinburgh: Oliver.

————. 1932. The bearing of genetics on the theory of evolution. *Science Progress* 27:5.

————. 1954. Retrospect of the criticisms of the theory of natural selection. In *Evolution as a Process,* ed. Julian Huxley *et al.,* London.

FLOURENS, P. 1864. *Examen du libre de M. Darwin.* Paris.

FOTHERGILL, P. 1952. *Historical aspects of organic evolution.* London: Hollis & Carter.

GALTON, FRANCIS. 1869. *Hereditary genius.* London: Trubner.

————. 1875. Heredity in twins. *Journal of the Anthropological Institute* 1 (DRC #1045).

————. 1875. A theory of heredity. *Journal of the Anthropological Institute* 1: 329–348 (DRC #1046).

————. 1877. Typical laws of heredity. *Proceedings of the Royal Institution* (DRC #1246).

————. 1889. *Natural inheritance.* London: Trubner.

GEISON, G. L. 1969. Darwin and heredity: the evolution of his hypothesis of pangenesis. *Bulletin of the History of Medicine* 24:375–411.

GILLISPIE, C. C. 1959. *Genesis and geology.* New York: Harper.

GLASS, BENTLEY. 1963. The establishment of modern genetical theory. In *Scientific change,* ed. A. C. Crombie. London: Heinemann.

————, TEMKIN, O., and STRAUS, W., eds. 1959. *Forerunners of Darwin: 1745–1859.* Baltimore: Johns Hopkins Press.

GRAY, ASA. 1861. *Natural selection not inconsistent with natural theology* [pamphlet]. London: Trubner.

GRUBER, J. 1960. *A conscience in conflict: the life of St. George Mivart.* New York: Columbia University Press.

HAECKEL, E. 1907. *The history of creation.* 2 vols. New York: D. Appleton & Co.

HALDANE, J. B. S. 1932. *The causes of evolution.* Ithaca: Cornell University Press.

————. 1934. A mathematical theory of natural and artificial selection. *Genetics* 19:412–429.

HARDIN, G. 1959. *Nature and man's fate.* New York: Rinehart.

HARRISON, J. H. 1959. The origins of isolation. *New Biology* 28:61–75.

HUXLEY, SIR JULIAN. 1957. The three types of evolutionary process. *Nature* 180:454–455.

————. 1958. The emergence of Darwinism. *Journal of the Linnean Society* 44:1–14.

HUXLEY, T. H. 1863. *Evidence as to man's place in nature.* London: Murray.

————. 1901. *Darwiniana essays*. New York: D. Appleton & Co.

HIMMELFARB, G. 1959. *Darwin and the Darwinian revolution*. New York: Doubleday.

IRVINE, W. 1955. *Apes, angels, and victorians*. New York: McGraw-Hill.

JUDD, JOHN W. 1912. *The coming of evolution*. Cambridge: University Press.

KETTLEWELL, H. B. 1959. Darwin's missing evidence. *Scientific American* 200: 48–53.

LERNER, I. M. 1959. The concept of natural selection. *Proceedings of the American Philosophical Society* 103:173–182.

LEROY, J. F. 1966. *Charles Darwin et la théorie moderne de l'évolution*. Paris: Seghers.

LOEWENBERG, B. J. 1959. The mosaic of Darwinian thought. *Victorian Studies* 3:1.

————. 1965. Darwin and Darwin studies. *History of Science* 4:15–54.

LOVEJOY, A. O. 1957. *The great chain of being*. Cambridge, Mass: Harvard University Press.

LUCAS, P. 1847–50. *Philosophical and physiological treatise on heredity*. 2 vols. Paris: Huzard. (DL)

LURIE, E. 1954. Louis Agassiz and the races of man. *Isis* 45:226.

————. 1959. Louis Agassiz and the idea of evolution. *Victorian Studies* 3:87–108.

————. 1960. *Louis Agassiz: a life in science*. Chicago: University of Chicago Press.

LYELL, SIR C. 1830–32 and 1837. *Principles of geology*. London: Murray.

————. 1863. The geological evidences of the antiquity of man with remarks on theories of the origin of species by variation. London: Murray.

MCKINNEY, H. L. 1966. Alfred Russel Wallace and the discovery of natural selection. *Journal of the History of Medicine and Allied Sciences* 31:4.

MASON, S. F. 1953. *A history of the sciences*. New York: Schuman.

MASTERS, M. T. 1869. *Vegetable teratology*. London: Hardwick.

MAYR, E. 1959. Isolation as an evolutionary factor. *Proceedings of the American Philosophical Society* 113:221–230.

————. 1959. Agassiz, Darwin, and evolution. *Harvard Library Bulletin* 13:2.

————. 1960. The emergence of evolutionary novelties. In *Evolution after Darwin*, ed. Sol Tax. 3 vols. 1:349–380. Chicago: University of Chicago Press.

MIVART, ST. G. 1871. *The genesis of species*. London: Macmillan. (DL)

————. 1873. *Man and apes*. London: Hardwick.

————. 1876. *Lessons from nature*. London: Murray.

————. 1881. *The cat*. London: Murray.

MOQUIN-TANDON, A. 1841. *Éléments de tératologie végétale*. Paris. (DL)

MÜLLER, F. 1869 [German ed. 1864]. *Facts and arguments for Darwin*. London: Murray.

MÜNTZING, A. 1959. Darwin's views of variation under domestication in the light of modern knowledge. *Proceedings of the American Philosophical Society* 103:190–220.

MURPHY, J. J. 1892. *Habit and intelligence*. 2 vols. London. (DL)

MURRAY, R. H. 1925. *Science and scientists in the 19th century*. London: Sheldon Press.

NÄGELI, K. VON. 1865. Enstehung und Begriff der Naturhistorischen Art. *Sits. Königl. Akad.*

————. 1866. *Theorie der Bastardbildung.* Munich.

————. 1875. *Über den Einfluss äusserer Verhältnissee auf die Varietätenbildung.* Munich.

NORDENSKIÖLD, E. 1946. *History of biology.* New York: Tudor.

OLBY, R. C. 1963. Charles Darwin's manuscript of pangenesis. *British Journal for the History of Science* 1:251–261.

————. 1965. Francis Galton's derivation of Mendelian ratios in 1875. *Heredity* 20:636–638.

POUCHET, G. 1864. *Plurality of the human race.* 2nd ed. London. (DL)

POULTON, G. 1896. *Charles Darwin and the theory of natural selection.* London: Cassell.

PLOCHMANN, G. K. 1959. Darwin or Spencer? *Science* 30:1452–1456.

RÁDL, E. 1930. *History of biological theories,* trans. E. J. Hatfield. Oxford: University Press.

RENSCH, B. 1959. *Evolution above the species level.* London: Methuen.

————. 1960. The laws of evolution. In *Evolution after Darwin,* ed. Sol Tax (3 vols.), 1:95–116. Chicago: University of Chicago Press.

RIBOT, T. 1875. *Heredity.* London: King. (DL)

ROBERTS, H. F. 1929. *Plant hybridization before Mendel.* New York: Hafner.

ROMANES, G. J. 1869. *Darwin and after Darwin.* 3 vols. London: Murray.

RUSSELL, E. S. 1916. *Form and function.* London: Murray.

SEMPER, K. 1881. *The natural conditions of existence.* London: Kegan Paul. (DL)

SIMPSON, G. G. 1949. *The meaning of evolution.* New Haven: Yale University Press.

SINGER, C. 1931. *A short history of biology.* Oxford: Clarendon Press.

SMITH, J. M. 1958. *The theory of evolution.* London: Penguin.

SMITH, SYDNEY. 1960. The origin of the *Origin. Advancement of Science* 64: 391–401.

SPENCER, HERBERT. 1864. *Principles of biology.* London: Williams & Norgate.

STAUFFER, R. C. 1960. Ecology in the long manuscript version of Darwin's *Origin of Species* and Linnaeus' *Oeconomy of Nature. Proceedings of the American Philosophical Society* 104:235–241.

STERN, C. 1959. Variation and hereditary transmission. *Proceedings of the American Philosophical Society* 103:183–189.

TAX, SOL, ed. 1960. *Evolution after Darwin.* 3 vols. Chicago: University of Chicago Press.

THOMPSON, W. P. 1960. The cause and mode of evolution. In *Evolution: its science and doctrine,* ed. W. P. Thompson. Toronto: University of Toronto Press.

TURRILL, W. B. 1963. *Joseph Hooker.* London: Nelson.

VORZIMMER, P. J. 1963. Charles Darwin and blending inheritance. *Isis* 54:371–390.

————. 1965. Darwin's ecology and its influence upon his theory. *Isis* 56:148–156.

————. 1968. Theories of inheritance before Mendel. *Acts of the XIth International Congress in the History of the Sciences* 5:34–40. Warsaw.

————. 1968. Darwin and Mendel: a historical connection. *Isis* 59:77–82.

————. 1969. Darwin's questions about the breeding of animals. *Journal of the History of Biology* 2:269–281.

————. 1969. Darwin, Malthus, and the theory of natural selection. *Journal of the History of Ideas* 30:527–542.

————. 1970. Darwin's "Lamarckism" and the "Flat-Fish Controversy" (1863–71). *Lychnos* 34:1–37.

WAGNER, M. 1868. *Die Darwin'sche Theorie und das Migrationgesetz der Organismen.* Munich: Straub.. (DRC)

WALKER, ALEXANDER. 1838. *Intermarriage.* London: John Churchill.

WALLACE, A. R. 1871. *Contributions to the theory of natural selection.* 2nd ed. London: Macmillan.

————. 1889. *Darwinism.* London: Macmillan.

WEISMANN, A. 1872. *Über den Einfluss der Isolierung auf die Artbildung.* Leipzig: Engelmann. (DL)

————. 1882. *Studies in the theory of descent,* trans. R. Meldola. London: Sampson.

————. 1893. *The germ plasm: a theory of heredity,* trans. W. Parker. London: Scott.

WICHURA, MAX. 1865. *Die Bastardbefruchtung im Pflanzenreich.* Breslau. (DL)

WILLEY, B. 1960. *Darwin and Butler.* London: Chatto & Windus.

WOLLASTON, T. V. 1856. *On the variation of species: with special reference to the insecta, followed by an inquiry into the nature of genera.* London: Van Voorst. (DL)

YOUNG, R. W. 1969. Malthus and the evolutionists. *Past & Present* 43:109–145.

ZIRKLE, C. 1935. *The beginnings of plant hybridization.* Philadelphia: University of Pennsylvania Press.

————. 1941. Natural selection before the *Origin. Proceedings of the American Philosophical Society* 84:106.

————. 1946. The early history of the idea of the inheritance of acquired characters and of pangenesis. *Transactions of the American Philosophical Society* 35:91–151.

————. 1951. Gregor Mendel and his precursors. *Isis* 42:93–104.

Index

Inheritance, laws of, 23, 33, 214, 223; mechanism of, 19, 21–42, 254
Inheritance of acquired characters, 29, 40, 90, 238, 258, 265
Instinct, 84
Intermediate forms, 6, 68, 141, 143, 145, 148, 150, 156, 204, 215, 239
Irvine, William, xvi, 21
Isolation, ecological, 111, 134, 141, 160, 163, 173, 174, 177, 183, 184; geographical/physical/spatial, 19, 104, 107, 111, 120, 126, 160, 163, 170, 173, 177, 178, 182, 185, 209, 220, 223, 225, 262, 264; physiological, 160, 177, 203, 209

Jenkin, Fleeming, 67, 97–99, 120–127, 148–154, 157, 173, 177, 178, 182, 196, 206, 211, 228, 231, 270
Johanssen, William, 149, 156
Juffruticose thesiae, 58
Juste milieu, 118

Knight, Thomas Andrew, 22, 23, 30–32, 116
Kolreuter, Joseph, 23–25

Lamarck, J. B. M. de, 15, 40, 90, 94, 97, 98, 120, 126, 235, 238, 264, 265
Law of balance. *See* Compensation
Law of necessary development, 216. *See also* Orthoselective speciation
Lawrence, John, 33
Leptomeriae, 58
Linnaeus, 33
Living mosaic, 117. *See also* Naudin
Lucas, Prosper, 34, 39
Lurie, Edward, 112
Lyell, Charles, 4, 51, 57, 73, 106, 129, 160, 179, 190. WORKS: *Antiquity of Man,* 190, 227; *Principles of Geology,* 8f, 129, 160, 179

MacKnight, Charles, 118
Madden, H., 118
Malayan fauna, 191, 204
Malthus, Thomas, 4, 8
Masters, Maxwell, 58, 59
Mayr, Ernst, 159
Mendel, Gregor, 21, 22, 32, 258, 259, 261, 267
Migration of forms, 175, 176, 180, 181, 262
Mimicry, 192, 196, 198–200, 232, 265
Mivart, St. George, 2, 209–211, 227–229, 232, 253, 261, 264, 267, 270. WORKS: "Review of 4th *Origin* and *Variation,*" 226; *Genesis of Species,*

226–233, 242, 244–246; "Review of *Descent of Man,*" 226; "Reply to Huxley," 226; *Specific Genesis,* 226; *Lessons from Nature,* 226; *The Cat,* 226
Monstrosities, 25, 47, 50–52, 55, 56, 58, 69, 81, 106, 111, 113, 136, 137. *See also* Saltation
Monstrous forms. *See* Monstrosities
Month, 241
Moquin-Tandon, A., 25, 36–39
Murray, John, 72, 73, 254
Mutation, 60, 113. *See also* Saltation

Nägeli, Karl von, 25, 59, 215–219, 228
Natural selection, 14, 17, 19, 20, 106, 107, 221, 223; mechanism of, 6, 14, 105, 145, 148, 161, 210; motive force for, 8
Naudin, Charles, 25, 116–118
Negative selection, 7, 9, 91, 95, 109, 110, 133, 134, 161, 163–166, 171, 178, 182, 264
Newtonian law, 28
Newtonian world-machine, 269
Nisus formativus, 86, 87
Non-heritability and non-transmissibility, 27, 28, 45, 51, 135, 231
North American Review, 250
North British Review, 124, 125, 127, 148

Ornithology, 194
Orthoselective speciation, 174, 185
Orton, J., 34
Owen, Richard, 112
Oxford debate, 138

Paint-pot metaphor of inheritance, 110. *See also* Blending inheritance
Pangenesis, 22, 41, 98, 120, 146, 156, 255, 257, 261
Parsons, Theophilus, 56, 57, 135, 137
Phenotype and somatoplasm, 17, 19, 43, 44, 77, 155, 257
Pigeons, Darwin's breeding of, 36
Pisum, 22, 116
Place, concept of, 162, 163
Pouchet, Georges, 66, 114, 211, 225, 270
Pre-adaptation, 134, 172, 182, 183
Primula, 254
Progressionism, 216, 232
Protective resemblances, 193, 195. *See also* Selection-for-protection

Quarterly Review, 139, 210, 234, 243–246